I0419410

The Great Airship

F. S. Brereton

[ZHINGOORA BOOKS]

This edition is published by
Zhingoora Books.

Apart from any fair dealing for the purposes of research or private study, or criti-cism or review, this publication may only be reproduced, stored or transmitted, in any form or by any means, with the prior permission in writing of the publishers. All disputes are subject to exclusive jurisdiction of Mandsaur Courts only. For any suggestions and feedback or book on new concept/domain, please contact us at the email given below.

contact@Zhingoora.com

"AIRSHIP IN SIGHT, SIR!"

Contents

CHAPTER I

The Fame of the Zeppelin

There are exceptions, we suppose, to almost every rule, and this particular Friday towards the end of June was such an exception. It was fine. Not a cloud flecked the sun-lit sky. A glorious blue expanse hung over a sea almost as blue, but criss-crossed in all directions by the curling white tops of tiny wavelets, all that remained to remind one of the atrocious weather which had prevailed. For the North Sea, Europe, Great Britain, everywhere in fact, had been treated to a succession of violent gales, to a continuous deluge of rain, to bitter hail, and squalls of snow in some parts. And here and now, off the mouth of the river Elbe the sun shone, the sky was a delight, a balmy breeze fanned the cheeks of the passengers crowding the decks of the Hamburg-Amerika liner.

"What a change! I began to wonder whether there was such a season as summer. Have a cigar?"

Mr. Andrew Provost drew from an inner pocket of his jacket a silver-mounted case, pulled the lid off and offered one of the contents to his nephew.

"Not that one, Joe," he said, as the young man beside him placed his long fingers on one of the weeds. "It's Dutch. Not that they're not good smokes; I like 'em sometimes. But give me a Havana, and offer one to your friends. There! That one! You'll like it."

"Thanks! I know 'em, Uncle. You always give me your best."

There was a smile on the handsome face of the young man as he obeyed the directions of his Uncle Andrew. It was obvious indeed from their smiles, the manner in which they paced the deck arm in arm, and from the intimacy of their conversation, that the two were on the best of terms. And why not? They were related, as we have stated. Then they had for long been separated. Mr. Andrew Provost had not always been the comfortable-looking individual he now appeared. For prosperous and comfortable he looked without a doubt. Florid and sunburned, with white hair and moustache which made his complexion seem to be even more ruddy, he was tall, and slight, and gracefully if not robustly built. There was something of a military air about him, and we whisper the truth when we say that he was often enough taken for an old soldier, much to his own secret gratification. Dark grey eyes looked out genially from a smiling face upon the world and his fellows. His forehead was hardly seamed. Care, in fact, seemed to have failed in its effort to reach him, or, more likely perhaps, his genial, plucky nature had caused it to fall easily from his shoulders. For the rest he was exceedingly well groomed, and looked what he was, a prosperous, healthy gentleman.

"But it wasn't always like that, Joe," he told his companion, as they paced the deck, basking in the sun. "Your Uncle Andrew wasn't always the stylish dog he looks now. Not by a long way. I've been on my beam ends."

"Ah! Exactly."

"Know what that means?"

"To a certain extent. When you came home last Christmas I was down in the dumps. Absolutely on my beam ends."

Andrew Provost turned to look with some astonishment at his nephew. He inspected him critically from the top of his glossy Homburg hat to the well-polished brown shoes which he wore. And the face finally drew all his attention.

"Impossible!" he declared politely. "Joe on his beam ends! Joe in the dumps—never!"

"True as possible, sir—I was desperate," repeated Joe, his face grave for that moment.

"Well, well, perhaps so. I'm forgetting. I was young like you when I was down. Young fellows make light of such matters. It's as well, perhaps, or the world wouldn't go along half so easily. But I'd never have thought it, Joe. You never said a word to me; you look so jolly."

No one would have denied the fact. Joe Gresson looked what he was, a handsome, jovial fellow of twenty-seven. Fair and tall, and broader than his uncle, he had deep-set eyes which gave to his smiling face an air of cleverness. And the young fellow was undoubtedly clever. An engineer by profession, he had graduated at Cambridge, had passed through the shops, the drawing office, and other departments of one of the biggest engineering concerns in England, and had finally struck out a line for himself. He had been experimenting for the past four years.

"What's the good of being miserable because things don't go right, Uncle?" he said with a smile. "I've told you how I took up engineering. Well, I thought I had a good idea. I left the shops at Barrow and worked on my own. Thanks to the few thousands I possessed I was able to carry out some important experiments."

"Ah, my boy! Well, you succeeded?"

"Yes and no; I went so far with the work that I was sure that success was possible. Then there was an accident. The whole affair was wrecked, and I woke up to find myself without funds and in a terrible condition of despair."

"On your beam ends, in fact—well, like me," said Mr. Andrew. "I'll tell you about myself; then you'll give your yarn. I'll have to hear what this work was. But my tale don't take long. Let's step up and down again and I'll give it to you. Let's see—yes, I was a fiery, unmanageable young idiot."

"Never!" interjected Joe.

"Like many other young fellows," proceeded Andrew, as if he had not been interrupted. "I bluntly refused the post which my father offered me, and cut away from home. I went to Canada, worked my way out aboard the steamer, a cockleshell in those days, and half starved for the next few months, for it was in the winter and there was no work to be had. But I learned something. In the six months which followed my landing I acted as a cook's boy, a porter, a fireman, and a clerk in a grocery store. That's where I had my eyes opened. The country was opening up. I had saved a few dollars. I set up a store of my own in one of the nearest settlements, a mere hut knocked together with the help of a hammer and some nails. But it paid. I saved all along. I built a real brick house, and the sales went up like wildfire. Then I chose a manager and opened up a second store away in the nearest settlement. It went on after that almost by itself. I got to own a hundred stores. I bought property right and left. Then I sold out. Now I'm merely an idler, come home to take a long look round. On my beam ends one day, you see; up and prosperous in the years that followed. Now, my boy, let's hear your yarn. Hallo, what's the excitement? People are crushing over to the far side of the ship."

The two had been so engaged in conversation that they had not noticed the exodus of the other passengers, and now awoke to find themselves the only tenants of that side of the deck. Arm in arm still they hurried round the long deck cabin to join their fellow passengers. They found them massed together on the starboard side, crushing towards the rails, and for the most part with their eyes cast aloft.

"Wonderful! Marvellous! Extraordinary!" were some of the remarks they overheard, emanating from the English people present. From the many foreigners there came guttural cries of delight and shouts almost of triumph.

"What is it? What's the fuss?" asked Mr. Andrew eagerly, craning his head and looking aloft. "I can see nothing to cause such excitement."

"Nothing, mein Herr! Is that nothing—no?" asked a stumpy little passenger against whom Andrew was leaning, twisting his portly frame round with an effort. He shot a short, plump arm above his head, and held a stumpy finger aloft. "Nothing?" he asked indignantly. "You call that nothing at all, mein Herr? It is marvellous! It is magnificent!"

"But—but, what is? I—I—er—beg your pardon," said Andrew politely, "but really I can't——"

"Look, Uncle," cried Joe sharply, pointing upwards himself. "It's a little hard to see perhaps. That's what they aim at, of course. But there's an airship there—a Zeppelin."

"Ah!" gasped Andrew, while the stumpy little foreigner, who had now contrived to twist himself entirely round, stared angrily at him. Then a broad, beaming smile of pride seamed his face, a fat, good-natured face to be sure, while the light of recognition danced in his eyes.

"Ah! Mr. Andrew Provost," he exclaimed in thick but urbane tones. "We have met again. This is fortunate. But you see now; you see the German triumph. You see the Zeppelin with which they have conquered the air. Ah, it is magnificent!"

Andrew had scarcely time to shake his hand and recognize this plump little person. He was vastly impressed at the sight some four thousand feet above him, and away to the left. He could have shouted with delight himself. The object, in fact, claimed his whole attention.

"A Zeppelin!" he cried. "A real Zeppelin! One of Germany's air dreadnoughts—magnificent!"

It was magnificent. Seldom yet have Englishmen had the opportunity of seeing one of those leviathans of the air. At a period when balloons have become common objects in the sky, when the whole world almost has become accustomed to aeroplanes scooping through the air, the people of most countries are still strangers to the sight of a mighty airship swimming in space. And there was one, a long, sinuous hull of neutral colour, so that even in broad daylight it was not too easily visible, floating horizontally in the sky, like some gigantic cigar, while fore and aft, immediately beneath the hull, were two boat-shaped objects, a little darker than the mass above supporting them. There was the dull hum of machinery too.

"Moving along slowly," gasped Andrew, still wonderstruck at such a sight. "What's she doing?"

"Finishing a continuous run of twenty-four hours and more," declared the little stranger, whom we will now introduce as Mr. Carl Reitberg. "Just showing us how fresh she is, and how easy the task has been," he cried in tones of the utmost pride. "See! She has more to show us. She has taken in fuel from the steamer yonder, and could sail again for another twenty-four hours. But she wishes to experiment with her bombs. Look, mein Herr! There is a float down below her. She will pulverize it. She will smash it. She will drop a bomb plumb into it, and, piff! it is gone. That, mein Herr, is the work of the latest Zeppelin." Perhaps a thousand passengers crowded the rails and watched the monster of the air, and it was as Mr. Reitberg had so proudly announced. The Zeppelin was manœuvring away from the Hamburg-Amerika liner. Ahead of her, some five miles to the east, was a dot upon the ocean. Andrew swung his glasses to his eyes and fixed them upon that object.

"A float of some sort—yes," he said. "She is motoring towards it. Then she will stop above it."

"No—not at all," declared Mr. Reitberg. "She will continue at her fastest pace. Yet she will strike it. Watch. See—ah! Did I not say so? It is marvellous! There!"

Was it imagination? Andrew fancied he saw a small, dark object fall from one of the boat-shaped cars beneath the long Zeppelin. In a twinkling he swung his glasses down upon the float half-immersed in the sea below. Then a loud detonation reached his ears, while the float disappeared miraculously, the sea being churned up and splashed all about it. Nor was that all. There came from the ship above a succession of sharp reports, while bullets of large size struck the sea immediately over the spot where the float had been. Then another object dropped from the airship. It burst into flames within two hundred feet of leaving the hand which had projected it, and almost at once sent out a vast, spreading mass of dense smoke, that spread and spread and spread till the sky was obscured, till the airship was utterly hidden.

Mr. Carl Reitberg chuckled aloud, and danced with delight.

"Magnificent! Cunning! The latest thing!" he declared. "You see the reason, Mr. Provost? No; then I will tell you. The ship, the air dreadnought, you understand, discovers an enemy's ship, or shall we say the enemy's war harbour, or arsenal, or magazine, or what you will? She sails above it. She drops a bomb. Then, piff! the thing is done. The ship is destroyed; the harbour is wrecked; the magazine explodes. Men rush to and fro in panic—those who are left. For some are poisoned. Yes, some die not from the effects of the explosion, but because the airship has dropped also chemical bombs which burst and spread poisonous fumes everywhere. But men are left, we will allow. There are gunners there. They rush to the aerial guns. They load them; they attempt to take aim. But—where is the ship? Gone? No—but where? The sky is all smoke. There is no sign of her. She is invisible. *Nicht wahr?* It is too late; all the damage is done. The Zeppelin escapes to wreck more ships, more harbours, more magazines."

He puffed out his stout little chest, gazed aloft at the dense and spreading cloud of smoke, and waved his hands excitedly.

"It is magnificent!" he repeated for perhaps the tenth time. "It is a triumph! None can approach it. Many have watched and scorned the idea. Count Zeppelin has persevered. Germany has backed his efforts, and now, *voila!*— there is the result. Triumph! The conquest of the air. Mastery of the upper element; with none to gainsay us."

"But—but there are limits to the power of these ships," suggested Andrew, his words almost faltering. "There are limits to their range of travel."

Mr. Carl Reitberg put one fat finger artfully to the side of his nose. It was perhaps a little peculiarity he had picked up in England, for we hasten to explain that he was cosmopolitan. Carl Reitberg had spent many of his fifty-three years in South Africa. There he had enjoyed the protection of the Union Jack. He had a house in London now, and one also at Brighton. It may be said that he had made his fortune, thanks to his own astuteness and the opportunities given him by our British colonies. But he was not English. He was not entirely German. He belonged to the world. One day he was resident in Berlin, a second found him in London or in Brighton, while as likely as not the following weeks saw him parading the Champs Élysées in Paris, the Boulevards of Buenos Ayres, the streets of Mexico, or Broadway, New York. In fact, and in short, he was cosmopolitan.

"Limits, mein Herr!" he cried, still in those tones of pride, still dancing on his toes. "None! That ship can sail continuously over a thousand miles. Her wireless telegraph will reach within a hundred miles of that distance. She can manœuvre easily over a ship at sea and take in further supplies. She is, in short, a cruiser. Do you wish to sail in luxury to St. Petersburg? Hire, then, a Zeppelin. Do you desire to escape *mal de mer*? Call for one of these huge airships and sail for London. Do you fancy the conquest of some island kingdom? Mr. Provost, you are rich; buy one of the air dreadnoughts and blow your enemies sky high."

Andrew took his eyes from the spreading cloud of smoke overhead and glanced at the excited orbs of the little fellow. Then he looked at his nephew. And we tell but the truth when we say that his own eyes were troubled.

"It is magnificent, but it is terrible," he said slowly. "Terrible for those who have no aerial dreadnoughts. Yes, terrible. Their danger is greater than I could ever have imagined. And you say that these Zeppelins stand alone. There are no others?"

"None. But wait. Yes, there are others, also German. There are the Parseval, the semi-rigid ships of the air," said Mr. Reitberg with a truculent smile. "There are also the Gross ships; but the Zeppelins are infinitely superior. Elsewhere there are none. France, what are her ships? Russia, poof! we will not waste breath in discussing them. England—mein Herr, she has the Alpha, the Beta, and the Gamma, mere toy airships. They do not count."

There was a wide smile on his face now. Andrew winced at his words; there were even beads of perspiration on his forehead, while lines had knit themselves across his brow.

"You say that England has no such ships. Then she can build them, must build them," he said.

"Must—yes! But can she? Impossible!" Mr. Carl Reitberg looked his pity. "Impossible!" he repeated, while Andrew wiped his perspiring brow.

"I think not—hardly impossible, mein Herr," came in quiet tones from Joe, a silent witness of all that had been passing.

"Eh! Not impossible? You think that a bigger Gamma would suffice? You think that England could build such a ship as this Zeppelin without experiment, without numerous failures—all, we will say, within a year?"

"I am sure."

"Sure! You joke. The thing cannot be done; I know England. Men are clever there, but they have not studied these airships: they are ignorant."

"Not quite—I disagree. In six months, in three, perhaps, such a ship as sails above us could be erected; but better, with more power, a wider range, and a greater capacity for destruction."

Mr. Carl Reitberg gasped; he pulled an elegant silk handkerchief from his pocket and mopped his forehead. He was beginning to get annoyed with the calm, not to say idiotic, assurance of this young man. He looked Joe Gresson superciliously up and down, and then smiled urbanely.

"You are young," he said. "When you arrive at my age you will see your error. I, who know, say that such a thing is impossible."

"And I, Herr Reitberg, while thanking you, say that it can be done. It has been done, on a smaller scale. To-morrow, or let us say within three months, England could possess an aerial dreadnought superior to any Zeppelin. I am positive."

The smile left Mr. Reitberg's face. He looked at Joe as if he thought him mad. As for Andrew, at first he had watched his nephew with every sign of surprise, if not of disapproval. But now he smacked him on the back encouragingly.

"Bravo, Joe!" he cried. "Stick to your guns. You say England could build such a ship. Well, she's tried?"

"Yes; the Admiralty tried through their contractors, and failed."

"Ah, failed, yes!" lisped Mr. Reitberg. "So did Zeppelin. But he carried on his experiments; he succeeded. Your people did no more."

"Others took on the work."

Joe returned the looks of his two companions firmly. "And succeeded," he added.

"Who? You?" demanded Andrew eagerly.

"Yes; I did."

"Then I'd back you to do as you say. You declare that you could erect such a ship as we have just lost sight of, but better, with greater powers of movement, with greater range?"

"Certainly."

"Then why has mein Herr not done so?" asked Mr. Reitberg, with a lift of his eyebrows and outspread hands. He was the essence, in fact, of polite incredulity.

"I did on a small scale; then funds failed."

"Ah, yes! they always do, fortunately, mein Herr. Then your experiments are ended. This ship is but a creation of your brain. It must remain so; for funds are done with."

There was sarcasm in the voice. Andrew Provost resented the tone. He had never liked Mr. Reitberg overmuch, though they had met in more than one country and had dined together frequently. Besides, it roused his gorge to feel that here was an example of British ineptitude. He knew his nephew well enough by now, knew him to be a young man worth trusting. If he said he could do this thing, then he could.

"By Jingo, I'll give him the opportunity!" he cried. "Joe, how much'd it cost?"

"One hundred thousand pounds, perhaps. Not more; very likely a great deal less."

"And within three months? Well, let us say, within six months?" asked Mr. Reitberg incredulously. "Impossible! The money would be wasted. A ship be built in that time, by men inexperienced in such work, a ship, moreover, of almost unlimited range! You are dreaming, sir!"

Joe Gresson might have been excused if he had lost his temper. Instead, he smiled at the little foreigner. "I am all seriousness," he said. "If I had the means I would erect this ship, and prove her capacity to you. She would sail where you wished; no part of the earth would be too far for her."

"And I back him up in what he says. What this young fellow cares to declare as in his power I feel is not impossible. Now, Mr. Reitberg," cried Andrew with no little warmth, "I'll stand by him."

Mr. Reitberg did nothing in a hurry. It was his very slowness which had sometimes proved his success. But this discussion irritated him. He liked to feel that the Zeppelin was beyond all attempts at imitation. He considered that Joe was mad, or suffering from too great a shock of confidence. In any case, it seemed to him that what he described as possible was hopelessly out of the question. He tucked his short neck deep into his collar, screwed his head on one side, and then began to smile urbanely.

"Well, well," he said at last. "One hundred thousand pounds. What is it to me, or to you, Mr. Provost? Build this airship. Prove her to be better than a Zeppelin. Sail her round the world and then return to England. If you do all this, say within nine months of this date, then I return the cost of the venture. Is that a bargain?"

"Done!" shouted Andrew. "I'll back the boy. I'll find the money for him. If we succeed within nine months, then the loss is yours. The ship remains ours, while you pay for it. Let us step into the cabin. We'll draft out a form of agreement. When that's signed we'll set to in earnest."

It took but a half-hour to complete this necessary preliminary, so that when they returned on deck again the huge cloud of smoke had disappeared, while the Zeppelin was again in sight, a mere speck in the distance.

"Like that, but better, faster, stronger, with greater range," said Andrew, pointing up at her.

"Quite so—the impossible!" smiled Mr. Reitberg. "Do not blame me if you fail, Mr. Provost. I hate taking other people's money, or running anyone into large expense. Good luck to you!"

They shook hands on leaving the steamer at Southampton and parted. Joe and his uncle took train for London, and that same evening found them seated before the window of their private room at the hotel quietly discussing the exciting future before them.

CHAPTER II

Andrew Provost's Resolution

Andrew Provost was not the man to shirk his liabilities, or to shrink from an undertaking however difficult it might appear, and however impetuous he may have been in his decision.

"No, siree," he exclaimed, sipping his after-dinner coffee, and then pulling at a big cigar. "No, my boy, I ain't the one to back out, you bet. That fellow Reitberg got my monkey up with his sneers and his crows about those German Zeppelins. Boy and man I've lived under the Union Jack, and what folks can do elsewhere, why, they can do 'em as well where I've lived. Fire in at that agreement, Joe."

For the moment he had allowed a decided Yankee drawl to betray the country from which he had so recently come, for in Canada they speak much as they do in America, though the drawl and the accent are not so accentuated. It showed that Andrew was stirred. In moments of excitement he always developed a drawl; but if excited, he was also practical.

"Read that document, Joe?" he asked again. "Mind you, I admit that there are many of my old friends who would call me a fool over this business."

"Impossible, Uncle!" his nephew interrupted.

"Fiddlesticks, my boy! No offence, mind; but look at this matter squarely. How do we stand? It's like this. We're aboard a Hamburg-Amerika liner. We see a Zeppelin, and get a fine display, all free and for nothing. We run up against a fat little fellow named Reitberg, who's neither German nor English, nor anything in particular. Anyway, he's made his money like me under the Union Jack. Well, now, he crows about that ship, says there's not another nation could build one. Gets riled too, when you say that England could, that you yourself could. Shows plainly, though with some amount of politeness, that he don't believe you, and then gets to crowing again. Isn't that enough to put up a Britisher's back? Eh?"

"Well, it wasn't very pleasant certainly, rather riling. Made one wince."

"Wince! Squirm! Look here, Joe, I never liked being beaten. If I did I'd never have got to the position I have. I'd have been still running that small store away outside Toronto, with its tin roof and its walls tintacked together. It's because I didn't like being beaten that I'm not there. And I don't like to think that

Britishers are beaten. When you said that you could build an airship better than a Zeppelin I believed you."

"Awfully kind of you, too, Uncle," Joe declared, gratitude lending unusual warmth to his tones.

"It *was* mighty kind," came the half-smiling answer. "Then and there I let myself into an expenditure of a hundred thousand pounds, and all because I couldn't stand that fellow Reitberg's crowing, and, from a mighty long experience, had confidence in my own countrymen. You'd said that you could do it—that was enough for me. But it's very small reason for such an expenditure when you come to look plainly at it. No offence, Joe, mind that. You're my nephew; I've heard big things about you, and if you've said you can succeed, why you shall. Your Uncle Andrew'll help you."

They shook hands on it, exchanging a firm grip. But it must be allowed that Andrew was really only putting the true facts before his nephew. After all, what hard-headed business man—and Andrew was that if anything—would promise such a huge sum simply because a nephew had declared that he could build a ship of similar class to a Zeppelin, that is, one lighter than air, but more powerful, more perfect, in every way more desirable? Why, the fat, comfortable-looking Mr. Reitberg was even then detailing the incident to a few of his cronies who were seated in the smoking-room of his luxurious town house. There were five of them present, none of whom would again see a fiftieth birthday, comfortable-looking gentlemen, robustly built, running to fat if we were asked for a concise description. They discussed the matter in English, though all betrayed some accent. In fact, they had without exception been foreigners, only three at least were naturalized Englishmen.

"It made me laugh afterwards," declared Mr. Reitberg, sitting up, and withdrawing his cigar from between a pair of short, stumpy, fat fingers. "You've met Andrew Provost?"

They had: all nodded. "From Canada—stores," said Mr. Julius Veldtheim laconically. "Rich man—very."

"Said to be one of the wealthiest," added Mr. Herman Schloss, puffing a cloud of smoke in the direction of the table bearing decanters and glasses.

"Has a reputation for sagacity. Buys heavily from us," ventured a third, whose name is of no consequence.

"And yet laid himself open to an expenditure of a hundred thousand pounds—one hundred thousand pounds, gentlemen, on the word of a young nephew who, whatever his merits, won't languish for want of self-confidence."

"Ah! How? Why? He had a reason. Provost always has a reason. He's sharp."

The questioner looked languidly across at Mr. Reitberg, and smiled as that complacent gentleman smiled. He chuckled even. "I'll tell you," he said, turning to them all. "There was a Zeppelin overheard as we crossed from Hamburg. Well, its manœuvring was wonderful. Provost was amazed. He began to think that he would feel queer in this country if one were to sail overhead. You see, this one dropped bombs, so we were able to watch the actual thing that will occur in war. It frightened Provost. He wondered why they hadn't any here. I told him."

"Ah! Why?"

"Because they can't build 'em. No one can."

"You are sure?" asked Mr. Veldtheim.

"Positive; I said so plainly. Provost got quite hot at the news. But his nephew declared he could build one, that he had done so. Well, you know, I could see what it was. I smiled; the young fellow's confidence was really too pronounced. But Provost was too riled to notice. 'He says he can build one. Then he can and will,' he sings out. 'I'll pay.'"

"Ah! One hundred thousand pounds," lisped Mr. Veldtheim.

"Yes, one hundred thousand pounds. 'You'll lose it all,' I told him, or rather, I intimated that as politely as was possible. 'You'll never succeed. I'm so positive, that if you do, and build a ship which can sail round the world, all within nine months of this, why, I'll pay the bill.'"

"Bravo!" cried Mr. Veldtheim. "Your money's safe. Zeppelins aren't built in nine months, even by those who know all about 'em."

That seemed to be the general opinion of the company present. In fact, one and all looking at the matter from their own point of view considered that Andrew Provost had been guilty of a species of madness.

"Better by far hand his nephew a handsome cheque and have done with the matter," observed Mr. Veldtheim. "It'd be easier and cheaper."

But, as we have intimated already, Andrew Provost was made of stubborn material. Also, he had seen sufficient of Joe during their travels on the Continent since his coming from Canada to assure him that he was not overstocked with confidence. Or rather, to assure him that he was a clever, painstaking fellow, who seldom declared his powers, but who, when induced to do so, never overshot the mark. Consequently, when he said that Mr. Reitberg was misinformed, Andrew Provost believed him. But a statement was one thing; hard facts another.

"Just get to and read that agreement between Reitberg and myself," he said again. "Then tell me all about this ship of yours. Recollect, I've never seen it, nor heard of it either."

"Pardon, you've heard of it," said Joe shortly.

"Eh, heard of it? Come!"

"A year ago. There was a scare in England," Joe reminded him. "There was even an airship scare in Germany. The papers were full of reports. Brilliant lights had been seen in the sky. The noise of aerial motors was heard. It was feared in England that a foreign spy was manœuvring over our magazines and arsenals."

Andrew looked sharply at his nephew over the rim of his cup. "Airship scare? Yes, I remember; the papers in Canada were full of it—well?"

"That was my ship. People said that a mistake had been made; that folks had imagined the ship. They said the same in Germany. But it wasn't imagination: it was a real ship, the one I had built."

"And—and what became of it?" gasped Andrew—for this was news—"Why didn't you sell it to the War Office authorities?"

Joe smiled. "War Office authorities! Know 'em?" he asked.

"Never met them—why?"

"They're too slow for words," declared Joe, laughing. "I'll tell you about them. I went there, to the War Office. I got lost in the place, it's so vast and has such huge lengths of corridor. And I'm inclined to believe that the folks who work there get lost. Anyway, they couldn't for an hour or more direct me to the department likely to have some knowledge of airships. But I reached it at last and told my tale."

"Ah! You got home. Then, what happened! They sent right off to investigate."

"The official who interviewed me, and who had, I imagine, as much knowledge of airships as I have of turnips, informed me that he was vastly interested and would put the matter before the authorities and communicate with me. I left my address; I waited; I got tired of waiting."

"What! How many days?"

"Six weeks. I wrote reminding them of my visit."

"Gosh! Six weeks! Then, what happened?"

"They sent a formal acknowledgment—the matter was having their consideration."

Andrew Provost leaped from his chair and stood facing Joe, biting his cigar fiercely. "You mean to tell me that that's the treatment you received? That I might expect the same to-morrow if I went to the War Office with a brilliant invention?" he demanded hotly. "Do you mean to say that I'd as likely as not be interviewed by a fellow who knew next to nothing about the matter, and that weeks would elapse before I heard from 'em again, and then only after sending 'em a reminder?"

Joe laughed. "That was my experience," he said. "I dare say others meet with the same. Tantalizing, eh, Uncle?"

"Tantalizing be hanged! If that's the sort of thing that happens, then the sooner the crowd inside that office is hauled out and booted the better. Guess live men are wanted—folks who can earn their pay—not dolls and dullards. But let's leave 'em. Tell me about the ship—go on."

"She was wrecked; a violent gale sprang up."

"Ah! Usual thing. That's the weak part about those Zeppelins," said Andrew. "They're unmanageable in a wind. A half-dozen and more of them have been wrecked; so you suffered in the same way."

"No! The gale wrecked my hangar; it was flimsily put together. That was the fault of having small funds. As to Zeppelins, I know that they have that particular weakness. Wait till you see my designs. I'm not afraid of a gale, and can manœuvre into my hangar when gusts are blowing at fifty miles an hour. Fact, Uncle! You'll see when we've finished."

Andrew Provost strode backwards and forwards before the wide-open window of the hotel. He was thinking deeply, and more than once he cast a shrewd, sharp glance at his nephew. This long-headed man was a little uneasy. And who can blame him? For, in the first place, solely on the strength of Joe's assertion, and because Mr. Reitberg had riled him, he had taken up a challenge. And now he heard his nephew declare that a fifty-mile gale was of no consequence, though to a Zeppelin airship it would prove easily disastrous. Was Joe romancing? Or was he so carried away by this work of his that his imagination made successes where they did not exist?

"No; certainly not. He looks and is clever. If he says gusts don't matter, they don't," thought Andrew, after another sharp look at his nephew. "What appears difficult to believe may very well be simple when one has seen his designs. Here, Joe," he cried. "We get drifting on; do read that document, then show me your plans. I'll pay a cheque for ten thousand pounds into your account to-morrow, and then you'll be able to go ahead. Now, the document."

Joe picked it up from the table on which it was resting. Unfolding the sheet, he disclosed at the top the arms of the Hamburg-Amerika Steamship Company, and in the right-hand corner the name of the ship they had so recently left. The date was scrawled in a firm hand beneath it, and then there appeared the following words: "I, Andrew Provost, of Park St., Toronto, Canada, and of 29 Fenchurch St., London, England, guarantee to build with the help of my nephew, Joseph Gresson, and others whom I may appoint, an airship similar to the well-known Zeppelin; that is to say, when inflated with gas the said ship shall be lighter than air. It shall be capable of lifting not less than thirty tons, of progressing against a wind at more than sixty miles an hour, and of traversing the world in any direction, keeping in the air for that purpose as long as shall be necessary, though she may be allowed to descend to the land for necessary supplies, renewals, and repairs. Should I succeed with the help abovementioned in building a ship capable of all this, and of circling the world, and should that voyage be completed within nine months of this date, then Carl Eugene Reitberg, of 42 Park Lane, London, England, guarantees to pay the full cost of the building of the said ship, and of her voyage, but not exceeding in all one hundred thousand pounds. It is further agreed that a special form of passport shall be obtained from the Foreign Office, and that the same having been initialled by the various authorities of the countries over which the ship may pass in her voyage shall be held to be proof of her voyage."

"Clear as crystal. And you can do it?" asked Andrew.

"Certainly."

"Then let's have the designs. How does your ship beat the Zeppelin? What's she made of? Tell me everything; remember I'm ignorant. I just know that an aeroplane is a heavier-than-air machine, and a Zepplin's a lighter-than-air; that is, once she's inflated with gas. Fire away. I'm dying to get in at the actual building."

Joe was a practical young fellow, and was not to be hastened. He unlocked a leather bag lying near his feet and abstracted a sheet of glistening paper. Spreading it out on the table, he showed his uncle a big detail drawing of the machine he proposed to construct.

"It's not easy to follow the outline here," he said. "Wait till the ship's finished. But you can see this much. She's long and pointed at either end, and looks like a flattened cigar. That's how she differs from the Zeppelins. She's built very flat, and extends on either side till the top and bottom half come together in what may be called a lateral keel."

"Why? Where's the reason?"

"To protect her against gusts of wind and gales. A Zeppelin can't escape. Every breath plays on her big lateral bulk. In my ship the wind strikes a thin keel on whichever side it comes, is divided there, and passes over and under the ship, sliding as it were upwards and downwards away from the gradually-sloping surfaces which lead from those keels. In fact, the ship is almost as flat as a tortoise, and as wide comparatively, though she's very much longer."

"And—and this flattening of the ship makes her laugh at gales?" asked Andrew, staring at the plans before him.

"Certainly—her shape, and other fittings. Now, let's return to the Zeppelin. It's a huge framework of aluminium, built very light and covered with a material of neutral tint."

"Which holds the necessary gas."

"No, Uncle. Which merely covers the aluminium skeleton. Inside the frame there are twenty or more balloonettes, inflated with gas. Thus if one bursts, or two, or more even, the ship still floats."

"Canny that! Smart!" declared Andrew. "Well, yours? It's a similar framework, I suppose? The same balloonettes? Where does the difference come?"

Joe bent again to his bag and produced a parcel, which he rapidly opened. He drew from the interior a sheet of shining material, which might have been glass but for the fact that it was folded half a dozen times. Placing it on the table, this sheet opened to its full capacity as soon as the weight of his fingers was removed.

"Flexible and elastic, you see, Uncle," said Joe. "And yet not extensible. See— it does not stretch. Transparent, of course—one of its least advantages—but yet one of great value in the construction of an airship."

"What! You don't mean to tell me you build the ship of that? How? What part does it form? I—look here, Joe, you're romancing."

Joe smiled; his deep-sunk eyes took on the clever expression, to which his uncle had become familiar. He placed two long objects on the table, and stood leaning the tips of his strong fingers upon them. He might have been a lecturer, and his uncle a student about to absorb his wisdom. As for the objects he had placed on the table, one was a long piece of the same transparent material, an eighth of an inch thick, perhaps, two inches wide before it was bent, and now bent all the way down its length into a right angle. In fact, composed of iron it would be known simply as "angle iron". The other object was a tube, perhaps half an inch in diameter, two feet in length, and of thinner material. Both were transparent, and exceedingly light in weight, as Andrew assured himself instantly.

"Go on," he said huskily. "What is the stuff? Not talc—that I can tell easily. Not celluloid either—you'd never be such a fool as to build a ship of such a highly inflammable material. That stuff's lighter, also. What is it?"

But Joe was not yet to be persuaded into an answer. He spread the thin transparent sheet out, caught the four corners, and taking a jug of water, poured some of the contents into the centre of the sheet. Not a drop penetrated it. Joe demonstrated the fact quietly and without show of haste. Then he stepped to the window and cast the water out. A moment later he was striking a match.

"Stop! Stop! How do I know that it isn't like celluloid?" cried Andrew in some alarm. "Supposing it fires. Supposing there's an explosion."

Joe smiled. "It won't," he said curtly. "Look there."

The flame was licking round one of the corners of this thin sheet of material. It blackened the surface above, while that below, immersed in the flame, gradually changed colour. It became a dull red, then got redder and redder till it was glowing. Slowly it changed its form, the corner curled up into a globule. The latter separated itself from the sheet and tumbled on to the glass-topped table, where it broke into a number of smaller drops.

"Glass! No—too light by far. Not celluloid. Not talc. Then what is it?" demanded Andrew impatiently, taking the various articles and examining them. "Why, this angle piece is strong—as strong as aluminium!" he cried.

"Stronger—stronger and tougher," asserted Joe. "You can bend it; it's flexible. You can bend it double, and still it comes back to its original formation. Aluminium would crack at once; even steel would. Now, try the tube. See, it kinks when you bend it, though it requires some strength to do that. Now, set it on its end on the floor; we'll put a book on the top end. Sit on the book, Uncle."

Andrew did so—gingerly it must be confessed—for this transparent tube with its small diameter and its walls less than an eighth of an inch in thickness looked as if it would at once succumb to his avoirdupois. But it did not. He sat boldly upon the book now. He balanced himself upon the frail support and jerked his feet from the ground.

"Jingo!" he cried. "What in thunder is the stuff? It's strong, strong as possible. Surprisingly powerful stuff. It bends if you use sufficient force, yet doesn't break. It's tough; you've shown me that, for a knife edge bites into it with difficulty. Then it softens and melts at a fairly high temperature, proving that it can be easily treated and moulded. Well?"

"I call it celludine," said Joe, not without some trace of pride in his tuneful voice." I dropped upon the stuff quite by accident, for at the 'Varsity' I was fond of working in a laboratory. Asbestos enters into its composition, that I can tell you. It is easily manufactured, the materials of which it is composed are inexpensive. It can be rolled into plates and bars and drawn into tubes. Better than all, perhaps, when bars and tubes and angle pieces are being built into a framework rivet holes can be punched with the simplest pneumatic tool, while the joins and the rivets can be instantly and securely welded together with an electric heating iron. Thus every joint becomes a solid piece."

Andrew wiped his forehead—this was something—he even chuckled.

"Reitberg'd have fits," he laughed. "He'd be beginning to get anxious about that money if he heard what you were saying. But get along. This stuffs fine. I can see that, and I'm quite a child in such matters."

"Then it is hardly necessary for me to explain that I build my framework of this celludine. That frame is wonderfully strong, stronger a great deal than if composed of aluminium, and constructed far more rapidly and at less cost. It has another advantage Zeppelins have broken up before now, simply because certain portions of their frames have fractured under great strain. With this material the flexibility is such that the frame gives before a strain, grudgingly it is true, but gives without receiving damage, and instantly returns to its former shape once the strain is removed. Now let us proceed. I cover the frame with the same material. It is waterproof and gas-proof. Note that, Uncle. I fashion partitions of the same material. Thus my balloonettes are formed. There is no need for the twenty and more balloonettes. All that weight is removed. There are merely the partitions and the outer covering, and since celludine is the lightest material of any that I have yet discovered, you can follow that here I have a material with which I can make a ship at once lighter than a Zeppelin, though of equal size, while it is stronger and more flexible. Add the important fact that the whole thing is transparent."

"Eh? Why? Where does the advantage come?"

It was natural, perhaps, that Andrew should not follow his reasoning so quickly.

"Imagine the ship to be inflated and in the air," said Joe. "Well, gas is transparent. So's the framework of the ship. She is invisible almost, except for engines and gear of a similar description."

This time his uncle mopped his forehead busily. He was glad that he had taken up that challenge. He was beginning to hope that some day it might be his turn to gloat over Mr. Reitberg. He could even conjure up the huge airship which Joe Gresson would build. Facts were in his case far easier of digestion than any amount of theorizing, and here his nephew was providing him with facts. As a practical man Andrew could decide that this celludine was essentially suitable for the building of a vessel to sail the air. Now he could realize better than ever that success was possible. But a few hours ago he had been content to take Joe's mere word for it. His own common sense now supported that belief. He drew in a series of deep breaths, while he handled the samples before him. Unconsciously it seemed his hand sought his handkerchief and he mopped his fevered brow. Then he drew a cheque book from an inner pocket, seated himself at a desk, and took up a pen.

"Pay Joseph Gresson ten thousand pounds," he wrote, and attached his signature.

"There," he said, with a beaming smile, smacking his nephew heartily on the back, "get to at the work, Joe. Call for more when you want it. Don't stint yourself; spend freely if necessary, for there's no time to waste. We've got to be up and doing. I'll teach Mr. Reitberg to have a better respect for Britishers. What others can do, we can. Gosh! We'll have that ship sailing before he's finished chuckling at our helplessness."

We leave him then for the moment, filled to the brim with enthusiasm, while we step aside to introduce a person of no little importance, namely, Mr. Midshipman Hamshaw, R.N., Dick Hamshaw, lately out of Dartmouth Naval College, and already known by officers and men as simple and plain Dicky.

CHAPTER III

Dicky Hamshaw, Midshipman

"Of all the little bantams 'e's it," quoth Able Seaman Hawkins of H.M.S. *Inflexible* in a deep, hoarse whisper, leaning over the tiller of the steam pinnace he was steering to place his thick lips close to the huge ear of his comrade. "That 'ere shaver's just it all the time and no mistake about it."

A long tongue of flame shooting out through the stumpy funnel of the vessel at that precise moment lit up the afterpart, disclosing the fact that Seaman Hawkins's face was divided by an expansive grin, while Able Seaman Hurst's rugged and none-too-handsome features seemed to be made up mostly of two rows of irregular teeth. The short stem of an extremely black pipe was gripped between those same teeth, while smoke was issuing from the nostrils. But a second later the pipe was dragged from its position and found its way with extreme rapidity into a pocket.

"Stop that talking, men! One can't hear. Silence aft!"

The command came in quick, decisive tones, and yet in a voice that betrayed the youth of the officer. For Dicky Hamshaw was young, painfully young, we must admit. When he stepped the decks of His Majesty's battleships no one deplored that fact more than Mr. Midshipman Hamshaw. It was a defect which time would undoubtedly eradicate, but for the moment it was annoying, to say the least of it. For ever on the faces of the tars beneath his immediate command there lurked a queer demureness, an indefinite something which he could never actually fathom, but which told him as plainly as words that he was almost an object of amusement. Not of ridicule, let us explain. No other officer's orders were obeyed more smartly than those of Mr. Midshipman Hamshaw, while your British tar is far too jealous of his good name to ridicule an officer, even if such a thing were not decidedly contrary to discipline. No; Dicky Hamshaw was very young, and looked younger than his seventeen and a half years. Not a hair yet adorned his upper lip, and there was not even a suspicious down budding from the square chin of which he boasted. He was merely disgustingly young in appearance, tall and slim and active, and full of a dash and jollity which had long since captivated the tars.

"Just it—nothing more," repeated Hawkins in a hoarse whisper to Hurst. "A bantam that's full of fight, and don't you make no mistake about it."

Precisely what "it" meant on this occasion the burly Hawkins did not stoop to explain, and apparently Hurst needed no enlightenment. He nodded, expanded his capacious jaws again, and then slowly introduced the stem of his clay between his strong teeth.

"Stop that smoking aft! There's someone smoking."

Once more the order rang out crisp and clear, and in those very juvenile tones. Let us say at once that it was Dick's boyish voice, perhaps more than his youthful appearance, which excited the smiles of his men. But in any case the crisp tones meant business. Hurst slid his pipe back into its receptacle with alacrity and grimaced through the gloom at his comrade.

"And 'e's got a nose," he ventured to Hawkins when a few moments had elapsed. "Here are we away aft, and you'd have said as all the smoke was blowed clear away behind us. But Dicky's got a nose for it. Blest if he couldn't tell you what 'bacca it was. Not ship's I can tell you, mate, but a bit of cake bought ashore at a place I knows of. What's he up to?"

"Keep her away a point to starboard," suddenly came from the midshipman. "That'll do. Hold her so and keep her steady on that course. I fancy we must be somewhere near the spot Anyone hear anything?"

"Nothing, sir?" came from Hurst, while Hawkins opened his thick lips to cry "Aye! aye! sir," in recognition of the order given him. "Steady it is, sir. Fancied I heard a cry away over here a minute or more ago, but I ain't sure. There's no sayin'."

"Then keep your ears open, men, and—Hawkins."

"Aye, aye, sir."

"As we're away from the ship and it's dark I've no particular objection to Hurst's smoking. All you men can smoke; but please don't forget to listen carefully."

Had it not been dark expansive grins could have been seen on the faces of the half-dozen tars manning this steam pinnace. For here was a privilege granted without the asking, and one, too, which every one of the men could fully appreciate. It was just one of those thoughtful actions for which Dicky had become almost famous since he became a full-fledged midshipman, and which added so much to his popularity. As for Hurst, the mention of his own name caused him to bring one broad palm with a resounding smack against his thigh. Hawkins could hear him gurgling, and then listened to his low-toned whisper.

"Did you hear that? Spotted who was smoking. Spotted it was me," he said hoarsely, his tones betraying delight if anything. "If that don't beat me handsome! Here's he away for'ard a-listening for shouts and cries, while the pinnace steams against the wind. He spots as someone's smoking. And he says as sure as he can make it that it's me. That's smart, mate, ain't it?"

"It's jest common sense, that's all," came the rejoinder. "Dicky ain't asleep, not by a long way. He knows his men better perhaps than a sight of the orfficers. And he knows you, Bill, and the smell of that 'ere pipe. That's where his smartness comes in. He puts things together quick, same as he'll clear up this here little business that's brought us away from the ship at a time when we ought to be turnin' down and alookin' forward to our suppers. Did you hear what it is exactly? They was mighty quick in pipin' us away. It's something particular."

"Someone lost away out beyond the Needles, that's all I heard," came Hurst's answer. "Anyways, there ain't much chance of our being able to help. It's blowing hardish out here, and if a boat has foundered and left her crew in the water, why, they'll stay there I'm afeard. It don't take long to drown a man, even with the little sea there's running."

A sudden order had in fact disturbed the peace of shipboard life late that evening. Mr. Midshipman Hamshaw, in all the glory of his mess kit, was on the point of making his way to the gunroom, there to sit down to an appetizing dinner, when he received an unexpected order.

"Mr. Hamshaw! Mr. Hamshaw!" he heard someone calling. "Pass the word to Mr. Hamshaw, please. Ask him to step up on deck at once, bringing oilskins with him."

Dicky's servant conveyed the tidings to him. Dicky himself tore off his mess jacket with no very pleasant expression, dived into a workaday costume, and grumbling at the ill fortune which had befallen him stumbled up on deck.

"Yes, sir," he cried, halting before the officer of the watch and displaying that smartness for which he was notorious. "Here, sir."

"Ah, Mr. Hamshaw, there's a Marconi in to say that someone's been lost just outside the Needles. I can't get further information, and don't know what sort of a craft it is that has foundered, nor how many were aboard. But it's urgent. Tumble into the pinnace and get out as fast as you can steam. Don't return till you have thoroughly searched the water out there."

"Yes, sir." Dicky's youthful heart leaped with delight. True, he longed for that dinner which he was leaving. But this order entailed an independent command, and Dicky loved that more than anything. "Yes, sir!" he repeated.

"And keep a lookout for another pinnace. The Admiral's sending one from another ship. There, off you go. I'll send down to the mess steward to tell him to keep things going hot for you. Smartly does it."

Smartly was always the way aboard that ship, and particularly when Dicky Hamshaw was the officer. He tumbled down into the pinnace with the rapidity almost of lightning. An active monkey would have been hard put to to beat him.

"Push off there for'ard!" he shouted. "Now, ahead. Give her steam, Perkins!"

The low-built pinnace went away from the ship's side into the night like a sleuthhound, and but for the light she carried at her bow was quickly invisible. They steamed out to the Needles at their fastest pace, and then began slowly and thoroughly to circle the water outside, searching every yard of it as far as they were capable. And had they heard a cry?

"Sartin," declared Hawkins, when Dicky appealed to him after the space of a few minutes, and when the red glow from half a dozen pipes told that the men were taking advantage of the privilege of smoking. "I heard one a moment ago, faint-like, sir. Someone almost drowned already."

"Then give 'em a call. Perhaps that'll rouse an answer," said Dicky anxiously. "Now, all together!"

A deep gruff call was sent up by the crew of the pinnace, Dicky's shrill treble merging with the bass of the men. Then all listened, while Perkins shut off steam and silenced his throbbing engines. Ah! A faint cry reached their ears.

"Starboard, sir, starboard," called Hawkins. "I'm certain."

"Sure," grunted Hurst, snatching his pipe from between his teeth. "There again, sir—listen."

There could be no doubt that Mr. Midshipman Hamshaw and his men had heard a call for help, and the sound, faint though it was, set them in a fever. At a command from the officer, Perkins sent steam whizzing and hissing into his cylinders. Flames roared up the stumpy funnel of the pinnace, while the propeller thrashed the water into white foam at the stern, foam that could easily be seen in spite of the surrounding darkness.

"Keep her away a couple of points then," shouted Dicky, leaning with both hands on the gunwale of the craft and staring into the darkness. "Keep a bright lookout forward there, and give me a shout if you see anything. One thing's in our favour. There isn't another craft about here, so we can plug along at our fastest."

Perkins had no hesitation in giving all the available steam to his engines. By then, the pinnace having been the better part of an hour on her journey, there was a fine head of steam, the gauge showing a pressure which promised something approaching full power. It was not to be wondered at, therefore, that the whole pinnace vibrated. The engine roared. The propeller behind even threw white foam into the after portion of the vessel. And so, for perhaps five minutes, they continued plunging into darkness, each man of the crew straining his eyes to detect something.

"Stop her! Let's listen again. Wait though—give another shout," directed Dicky, and at the command once more a hoarse growl was sent across the heaving water.

"Nothing, sir—not a sound," cried Hawkins, when they had listened a full two minutes. "Whoever it was who answered us before is drowned."

"No—I heard something. Silence!" called Dicky. "There! Hear it, any of you men?"

"Yes, sir. There it is again," cried Hurst, now filled with eagerness. "Listen, sir—there again! Well, I'm blistered!"

It was one of the seaman's choicest expressions, reserved for moments of unusual excitement. He let his still-smouldering pipe drop into a pocket and scratched his head with one rugged forefinger. And no wonder that he was puzzled. A moment before he and Hawkins, and Dicky Hamshaw and the remaining members of his crew would one and all have declared that they heard a shout come from a point almost directly ahead. They felt sure of the fact, could have made an oath upon it. And now it came from aloft, from the sky in fact.

"I'm blistered!" repeated Hurst, stupefied at such a strange occurrence. "Must be a sort of echo, sir."

"Hardly likely. Why, there it comes again, and from the sea this time without doubt. Dead ahead, too. Put her at it, Perkins."

Once more the process of giving steam to the engine was repeated, and presently the pinnace was tearing along through the water. Then of a sudden her onward progress was arrested. She struck some object heavily, canted to one side till the water poured in over the gunwale, and righted all in a moment. There was a tearing, grating noise for'ard, followed almost instantly by the hiss of water meeting something intensely hot, and by dense clouds of vapour.

"Holed, sir!" shouted Perkins. "There's water pouring in and flooding the furnace. I'm up to my knees in it already."

"Stand by there! Get hold of that light, Seaton, and let's see what's the damage. Stand by there, men. This looks like a bad business."

Dicky did not plunge into hysterics. On the contrary he was as cool as one could possibly have wished. That the matter was serious he guessed at once, though his inexperience left him doubting what had actually happened. However, the rapidly rising water within the pinnace, the fact that he already stood knee deep himself, went a long way to convince him that his little command had met with an unfortunate accident. But he was hardly prepared for the amazing swiftness of its termination. Hardly had one of his men seized the light for'ard and held it aloft when, as if that was the prearranged signal, the pinnace filled, waves washed in over the gunwale while clouds of steam were shot from the furnace. Then, with a heave and a wriggle and an almost audible sob the pinnace shot away from beneath the feet of the crew who had manned her. Perhaps one half-minute later Dicky's head appeared from beneath the water which had submerged him. He opened his mouth and shouted:

"Stand by there, men! There's wreckage here. Hold on to it."

"Aye, aye, sir," came from Hawkins, his deep tones easily recognizable. "Now, lads, answer to your names as I call 'em. Hurst."

"Here, sir."

"Perkins."

"Here, sir."

The answer was given with a gulp. Perkins was endeavouring to eject the volume of water which he had so recently swallowed.

"Seaton, Carew, Tomkins."

"Here, sir! here, sir! here, sir!" came with varying degrees of quickness, and for the most part in distinctly gasping fashion.

"All present and aboard, sir," cried Hawkins, using that formula by force of habit. "All clinging tight, sir."

"But to what? And there's that shout again. This is getting beyond me," declared the youthful Dicky, not in despondent tones it must be declared, for never was there a lighter-hearted nor more courageous individual. But in a manner which showed that the speaker was sorely puzzled. No wonder, too, for that elusive call sounded now as if it came from the sky again. It made the bulky Hurst actually tremble. He was shivering already, for the water was cold, and this sudden immersion was no joke under the circumstances. But now that call, three times repeated, sent a cold shiver down his back, as if someone had suddenly added a huge block of ice to the water.

"I'm jiggered," he stuttered, his strong teeth chattering. "From away up aloft. Why, there's a man here, sir, tied up to this here wreckage."

It was too dark to see more than an inch in front of one's nose, but Hurst could feel, and rapidly ran his fingers over the form of a man supported on the wreckage to which he and his companions were clinging. Was that wreckage the remains of a boat? Undoubtedly no. Then what was it? Both Hawkins and Hurst endeavoured to elucidate what had become a mystery. They ran their hands far and wide over spars and timber. They stretched as far as they were able, while Dicky Hamshaw did likewise, puzzled beyond expression by the strangeness of his immediate surroundings. And then that far-away cry again fell on his ear.

"Silence, men," he commanded, in his most peremptory manner. "Now, give 'em a call—all together!"

The bellow which the half-submerged members of the crew sent out must have penetrated some considerable distance. They waited for an answering cry, and then were more completely bewildered. For of a sudden the darkness overhead was split in twain by a beam of brilliant light, which shot from a point far above them, a point so brilliant that they dared not gaze at it. A moment before they were struggling in the water surrounded by the densest darkness. Now, they and a huge circle about them were brilliantly illuminated, showing seven forlorn figures bobbing in the ocean about a mass of wreckage of curious formation secured to which was the body of a man more forlorn than themselves. Dicky Hamshaw wondered whether he were dreaming. He stretched out a hand and pulled at the sleeve of that unconscious figure. And then he gazed aloft, wondering from whence that light came, who could have cast it upon them, and what manner of ship it was that floated there, invisible and stationary yet a ship for all that; for a man or men were aboard it. Cries had come from that direction, while their own shouts had been followed by the sudden jet of light which now played about them. Was he dreaming indeed? or could that actually be the figure of a man descending through the very centre of the beam towards them, descending at a speed which made him giddy, treading steps which there was no seeing?

"Jingo!" he gasped. "This is getting too hot for anything. Why—why, the man's on a rope. Now, what in the dickens supports him?"

What indeed? Not one of the men clinging to that strange wreckage in the water illuminated so wonderfully could guess to what class of vessel that rope could be attached. For nothing was visible aloft save that one penetrating eye, that brilliant orb which shot down upon them its dazzling beams. Hurst shivered yet again. Even Mr. Midshipman Hamshaw was decidedly disconcerted and nonplussed by the uncanniness of the situation. For that man, dangling from a rope, turning like a spider hanging by a single thread, and swaying from side to side as the wind caught him, appeared to be supported by nothing in particular. And yet he was descending towards them at an amazing rate, and that too with no effort on his own part. Someone above must be paying out the rope to which he was attached. But who? Where was the spot from which he had started? What sort of vessel hovered aloft?

"I'm hanged," ventured Dicky.

"It's just the queerest thing as ever I seed, sir," admitted Hawkins. "But there's one thing I'm sure of. This here wreckage is what's left of a waterplane. See there—one of the floats is on the top of the water. There's generally two, so one can guess that the other's foundered, and if it wasn't for this here one the whole affair would have sunk. It's lucky for us and lucky for the man here. French, sir."

"Yes," agreed the young officer. "Looks it. Hallo!"

His last exclamation had been drawn from him by the sudden discovery that the man at the end of that strange rope was now within a matter of ten feet of him, swaying just overhead. In fact, in those few seconds during which Dicky had turned to inspect the wreckage to which he was clinging, the newcomer, descending as it were from the sky, had dropped to within speaking distance. Who was he? Of what nationality?

"Ahoy!" shouted Dicky, nothing daunted. "Where do you come from?"

A face looked down upon him, a face cast into shadow by that brilliant beam from above, and yet distinguishable to some extent by reason of the reflection from the water. It was a bearded face, that of a man in his early prime, strong, reliant, and dauntless, and bearing an expression familiar to the young officer. Did he know this man? Impossible.

"Who's that?" came in stentorian tones.

"Mr. Midshipman Hamshaw, sir," bellowed Hawkins, taking upon himself to answer; "he and the crew of the steam pinnace away from the Solent. We've struck against the wreck of a waterplane, and the pinnace has foundered."

"All present, I hope?"

"Aye, aye, sir!" shouted Dicky, for without a doubt the man above was a naval officer. He had the cut of a nautical man from head to foot, while whoever saw a man hang so comfortably in midair at the end of but a single rope but a sailor?

"And you can stick tight for a while?"

"Certainly," answered Dicky.

"Then hang on; I'll be down again in a minute."

The man waved his hand. There came a cry from far up aloft, and then the dangling figure was whisked upward at express speed, for all the world as if he were seated in an elevator going aloft in a New York skyscraper.

"I'm jiggered!" gasped Hurst, silenced up till now by the novelty of the situation. "Why, look what's coming."

Down through the very centre of the beam, appearing once more to have actually no point of support, there dropped a wide platform, over one edge of which a man's head protruded. At lightning speed it fell towards the wreckage, halting abruptly within two feet of the water as the man signalled. Then it dropped a few inches lower, while a hand was stretched out to Hawkins.

"Come aboard," that same cheerful, brisk voice commanded. "Where's the officer?"

"Here, sir," shouted Dicky.

"How many men are you responsible for?"

"Six, sir; and this fellow lashed to the wreckage."

"Good! Then we'll soon finish this business. Now, on you come."

Very rapidly was the crew of the pinnace transferred to this strange platform, and following them the unconscious figure of the man they had come out to rescue.

"Hold tight!" came the order.

"Tight it is, sir," responded Hawkins.

"Then hoist."

The stranger signalled. Dicky felt the platform move upward. Then it shot towards the sky, while of a sudden the beam died out, leaving them all in darkness. It sent a chill down his back. Even the jovial and careless midshipman was impressed by the uncouthness of this adventure. Where was this stranger bearing them? What was to be the end of this amazing rescue?

CHAPTER IV

The Great Airship

"Hold tight all! Don't move or you will make the platform sway, and then it will be a job to keep your footing. Ah—up we go!"

The cheery individual, who had dropped so suddenly as if from the sky, bringing help to Dicky and his crew, called out loudly, once he had contrived with their help to cut asunder the lashings that bound the unconscious figure of the man they had come to rescue, and had lifted him aboard the platform which had borne him from aloft. He signalled at once, and then, as we have recorded, the platform shot upward at tremendous speed, while the brilliant light shedding its beams upon them went out of a sudden.

"I'd as soon be aloft in a gale on a dirty dark night, so I would," the bulky Hurst began to grumble, while he clutched at the smooth floor of the platform, and finding no hold there, sought for the edge and gripped it. For all had sunk upon their knees, standing being almost out of the question, and in any case hardly a position to attract any of the company. "There ain't no sayin' where this here platform ends and where it begins, and if you was to fall where'd you go to!"

"Where? Davy Jones's locker!" laughed Hawkins, though his hoarse tones told how the situation impressed him. "Right slick down to Davy Jones. Just you quit grumblin', my lad, and get a hold on with your eyebrows."

"Silence, men!" came sharply from Dicky. The precarious position in which he found himself, his unusual surroundings, and the uncertainty of the future making him quite irritable. "Now, sir, will you kindly explain where you are taking us. And first, let me thank you for turning up just in the nick of time."

"Not at all! Not at all! Delighted to be able to lend a helping hand to some of my own service."

"Navy, sir?" asked Dicky, though he felt sure of that fact from the very first.

"What else, my lad? Commander Jackson, at present engaged in experimental work."

"Aeronautics?" ventured Dicky.

"Perhaps; you'll see. Hold tight! Now that the light has been switched off it makes this platform none too safe. That is, for anyone not a sailor. Ah! They're slowing down the motor. We'll be aboard in a jiffy."

Their upward flight had indeed taken but a matter of a minute, and already they were hundreds of feet above the sea. Not that they could tell that for certain. But every one of the rescued crew had the uncomfortable feeling that they were poised high in the air, with but this flimsy platform between them and destruction. However, a few seconds later they became aware of a dull, droning noise, hitherto inaudible, while the speed of their strange lift had slowed considerably.

"Keep your hands off the edge of the platform!" shouted their rescuer. "Ah! Here we are! Come aboard, Mr. Provost."

The change from darkness to brilliant light was positively stupefying, even more than it had been in the reverse direction. For now, as Dicky and his crew crouched on the platform, fearful of moving to right or left lest they should lose their footing, there was a gentle bump, a flooring above their heads lifted, and in an instant they found themselves in a wide gallery blazing with light and occupied by three individuals. Another second and the platform came to a rest on a level with the flooring of this gallery, while a well-groomed, white-headed man stepped forward to greet them.

"Welcome!" he cried. "Well done, Commander Jackson! I was in a fever till I saw you had them all on board. Gentlemen, allow me to welcome you on your arrival."

It was Andrew Provost, well set up, thin and spare, and exceedingly well dressed. More than that it was Andrew Provost with a new light in his eye. He was almost truculent, and none who took the trouble to look at him could doubt the fact that if ever there were a successful and a contented man it was Andrew Provost.

"Permit me," he said, "to introduce my nephew, Mr. Joseph Gresson, the inventor and builder of this wonderful ship. Step in, gentlemen, and let us provide you with dry clothing and refreshment."

"And allow me to introduce Mr. Midshipman Hamshaw," cried Commander Jackson, beaming upon the party. "Now, Mr. Provost, I think we had better do something for this poor fellow who was lashed to the waterplane. Let Alec take care of our guests for the moment."

"Alec! Alec! Of course; where is the fellow? Ah! There you are! Come here, sir," cried Andrew, in mock tones of severity, beckoning to a youth who till now had stood in the background. "This is Mr. Midshipman Hamshaw, in command of the rescued party. Take him along to your cabin and provide him with clothes. Hand the six men over to Sergeant Evans, and ask him to see at once to their wants. There! I leave it to you. We'll see what can be done for this poor fellow."

With his head still in a curious whirl, and his eyes turning from one strange object to another Dicky obediently followed the young fellow who had just been introduced as Alec, while Hawkins and the remainder of the crew stepped along the curiously smooth, elastic floor of the gallery after them. They reached a door, opened it and passed through, finding themselves in a second wide gallery. But this was different from the other; for it had doors on either side, while a railed-in square of flooring near the centre showed a hatchway, leading by a shallow flight of steps to a deck below, from which came the low hum of a motor.

"Sergeant Evans!" shouted Alec, and repeated the call.

"Here, sir!"

One of the many doors opened, and a tall, soldierly man appeared dressed in the smart livery of a mess waiter. "Got something hot, sir," he said brusquely. "I guessed food would be wanted, and so I set the cook to work to prepare it. But they're wet, sir."

He nodded to the young naval officer and his men, and looked at them with interest.

"Drenched," said Alec. "Pass the men along to Peters. Tell him to ferret out clothing for 'em, and give 'em a meal. I'll take the officer to my cabin, and we'll be in the saloon in five minutes."

The sergeant went off at once along the gallery, motioning to Hawkins and his comrades to follow; while Alec dived in through an adjacent door and ushered Dicky into as nice a cabin as he had ever seen. Indeed, it contrasted more than favourably with his own quarters aboard the vessel from which he had so recently parted. It was flooded with light from a couple of electric burners, and heated by a stove fitted in the far corner which was also operated by electricity. There were pictures on the walls, secured in a manner which he had never observed before, while the walls themselves were of a milky-white colour.

"Sit down over here," cried Alec, doing the honours with obvious pride. "You see, this cabin communicates with the next, and there's a common bathroom. That'll be the place in which to pull off your wet togs. Hop into a hot bath as soon as you've got 'em off. By then I'll have a complete rig-out for you. We're about the same height and size, eh?"

He had been looking his guest up and down sharply, admiring his uniform, in spite of its drenched condition. And short though his scrutiny had been Alec had come to the conclusion that Mr. Midshipman Hamshaw was a right good fellow. As for Dicky himself, the novelty of his surroundings and the strange adventure through which he had passed had altogether kept his attention from his new comrade. He had merely noticed that Alec was a straight, active-looking fellow, with a pleasant smile and a jolly manner about him. Now, as he thanked him for his kind attention he gave the young man a quick, frank glance, which missed very little.

"I say, thanks awfully," he began. "What's—what's your other name?"

"Jardine—Alec Jardine. But Alec's good enough. Yours is Hamshaw, isn't it, Dicky?"

"Yes, Dicky," grinned the midshipman. "It's stuck to me ever since I was at Osborne. I hate it, I can tell you. Makes one think one is a girl. It's an awful nuisance looking so frightfully young, ain't it?"

They could condole with one another there, for Alec Jardine suffered from the same infliction. To be precise, he was within two months of the midshipman's age, no longer a boy, and not yet a man. And as is often enough the case with youth, he resented the position, found his age embarrassing, and his obvious juvenility a nuisance to say the least of it. But he did not allow it to damp his good spirits.

"We'll get over it, that's one good thing," he laughed. "I say, this is simply a ripping ship. You'll have an eye opener. But pull those togs off; I was thinking that mine would about fit you."

"To a T. Tell me about the ship—an airship I suppose? Something like a Zeppelin?"

"A Zeppelin! Why, that type of ship can't hold a candle to this one!" declared Alec loftily. "I've seen 'em. They're fine to look at, fast, and have big lifting capacity. But see how they behave. Let it blow just a little hard, and they're done for, that is if they happen to be outside their sheds and run out of petrol. It's only a week or more ago since one of them lost her way in a fog, ran out of spirit, and was forced to descend. She dropped into the hands of the French, my boy, and they soon had every one of her cherished secrets laid bare. Don't you make any mistake. This ship's not a Zeppelin. She's in a different street; she's just splendid."

The unstinted praise of a vessel with which he was as yet unacquainted whetted Dicky's appetite for a complete inspection. But not yet. He was wet and cold, and decidedly hungry. The news that Sergeant Evans had imparted had made his mouth water. Dicky reminded himself that there was a hot meal in prospect, and so that it might not be delayed he dragged off his wet clothes, and immersed himself in a bath of steaming hot water that Alec had made ready for him. In about ten minutes he announced that he was fully dressed.

"And as hungry as a hunter," he told his new friend. "You wait and try the same experience. I was almost in our gunroom. In any case I could tell you what we were to have for dinner, because in a ship you can't keep all galley smells away from your messroom. Then they passed the word for Mr. Hamshaw. Of course I had to go, leaving the other fellows to sit down to a meal which I really wanted. An hour's steaming made me ravenous, and then came our ducking. I say, lead the way there's a good fellow. But I'd like to see my men before I take a bite myself. Eh?"

"Quite right. Look to your command first, then to number one. Follow down the passage."

Dressed in Alec's clothing, and looking spruce and smart, Dicky followed his friend down the gallery, through the door by which Hawkins and his comrades had departed, and so into the quarters of the crew of this strange vessel. Nor did there seem to be need for anxiety for the welfare of the gallant fellows who had accompanied him upon the steam pinnace. Already they were changed and dressed in clothing hurriedly dragged from lockers. Surrounded by swinging bunks on either side, with one huge electric lamp shedding its light upon them, they were seated about a long table with half a dozen strangers amongst them.

"All aboard and comfortable, sir," grinned Hawkins, standing as his officer appeared. "We've fallen amongst friends, and liberal ones too, sir."

"And have got a meal here what ain't supplied every day of the week by the Admiralty, sir," gurgled Hurst. "Not by a long way."

Dicky grinned his delight; and then, suddenly recollecting that it was not exactly the thing for an officer to listen to what might be construed as abuse of the Admiralty, he turned on his heel and motioned to Alec to lead the way.

"And you mean to tell me that we're high up in the air, floating in space!" he cried.

"One moment. Here we are—three thousand two hundred feet up," said Alec, stopping just outside the door of the men's quarters to inspect a barometer affixed to the wall. "That high enough?"

Dicky was at once conscious of a creepy feeling down his back. "What!" he gasped. "Three thousand feet?"

"Every inch of it. As safe as if you were on land; safer, perhaps, because you never know what's going to pass overhead nowadays, do you? What with airships and aeroplanes, the land's beginning to be a dangerous place to inhabit. Come along. You wait till it's daylight and you can see below. You'll get used to the height in a jiffy, and you'll agree that flying's magnificent. Here we are. Sergeant Evans!"

He dived in through a doorway, ushering his friend into a large saloon, in the centre of which stood a table laid ready for dinner. And here again we record but the bare fact when we say that Mr. Midshipman Hamshaw positively gasped. He was dumbfounded at the luxury he found here, at the brilliant lights, at the huge table groaning with silver and glassware, at the laden sideboard, and at the richness of the decorations. Whoever heard of such things aboard a ship sailing in the air?

"Wonderful!" he cried. "Why, I imagined there would be nothing but machinery—huge, oily engines thumping and thudding away at one's side, with just an odd corner for the captain and crew to rest in. This is magnificent; there's nothing better in all London."

It was at least flattering to Andrew Provost's taste, since he had been the designer of all this magnificence. But who could expect Dicky Hamshaw to take notice of rich carpets, of glittering silver, of famous pictures clinging to silk-brocaded walls, when there was food before him? He was ravenous. Had Alec had any doubts about the matter before, this smart and jolly young sailor soon set them at rest. He tackled that meal with the same dash and energy with which he had undertaken the task that had sent him post haste away in the steam pinnace. It was, perhaps, half an hour later when, having eaten to his own and Alec's content, he leaned back in his chair, accepted with a wonderful assumption of coolness the cigarette which Sergeant Evans offered him, and setting a flaming match to the weed, tossed his head back and sent a cloud of smoke upward. A moment later he had leaped to his feet with an exclamation of amazement. He might have suddenly come upon a pin-point by the cry he gave. But undoubtedly something of real importance had created this excitement. He stood with his head tossed back, his eyes fixed upward, and his lips parted.

"What's that?" he asked. "It startled me. I—I've never seen anything like it. One appears to be looking through an enormous window into space. What's the meaning of it?"

His excitement caused Alec to smile, though he, too, looked his admiration as he gazed upward.

"Wait a moment," he said. "I'll switch off the light here and then the effect will be greater. Now, how's that?"

Well might Dicky give vent to exclamations of surprise and even of admiration, for, as he said, he had never seen anything nearly like this before. Up till now he had been far too busy with his meal to take note of anything but his immediate surroundings. But now, when he quite by chance cast his eyes upward, it was to become aware of the fact that this saloon apparently boasted of no ceiling. If it had one, then it was transparent; while, more wonderful than all, the supporting gas bag of this airship, which he imagined must be above, had all the appearance of being non-existent. Far overhead there burned one single electric lamp, casting its rays far and wide, illuminating the interior of the saloon brightly. But it appeared to hang to nothing, to be supported by no beam or rod, while the saloon itself in which he stood was, so far as he could see, attached to nothing. It was merely floating in the air, riding in space in the most uncanny and inexplicable fashion.

"Jingo!" he cried, feeling that strange, creepy sensation down his back again. "We're—we're safe, I hope?"

"As a house," laughed Alec. "But it does give one the creeps, don't it? The first night we were aboard and I looked upward it gave me quite a turn, even though I knew all the ins and outs of this wonderful vessel. Looks as if we were hanging here from nothing, eh?"

Dicky admitted the fact, with something approaching a gasp.

"And yet you're as sure as sure can be that such a thing is out of the question, absolutely impossible?"

"Well, yes," admitted the young officer, not too enthusiastically, for that uncanny feeling that he was high in the air, and might easily find himself falling with terrible rapidity, assailed him. And who can blame the midshipman? Who that has found himself suddenly at the edge of a tall cliff and looked over has not been assailed by a sensation of uneasiness, by the natural desire to reach firmer and more secure ground, to retire from a spot which might easily be filled with perils? Then think of Dicky Hamshaw high above the sea, aboard a ship the size and shape and contour of which were unknown to him, standing in a gilded saloon to all appearances open to the sky, with no ropes, no beams—nothing, in fact, to show him how it was supported. No wonder he shivered. Even Alec forebore to smile. The situation was unpleasant and uncanny to say the least of it.

"Place your two hands together and look between them," said Alec, suiting the action to the word. "Don't stare at the light up there, for it's so bright that it half blinds you. Look well to one side. Now. Eh?"

He expected an answer, but Dicky failed to give it. Gasps of astonishment escaped his wide-parted lips, gasps denoting pleasure and admiration. For up above, now that he had shielded his eyes from the glare and looked away from the light, he could dimly make out huge girders stretching from left to right, criss-crossing and interlacing with one another. Here and there they ended apparently in nothing. Elsewhere they could be traced to their junction with other girders. And on beyond them, far overhead, he could even see stars, blurred a trifle by the material through which he observed them.

"Well, of all the wonderful things of which I have ever heard, this beats all!" he gasped at last. "What's the thing made of? There are girders above there heavy enough to carry a 'Dreadnought'. There's a huge framework that looks as if it were constructed of solid bars of steel; and yet, to look at them in a half light, which just throws out their outline, one realizes that they are made of something else, something transparent—yes, that's the term—for when one stares direct at the light, knowing full well that there are more girders in that direction, none of them can be detected. George, this beats everything! What's the meaning of it all?"

"The meaning of it all! Why, that Joe Gresson is about the smartest fellow you ever heard of, that he's had the courage to employ a substance for the framework, and almost every part of this ship, which the average engineer would treat with scorn. In short, he's the discoverer of a substance which he calls celludine, which isn't celluloid, nor common glass, nor talc, and yet which is wonderfully like all three substances. You'll hear more about it, my boy. You'll get the same idea of Joe that I and all the others have. Look here! Just rap your knuckles against the wall of the saloon."

Dicky did as he was bidden, though he was still so astonished at the news given him that he did not even trouble to ask the reason.

"Well, how does it feel? Of course, there's a silk covering. Under that is the celludine. There's the same stuff here under the carpet."

"Hard, and yet it gives," said Dicky. "Appears to be very thin, and yet, I imagine, is very strong."

"That's celludine," cried Alec triumphantly. "Every wall, every door and frame is composed of it. Only here, where there are cabins—and one doesn't want to be stared at all day long—it's coloured a milky white, and so isn't transparent. But the ceiling is, that's why you can look aloft and see the stars floating overhead. But come along. We'll take a breather. I'll lead you to a spot that'll raise your hair, but will give you a better idea of this airship than you can possibly have imagined."

They left the saloon at once, and passing along the gallery paused to look into a room on the far side. There they found Commander Jackson, Andrew, and Joe comfortably seated, smoking and chatting quietly.

"Ah, comfortably dressed and fed, my lad?" sang out the Commander.

"Yes, thank you, sir," smiled Dicky. "And, I say, sir, what a ship we've got to!"

"You'll say so to-morrow, when you've looked over her," came the answer. "Where are you two youngsters off to?"

"Aloft," sang out Alec. "I'm going to give him a scare, and get him used to the situation. But how's the foreigner, please?"

"Conscious and tucked up in a warm bed," answered Andrew. "There, cut along, you two. But no mischief, mind. I don't care if I'm responsible for Alec, but I'll not be having the Admiralty pouring all their indignation upon my unprotected head because of the loss of a midshipman."

That set Dicky flushing, while the Commander laughed loudly.

"There, off you get," he cried. "Trust a midshipman to look out for himself."

They closed the door, hastened along the gallery, and passing through a second door found themselves in the gallery upon which Dicky had first set foot. Alec led him to the precise spot where the lift had finally halted, and pointed to an opening overhead.

"It's the main hoist," he explained. "If we want to pick something up from down below we lower that platform, just as we did to fetch your party. If we desire to get aloft to the top of the ship we step aboard the platform, now provided with rails; just so, Dicky, my boy, see that all's secure and safe, and then touch a button. Whiz! Up we go!"

It was a case of whiz with a vengeance. Dick had obediently followed his guide on to this lift, and now he felt his knees bend beneath him, while the smooth, elastic floor on which he stood shot upward at terrific speed, flashing through an oblong opening in the framework overhead, a framework quite transparent for the most part, with that arc light flashing down upon them without the smallest hindrance.

"Saves climbing, don't it?" shouted Alec, for the noise of a motor drowned the ordinary voice. "But if the thing refuses to work you can mount to the top of the ship by a stairway erected round the lift. Ah! Here we are. Hang on to your hat; it's blowing."

Dick felt a fresh gale of wind fanning his cheek, which alone told him that he was now in the open. He followed his friend across a flat, smooth deck and found himself clutching to a railing. And now for the first time he began to gather some information as to the contour and size of this amazing vessel. He might have been upon the upper deck of a second *Lusitania*, only this deck shelved off gradually on either side till it was lost in the darkness. That arc lamp, however, helped him wonderfully, and pacing beside Alec he began soon to wonder at the length of the ship as well as at her breadth. She was immense. It was hard indeed to believe that she was actually floating in space. And yet that must be so, for Alec bade him look downward.

"See for yourself," he said. "We're right forward, close to her nose, and there are no cabins beneath us. You can see clear through the ship down to the ocean. See the beacon lights along the shore, the lights of the vessels, and the blaze away there in the distance. That's where your ship is lying."

Even at night-time the sight was an amazing one, and left Dick stupefied. But what would it be in the morning, when there was no darkness to hinder his sight, and when he would be able to gaze directly downward from that terrific height?

"Let's go down," he said after a while. "I feel positively silly out here. I suppose it's because I'm not used to such a sight. How did you feel when you first attempted it?"

Alec laughed outright. "Feel? Awful!" he cried. "Everyone does at first, and wonders whether they're funking. Wait for the day. You'll get to love the view, particularly when you've learned how safe this vessel is. Come along; to-morrow there'll be a heap to show you."

They turned back toward the lift again and paused there for a moment. For beyond doubt there was at every turn something to attract the attention. A minute before it had been the lights about the Needles, the lamps on the shipping, the blaze from the Solent, where the warships were lying at anchor. Now it was the interior of the ship, seen through her transparent upper casing. Yes, there was the saloon, with Sergeant Evans and a helper clearing the table. Nearer at hand were Andrew Provost, Joe Gresson, and Commander Jackson, still smoking and chatting as they lolled in their chairs. While away aft, in the men's quarters, the figures of Hawkins and Hurst and his shipmates were distinctly visible. They were smoking heavily, and between the clouds of smoke Hawkins's arm could be seen moving with some animation.

"He's just it," he was reiterating, "that there midshipmite is as artful as a bag o' monkeys, and if he was to be left aboard this ship, why, there'd be mischief brewing, particularly with the young gent that's joined him."

And how Dick Hamshaw wished that he might remain. The first glimpse of this amazing vessel made him long for the day to come, so that he might investigate every corner. Then, he supposed, he'd have to depart. He and his men would take their places on that platform again and be lowered to terra firma. But the most unlikely things happen. He found that to be the case when he and Alec again joined their elders.

"Read that," said Commander Jackson, tossing a sheet of paper towards him. "We sent a wireless to your ship, and told 'em of your rescue. It seems they'd just heard of this airship through the Admiralty, and had orders to detail a party for her working. We've saved 'em the trouble. Read it."

Dick did, with flushing cheeks and beating heart. "Glad hear safety Midshipman Hamshaw and crew of pinnace," he read. "Have received orders from Admiralty to detail an officer and party for work aboard the airship. Keep Mr. Hamshaw and party if considered suitable."

"Hooray!" shouted Dick, filled with delight.

"One moment," interrupted the Commander with a quizzing grin. "If considered suitable, I think. Well, now, one has to consider."

"Don't scare the young fellow," cried Andrew jovially. "There, Dick, we'll take you. Just go along and tell your men, and then turn in. You've had enough adventure and excitement for the evening."

When, ten minutes later, Dick laid his head upon a soft pillow and pulled the clothes about him he could not believe that he was really aboard a flying vessel, could not credit the fact that he and his men were resting three thousand feet above the ocean.

CHAPTER V

A Tour of Inspection

"Hallo there! Turn out! It's a grand morning and there are things worth seeing." It was the cheery Alec who aroused Dick Hamshaw on the day after his rescue outside the Needles and his introduction to the airship. Dick wakened with a start, rolled over comfortably, and blinked at his new friend.

"Eh! My watch. Not it," he grumbled sleepily. "I was off late last night and have had the dickens of a nightmare since. Fancied I was aloft in a big airship. Leave a fellow alone to sleep, do."

Alec shook him, laughing loudly. "So you call our airship a nightmare!" he cried. "That's a nice thing to do when the Admiralty have offered you and your men as part of our crew and Mr. Provost has accepted you. I'll tell the Commander. You'd better be getting back to your ship, for there are dozens of fellows who'd be only too glad to come aboard here."

That brought the great Dicky to his senses. He sat up on an elbow, still blinking at Alec with half-open eyes. Then those sharp orbs of his opened widely, the light of full understanding returned to them, and in an instant he was out of bed.

"My word, but I've been dreaming the whole affair over again, and couldn't think it could be true. And it's real? Eh? Actually a fact that I'm on board an airship high in the air. How high did you say?"

Alec made no answer. He stepped across the carpeted floor of this roomy cabin, with its milk-white walls and furniture, and its pictures secured to those same walls by tiny cleats of transparent material, and turning back some hangings exposed a window three times the size of an ordinary porthole, and provided with a pane of what one would have imagined was glass. But it bent with the force of the wind. Half open, the frame projected into the room at an angle to Dick, and glancing at it he caught a reflection of the sun, now bright, and a second later blurred as the pane bent and the surface was altered. The simple fact brought him bounding after Alec. He ran his fingers over both sides of the pane, bent the material backward and forward, and then tapped it with his knuckles. That done he suddenly gazed upward, only to find himself disappointed.

"You don't expect to have transparent roofs to your cabins too, do you?" laughed Alec. "A fellow couldn't undress without half the crew seeing him. No, the ceilings of the dressing-rooms, cabins, and so forth are made opaque. But this window gives you a good idea of the stuff of which the ship's made. Now, take a squint below."

Dick did as he was bidden, and instantly clutched tight to the frame of the window. For down below, down a terrible distance, was a smooth, oily surface which he guessed was the ocean. And on it were a number of minute dots at irregular intervals, while away to the right was a blurred patch of white, which might be land or anything else. The sight made him absolutely giddy. A glance away to his right showed him the under-surface of this enormous ship, transparent, it is true, but of a bluish-grey colour owing to the shadows cast upon it. It was immense. It stretched away from him in an easily-curving line till it was lost in the distance. And beneath it there was nothing, nothing but thin elusive air, and far, far below that muddy ocean.

"Jingo!" he gasped.

Alec grinned. "Makes a chap feel queer at first," he said. "But, as I've told you before, it's as safe as houses. Here, tumble into a tub. It'll buck you up, and when you've been on top with me and had a general look round you'll feel as right as a trivet. Shave?"

"Eh?" asked Dick.

"Do you shave?"

"Er, no—that is to say, not always."

"Lucky beggar! I have to. A beast of a job, and takes half the morning. You pop into the tub. We've a bath between us, and I dare say by the time you've finished I shall have managed to get rid of this growth. Awful bore I find it."

Dicky couldn't help but grin. He stepped across to Alec, forgetful now of the strange sight he had witnessed outside, placed himself directly in front of him, and closely scrutinized his features, maintaining a gravity there was no fathoming.

"Poor beggar!" he said at last. "Awful hard lines, ain't it? You'll find it difficult to get down to breakfast."

To be perfectly truthful, there was not so much as a single hair on Alec's chin or lip, any more than there was on Mr. Midshipman Hamshaw's. And the gravity of his guest, his candour, and those twinkling eyes quite made up to Alec for any soreness he may have felt at this somewhat personal declaration. He flushed a rosy red, and then burst into loud laughter.

"Oh well, perhaps I imagined it a bit," he said. "If I stick to the razor things'll come along in time. There, into the tub. I'll be along in a jiffy."

Ten minutes later, in fact, they were dressed and ready to leave the cabin, Dick having found his own clothes dried, brushed, and neatly folded beside his bed.

"I say," he began, "how do you come to be aboard? Tell me."

"Cousin of Joe's: going to be an engineer one of these days. Accepted his invitation in a jiffy. Come on. Breakfast'll be ready in half an hour, so we've time to make a round of the ship. Now, up we go to the top deck of all; it'll give you a good impression of the vessel."

ARRIVED WITH A BUMP FACING COMMANDER JACKSON

They stepped into that strange lift again and were whisked on high. A minute later they were in the open, with a brisk breeze blowing about them and the genial rays of the sun pouring down upon them. Gazing in every direction Dick found himself stepping upon a flat deck of transparent material, immediately beneath which he could easily see the beams that supported it. Down lower still, beneath a deep space, which common sense told him must be filled with gas, were more beams, curving neatly to complete the shape of this ship, and beneath them again, stretching on either side of a central gallery a number of cabins, some with transparent roofs, others with opaque material let into the ceilings. And yet deeper, forming the lowest portion of the ship, was one long compartment, through the roof of which he could see engines, with a couple of men attending to them.

"Let's get along aft, then we'll make forward," said Alec, showing the various parts of the ship with pride. "I'll tell you something about her. She's longer than the latest Zeppelin, and equally deep from top to bottom. You can see that her shape is flattened from above downward, which makes her very much wider than a Zeppelin. Care to come out to one of the side keels?"

Dick hesitated. Then catching sight of a rail passing from this main deck down the easily-sloping side of the vessel he nodded. After all, he wasn't going to be beaten by Alec.

"Right," he said. "Get ahead."

They clambered over the main rail to find themselves on a narrow way provided with very shallow steps. This brought them after a minute right out to the farthest lateral edge of the ship, to that lateral keel, in fact, which Joe Gresson had made such a point of. And there the rail ended abruptly. Alec leaned over it and invited Dick to join him.

"Ripping, eh?" he asked. "Getting your balance at last, I expect. Don't seem so dreadful now, does it?"

It did not by a great deal. The midshipman was bound to confess that he was becoming accustomed to his surroundings. More than that, the huge bulk of this floating monster, the fact that she never even trembled, while the weight of himself and his comrade now brought right out to the farthest edge caused no sign of heeling, impressed him vastly with the stability of the vessel. He was beginning to catch some of Alec's enthusiasm. He was longing to peep into every corner, to get to understand every detail. And we must remember that Mr. Midshipman Hamshaw was not unacquainted with things mechanical. What naval officer can be in these days, indeed, when the old wooden walls have long since departed, and when your modern ship is composed of steel, while almost every movement aboard her, however trivial, is, where possible, carried out by some cleverly-contrived mechanical means? No, Dick had a fondness for mechanics. And here, aboard the airship, he guessed that his fondness was to be gratified to the utmost.

"Let's get back to the deck again," he said at last, when they had gazed below at the muddy ocean. "I'm dying to see more. Now, what are these rails for? It beats me your having a deck on top of the ship. But I suppose it's necessary. Why rails on the deck? That's what I can't fathom."

But he saw the reason a little later, for Alec took him to a sunken deck house, which, seeing that its roof was dead level with the deck, might be expected to offer no resistance whatever to the air. Opening a trap, he ushered his new friend in, though the contents were plainly to be seen without that manœuvre. And there, anchored to the floor, was a pair of spreading planes, as transparent as glass, strong and flexible, attached at their centre to a boat constructed of the same material.

"An aeroplane!" he gasped. "Here, on an airship? Why?"

"For scouting. To act as a messenger. To take passengers to and fro when it's necessary."

Alec spoke loftily, watching Dick's amazement with secret delight. "That's why there are rails on the deck outside," he explained. "She starts from 'em."

"But—but how does she return?" asked Dick, somewhat bewildered, for whoever heard of an aeroplane flying towards an airship and settling upon it? But Alec dismissed the question with a shrug of his shoulders, and a wave of his hands.

"Ain't there enough deck to please you?" he asked. "Do you want to provide a drill ground? You just operate a motor; this sunken hangar rises with the aeroplane, and there you are, ain't you?"

Dick felt the truth of the words. The huge monster on which he had found refuge presented a deck wide enough and long enough to provide safe landing for any aviator. As for this plane upon which he looked, it was obviously meant to float in the water, in fact, it was a waterplane, though the long, centrally-placed boat, to which the planes were immediately attached, was provided with wheels also, to enable it to roll upon the rails, and also to land either on this deck or on terra firma. It was, without shadow of doubt, the last word in the science and manufacture of a heavier-than-air machine.

"Ripping!" exclaimed Dick. "You've been in her?" he asked admiringly, with just a suspicion of jealousy in his voice.

"Once: I'm going again. You'll come too."

"From here? At this height?"

The possibilities of a swoop away from the broad deck of the airship, till a little while ago seeming to be so insecure, and now, compared with the machine he was inspecting, so broad and strong and trustworthy, was almost appalling. Dick wondered whether he could really screw his courage up to board this aeroplane, to sit in that flimsy boat and wait for the machine to move along the rails, to gather speed, and then to hurl herself over the side of the vessel. It made that old, creepy sensation return. Dick was one of those fellows gifted with an acute imagination, and consequently suffered on occasions. Here, then, was an occasion, and he was bold and open enough to admit the fact that he hardly viewed the prospect with enthusiasm.

"But you will soon," Alec told him. "It's simply a case of getting used to the sensation, and then you long to go out. But let's leave the deck. You can see that we carry guns. They're provided by the Admiralty. Yes, my boy, by the Admiralty. You see, both the War Office and the Admiralty have been stirred up by Mr. Provost. They had to move. They had to inspect this ship when she was completed. And inspection was enough for the two authorities. They began to stir, to get a move on with a vengeance, and, as a result, we've men aboard sent by the two services, guns up here, and on the deck below, a wireless apparatus, and an officer from either service, Commander Jackson for one, while the soldier is to come to us almost immediately. Of course, I ain't forgetting Mr. Midshipman Hamshaw."

He grinned a wicked grin at Dick and went racing away from him. As for the young sailor, he gave chase on the instant, so that presently the ship rang with their merry cries. And indeed, they made a race of it, for Alec made for the gangway built around the lift, racing down the steep stairs as fast as active legs could carry him. Dick, however, proved his salt and his training. Finding a smooth, central girder of that strange and transparent material, he wrapped his legs round it, and went shooting like a descending rocket to the deck below where he arrived with a resounding bump, to find himself directly facing Commander Jackson.

"'Mornin', sir!" he gasped, drawing himself up and touching the peak of his hat. "Fine weather, sir."

"For monkey tricks, yes," laughed the Commander. "Well, lad, how do you like the vessel? Seen the aeroplane? Eh? Like a trip aboard her? I'm the coxswain."

"Rather, sir," gasped Dick. "This is the finest thing I've had to do since I joined the Navy."

"Indeed! You've been an officer a long while I take it," smiled his senior. "Quite one of the older ones, Dick, eh? Come; I'll stop quizzing. Let's get along to the engines; Joe Gresson has gone there. There's no keeping him away from them. Come; you'll see the height of simplicity combined with the uttermost efficiency that has yet been attained."

Dick did indeed inspect a machine which, with its components, gave extraordinary power to the ship. To put the description with the utmost plainness, he found when he descended to the engine-room three sets of engines, of moderate size, and of the internal-combustion variety. There was nothing remarkable, perhaps, about the engines themselves, except that they were a modification of the Diesel.

"You see, a Diesel uses extremely high compression," Joe Gresson explained, leaning one hand affectionately on an engine which happened not to be working. "That can be managed easily ashore, and in the air also. But compressors are required in addition to the engine, for the explosive charge, consisting of the crudest oil, must be injected into the cylinders by pneumatic power at a critical moment, and that power must be at higher pressure than the contents of the cylinder. To me the most important question was the one of fuel. I barred petrol."

"Why?" Dick ventured to ask. "It's used on other airships."

"And other ships suffer from explosions and from fire. Petrol is too inflammable, particularly upon a ship which is lifted by a huge volume of gas. So I chose crude paraffin oil, the sort of oil that you can obtain in any part of Europe, almost in any part of the world. To discover a carburettor which would vaporize this crude oil was difficult. But a friend came to my help, and here you see the result. Our engines run steadily and strongly."

He pointed to the other two, which, as he said, were turning over noiselessly and with a rhythm that told its tale plainly. Even Dick had sufficient experience of this class of engine to know that the running was excellent. But beyond that he was somewhat fogged. For besides some machinery housed in at the end of each motor, and a certain number of switches and levers common to any engine-room, there was nothing to indicate in what manner the power of the engines was conveyed, nor in what direction. Where was the propeller? How did these motors operate it? By electricity? Perhaps, for he could see a large dynamo revolving at the far end of the cabin. But he was by no means certain. He asked the question instantly, causing Joe to raise his head, open a port at the far end of the cabin, and invite him to look through it.

"We're a little aft of amidships here," he explained, "and form the lowest attachment to the vessel. We're dead in the central line, and the weight of these motors and of other accessories housed in what compares with the keel of an ordinary ship, keeps her perfectly steady. Now, look yonder. That is the tail end of the ship. You can see the propeller, and as it is revolving and you cannot, therefore, distinguish its outline I had better tell you something about it. To begin, it's both propeller and rudder. See, I wish to turn the vessel. I press this lever to the right and at once the propeller swings in the same way, driving the tail of the ship to the left. See, I reverse the motion. Or, perhaps, I wish to descend or rise—hold tight, please, gentlemen, while I give our friend here a little demonstration! But first, let me say that the propeller itself is forty feet in diameter, presents half a dozen blades, the pitch of which can be instantly altered, while the blades are encircled by a tube some twenty feet in depth from back to front. Thus the air drawn into this revolving tube cannot escape to either side, and the blades lose no efficiency, while one can readily understand that when the ship is travelling quickly, particularly against a head wind, the alteration in the pitch of the blades makes for greater speed and more effectual use of the power. Now, hold tight, please. We'll show our friend of what we are capable."

At a touch upon a lever the propeller that Dick was watching, and which was rotating very slowly, suddenly gathered speed, till it was but a mere haze in the distance. He felt the whole ship move forward, while a touch on another lever bent the propeller downward, and to his consternation the deck he stood on canted badly, the vessel headed downward and went hurtling towards that muddy ocean which he could see below him. The sensation was in fact paralysing. It was worse, perhaps, when it was reversed, and the nose of the ship shot upward, setting the deck at such an angle that Dick had to cling hard to the railings fending the motors. But a moment later, at a touch from the inventor, she came to an even keel, the propeller ceased to rotate, while the vessel came to a halt.

"Now, see how we rise at will," said Joe, watching Dick's face with delight, for it pleased the young inventor to notice the open admiration with which the youthful sailor regarded everything. "Now, I pull this handle. We fall. I reverse the movement. We shoot upward, but always keeping the horizontal position."

It was really remarkable, for the mere touch of the inventor sent the ship up and down, for all the world as if she were suspended in space, and his fingers controlled the switch of some hoisting machinery.

"How's it done?" asked Dick eagerly. "How does the power get to that propeller, for instance? Your motors are here. There are no chains, no shafts, nothing save these cased-in things at the end of each motor, which might be pumps for all I know."

"And happen to be exactly what you have mentioned. They are pumps, of the rotary variety, and the material they deal with is that same common, crude paraffin on which our motors run. See those pipes. They are of the best, cold-drawn steel. They convey the oil from our pumps to the various propellers, to the lift and to any part where we have need for power. No corner is too sharp for them. They run anywhere, and, as you can imagine, convey the power of these engines with a certainty there is no gainsaying. Of course, at the far end we have other rotary motors. The oil pumped at this point, and under high pressure, is unable to escape from the steel pipes. At will we pass it into our distant motors, allowing some to escape back in this direction through a bypass. If the bypass is pulled wide open, the motors beyond do not turn; for the oil fails to reach them. If it is closed, there is no escape for the oil. It reaches the motors at its highest pressure, and operates them at full power, as powerfully, in fact, as if this engine down here driving the pumps was away up there close to the propeller with the shaft directly coupled to it. In short, and as an interesting fact, our propellers and other gear are operated by hydraulic power, applied after the latest principle."

"Which is a lesson that will keep you for a while," smiled the Commander. "Ah, there's our host, and I hear the breakfast gong sounding. Come, Dick, my lad, you could eat, you think? the great height at which we fly does not rob you of your appetite?"

Not by a long way. The young fellow was beginning to revel in his strange surroundings, and to quite like this residence at a height. More than all, he was vastly interested in the intricacies of the vessel. And we record only the fact when we say that he and Alec spent the whole of the morning in a close and thorough investigation, an investigation which disclosed, among other matters, the interesting fact that centrally-placed propellers, operating in tubes built transversely at either end of the ship, controlled her sideways movements, making entrance to a hangar easy, while she could be caused to descend or rise by others, located fore and aft likewise, with their tubes built in the vertical direction. As for the huge framework that held the gas, it was divided into twenty compartments, to each of which pipes of that strange transparent material led. These latter ended in one large branch which was attached to a machine at one end of the engine-room. Joe explained its action with a gusto that showed it to be one of his pet items, one on which he prided himself not a little.

"What's the good of a ship which has to constantly return to land for gas supplies?" he said. "We take ours with us. Not compressed and in steel cylinders. Anyone can do that. But in the form of fuel. We carry a matter of seven tons, and can get a further supply in any part of the world. A gas producer of my own designing deals with the stuff, and at desire we can supply gas to replace leakages. Not that we experience those. Otherwise it would not be safe to smoke. But each one of our compartments aboard the ship contains a proportion of air. When we want to go higher, or lift a bigger weight, we simply set the producer going, and by means of one of our motors pump gas to the top of the compartments. Simple, isn't it? But it makes us wonderfully independent. That's why we've undertaken to make a trip round the world."

"Round the world? When?"

"Now—to-morrow, that is to say."

"And—and I go with you?" gasped Dick.

"Of course; you've been detailed by the Admiralty."

The shout which the midshipman gave might have been heard at the far end of the vessel. The prospect filled him with delight, so that he was simply boiling over with enthusiasm and anticipation. Nor did his excitement evaporate as the day advanced. For the ship manœuvred over the ocean, and was put through her paces. Towards evening, however, her nose was turned to the north-east, and as night fell she hovered over England. Slowly she descended, obscured in darkness, till her pilot was able to pick up his bearings. A distant light of curious colour caught his eye and he sent the ship towards it. Then, when directly overhead that same brilliant light suddenly shot from the ship and flooded the buildings beneath. Dick found himself looking down upon a huge shed, placed in a wide-open place, and—could he believe his eyes?—the shed was moving, revolving, actually turning. It made him giddy. Or was it this wonderful ship which was turning?

"It's the revolving hangar, of course," Alec told him, with a laugh. "You see, if the wind's blowing, we head up to it. The hangar opens away from the point from which the gale comes. We manœuvre opposite it, and enter easily. You watch. No one is wanted to hang on to ropes. Our pilot can manage the ship in any direction. See, we've dropped opposite the shed; but we're not quite head on. We're getting near it, however, for those propellers located in the cross tubes are being set to work. Ah! that's better. See, we're creeping in. Now our huge lateral keels run into wide slots built into the sides of the hangar. They engage and run in farther. Right! We're home. Welcome to our kennel."

And what of the trip promised by Joe Gresson, and of the adventures it might and certainly should bring in its train?

"Jingo!" cried Dick, as he hastened to the post office to send a telegram requesting that his full kit might be sent to him. "Jingo, if we don't have a cruise worth talking about, well—well, my name ain't Dicky."

CHAPTER VI

Carl Reitberg, Sportsman

It may be imagined that the manufacture of an airship such as Dick Hamshaw had been introduced to, the child of Joe Gresson's clever brain, was not the work of a day. Four months had slipped by since that eventful day on which the young inventor and his uncle, Andrew Provost, had witnessed the flight of the Zeppelin outside Hamburg, and had accepted Carl Reitberg's somewhat arrogant challenge.

Nor did the trial flights of this wonderful vessel escape public notice, though, it is true, her hull was practically invisible. But the rescue of a naval party sent to help a foundered aviator was bound to be reported, so that on the very morning after Andrew and his friends reached their hangar, the journals were filled with this new mystery, while columns, indeed, were devoted to this new airship.

"Sensational rescue at sea by the crew of a strange airship," Dick read. "Mr. Midshipman Hamshaw and a party of six men aboard a steam pinnace were left struggling in the water owing to their craft colliding with a half-submerged waterplane. Who is the owner of the airship? To what nationality does she belong? Another air peril. Ship reported to be practically transparent and, therefore, almost invisible."

There was quite a furore about the affair, and no wonder, since England was still a laggard, and still employed her officers, capable and dashing enough themselves, in playing with toy airships—to wit, the Alpha, the Beta, and the Gamma. Other nations were pushing ahead. To us had belonged the mastery of the sea for years, the heavier element hemming our tight little island around. Now the lighter element was in danger of conquest by some other nation, by a nation which at any moment might prove to be an enemy, and which, within a few hours might have her air fleet hovering over our ports, our arsenals, our war harbours, even over London itself. Was this, then, a newcomer to add to our perils?

"I shall make it clear at once," said Mr. Provost, with that decision one expected of him. "I shall send a statement to the papers. You ain't afraid of the thing being copied, eh, Joe?"

Joe smiled at that. He was a young man of singularly few words; one read his answers often enough by his features. He shook his head vigorously now, and laughed outright.

"Afraid! no. Why should I be, Uncle? They can copy the design any time. But they can't manufacture celludine. That is my secret, yours if anything happens to me, the British nation's whenever we care to give it to them. Send along your statement. It will calm many who feel that another danger threatens."

And so the evening journals one and all contained a crisp statement from Andrew, a statement vouched for by one of the ministers of the realm. Thenceforward, as may be imagined, the curiosity of the nation was acutely stirred. Men walked along staring into the sky, as if expecting to see the airship. There were more taxi-cab accidents from this one cause in London that week than had happened in a similar period before. And far and wide people who were utter strangers to one another congratulated those they met at the news which had been published.

"Splendid! Magnificent! We'll be able to sleep peacefully in our beds now," observed Mr. Tobias Jones aloud to his fellow passengers as he travelled to the city. He omitted to mention that he never by any chance slept badly. His fatness, his red cheeks and blushing health proclaimed that well enough. But he was a patriot and the statement he had ventured upon, and which he repeated a dozen times that day under different circumstances, went only to prove his love for his country.

Meanwhile one may wonder how it was that Joe Gresson had been able to construct his ship in such a short space of time.

"Of course, the thing would have been impossible had I not had a great deal of the work already in hand," he told his uncle. "You see, a Zeppelin can be constructed in three months, though the first models took a year perhaps. But you must remember that I had a complete rolling mill installed here at my works, which was able to turn out the girders and sheets we wanted as fast as we could put them together. Then again, the bending and fitting of celludine is a different thing entirely from that of steel or aluminium. Moderate heat will easily make the stoutest girder we have used bendable, while the sheets require only the gentlest pressure. Then riveting is far easier. The electric iron has saved us numbers of hours. As for the engines, I had them by me, having taken them from my other model. So, after all, there's nothing very wonderful about the business."

But if Joe Gresson modestly thought there was nothing to comment upon and no reason for congratulations to be showered upon him, there were others who thought quite the opposite. Andrew was hugely delighted. The authorities at the

War Office and the Admiralty, sceptical as ever, took the thing up with a decision and an energy entirely foreign to them. And Mr. Carl Reitberg narrowly escaped a serious illness.

"What! Constructed their airship already! Rescued people at sea! Transparent! Able to hoist men into the air as if they were flies. This—this is incredible."

He didn't say it all quite like that, for he was troubled with a distinct accent, one, too, which had stuck to him all his business life in spite of the fact that he had spent so many years beneath the protection of the Union Jack. He blustered, fumed, and raged, and finally went to bed. The following day he carefully investigated his financial position.

"It will ruin me, this challenge," he declared in despair. "One hundred thousand pounds! It is a gigantic sum. I was an idiot ever to listen to Andrew Provost and his fool of a nephew. But—*himmel!* we shall see what we shall see. The ship is built, that is true enough. But can she circle the globe, and if she be able to do that, can she complete the journey in four months and a couple of weeks, all that remain now of the agreed-upon nine months? Ah! There is many a slip. She is fast, this ship. Eyewitnesses of her flight tell me that. She takes no notice of the wind. But Zeppelins have met with accidents: she may too!"

His fat little face was deeply puckered and seamed for the next half-hour. In fact, Mr. Carl Reitberg was considering matters very deeply and seriously. Then he took a sudden resolution. He donned a magnificent fur-lined coat, jammed a glossy hat upon his head, then, with a fat cigar protruding from his mouth, and wearing the ideal appearance of a very rich and prosperous financier, he stepped into his motor car and drove off to the place where the great airship had been constructed. Sergeant Evans himself conveyed his somewhat large and obtrusive card to Andrew Provost.

"A gentleman to see you, sir," he said in his well-trained voice. "H-m!"

Andrew could tell almost without lifting his eyes to the Sergeant's face what his private opinion was of Mr. Reitberg; for the card bore that gentleman's name. Not that Sergeant Evans was apt to forget his position. He was too good and too old a servant for that. But he happened to have served in many parts, and, strangely enough, Mr. Reitberg was known to him.

"Ever seen the gentleman before?" asked Andrew curiously.

"South Africa, sir."

"Ah!"

"Him and a crew of the same sort as himself, begging pardon, sir."

"Humph! I've thought as much myself," Andrew muttered, though exactly what his thoughts were he did not divulge. Still, from the curious manner in which Sergeant Evans spoke, from a queer inflection of his voice, Andrew gathered that he had not only met this Carl Reitberg before, but had little good to report concerning him.

"Long ago?" he asked laconically.

"Twelve years come Christmas, sir; during the Boer War."

"Ah! And my acquaintance has lasted for ten years perhaps. He was rich when I met him, and very pleasant. Was he, er—the same, Sergeant Evans? Please speak out; don't hesitate to tell me what you know. You must understand that Mr. Carl Reitberg is the challenger who declared that the building of this ship was impossible, and that we could not construct and sail her round the world in nine months. Well, we've done the first part. We've got only to circle the world."

"And you'll have to watch him all the while, sir," whispered the Sergeant. "He's got to pay if he loses, sir?"

"One hundred thousand pounds."

The Sergeant let go a little whistle. "Beg pardon, sir," he said, "but when I knew this Carl Reitberg, same gentleman as is waiting outside, he was a slippery fellow. He was trading near Johannesburg, and he was in with foreigners, spies anxious to see the British troops beaten. I know that, for I was one of the police corps, and we'd our eyes on him. Show him up, sir?"

"Certainly."

It followed that the magnificent, if small and podgy frame of Mr. Carl Reitberg was introduced to the airship, and that within five minutes, puffing heavily with the astounding wonders he saw, that same gentleman was seated in the saloon, staring upward through the transparent ceiling with positive amazement written on his face. An hour later he was back in the heart of London, when, dismissing his motor, he walked some distance up the street, hailed a taxi, and drove rapidly away in an easterly direction. Half an hour later, perhaps, he was closeted in a back room of a grimy house adjacent to Whitechapel, with an individual who looked the very opposite of himself. He was untidy, down at heels, even ragged, while his face with its half-sunken cheeks showed obvious traces of excitement. It was equally obvious also that Carl Reitberg and this individual were not entire strangers. To be precise, they had at one time been bosom companions,at the very time, in fact, when Sergeant Evans had had knowledge of them. Then they had parted, and the queer tricks Dame Fortune plays with various individuals had resulted in Carl Reitberg gathering wealth about him, while Adolf Fruhmann had become almost a pauper. And it had chanced that the wealthy and lucky man had caught sight of his old-time friend but a week before as he drove in his lordly motor down Whitechapel. He had seen Adolf Fruhmann hovering at one of the many corners; and though he passed him then without so much as a nod—indeed, shrinking back out of sight—he now remembered the chance vision he had caught of the down-at-heels man, and with the view of obtaining help from him sought him out.

"But I must go carefully," he told himself, as he drove in his taxi. "I'll leave the cab very soon, and then walk along the pavement. It shall be Adolf who shall recognize me, not I him. Then it shall be he who shall ask for help; I will give it."

The crafty little fellow followed out this plan to its successful conclusion. Looking the plutocrat admirably, he stepped briskly down the pavement of Whitechapel, and when he saw his man in the distance, gave vent to a grunt of pleasure. And yet he contrived matters so that it was Adolf who, looking up as the fur-coated man passed, recognized an old partner.

"Hallo!" he called, while a sulky cloud gathered upon his sickly face. "Carl Reitberg of all people!"

Now at any other time Mr. Carl Reitberg would, as we have hinted, not have been anxious to renew an acquaintance with such a man. His wealth had brought with it position. Carl Reitberg chose to forget his earlier days, and the people with whom he had consorted. But now he had an object in view, and halting at once he allowed first a look of amazement to spread over his fat and jowly face; and then a welcoming smile set his lips apart, while he stretched out a hand to grip Adolf's.

"You!" he cried. "Who could have thought it? And here of all places. Why, we parted in South Africa."

"Johnny'sberg—yes; because the police——"

"H-hush! That's done with; I've forgotten," said Carl hastily. "But—but you're down on your luck. I haven't forgotten that we were friends then, at any rate. This place is too public for a meeting. Take me somewhere where we can be quiet."

And thus it happened that they were closeted in that back room in the grimy house adjacent to Whitechapel.

"And so you're down, penniless," said Carl, eyeing his one-time friend narrowly.

"Absolutely; hopelessly."

The opulent individual who had sought this interview so craftily lifted ten fat fingers to show his concern. Then he dipped with difficulty into a waistcoat pocket, pulled out a crinkling note of the value of five pounds, and handed it across the dirty table.

"That'll tide you over for a little," he said. "After that——"

"Ah! That's where the pinch comes. What am I to do?"

"You want work?" asked Carl.

"Well, yes. Not hard labour, mind you. The class of thing we did out in South Africa wouldn't come amiss."

Whatever that task may have been one was not to hear it, for Carl held up a fat hand instantly.

"S-s-sh!" he said, somewhat angrily. "Least said soonest mended. We forget South Africa. But—yes, I might find a task for you, a congenial task. You've heard of this new airship?"

Adolf Fruhmann looked puzzled. After all, when a man has fallen upon evil days and finds it hard to discover from where his next meal is to come, he is not apt to betray much interest in passing events, nor has he, often enough, spare halfpence with which to purchase journals. But it happened that Adolf had seen an account in a paper, and since the story had now leaked out, and it was known how Mr. Carl Reitberg had issued a challenge to Andrew Provost and his nephew Joseph Gresson, he recollected that he had even noted the name of his one-time friend and associate in connection with this wonderful airship.

"Yes," he ejaculated. "One hundred thousand pounds, eh, Carl? A lot to lose if they win, and it looks as if they might do so."

A crafty look came across his face. He leaned farther across the table and whispered something. "Why don't you?" he asked.

"What! Impossible! I couldn't. It would be scandalous," came the instant answer, though Carl Reitberg's tones rather belied his words. "You don't mean to suggest that I should take steps to—to destroy the ship?"

He endeavoured to cast a tone of indignation into his speech now; but it seemed that Adolf knew his man well. He scoffed at that tone.

"Why not?" he asked quickly. "If they win, you pay one hundred thousand pounds. Eh? One hundred thousand sovereigns."

"True—but——"

"There is no but. They must not succeed. There are others who would willingly pay for the secrets of this airship, and who long to hear that she has been wrecked. Give me the job. Keep in the background yourself. Go down to the ship and wish them the best of success. Place yourself in a good light before them and the world. Let them believe you to be what is known to these fools as a sportsman. Yes, that is the word. A sportsman, almost anxious to see yourself lose, and ready at any moment to pay that hundred thousand pounds. Then leave the rest to me."

Carl Reitberg sank back upon the hard-wood chair he occupied and pondered deeply. Even Adolf Fruhmann with all his knowledge of Carl's cunning—and in former days the two associates had carried out many a rascally piece of business together, demanding no little acumen and cunning—even he failed to see to the depths of Carl Reitberg. For the plutocrat had skilfully planned this meeting with one object in view, and had so arranged matters that this proposal, which he listened to with pretended indignation, and which had been hatched in his own brain, came actually from Adolf Fruhmann. To appear too ready to fall in with it would be to weaken his own position. Therefore he sat bunched up on his chair, one fat hand over his eyes, but those same orbs closely scrutinizing his companion's crafty features from between his own fat fingers. He remained in that position for a full five minutes, while Adolf fidgeted and fretted. For the man was eager to undertake this work, a task after his own rascally heart. He had not been engaged in South Africa, in delving for British secrets and in selling them to the enemy without something resulting. A born schemer, those experiences had whetted his appetite for more conspiracy. Besides, it was a game which promised wealth, while it had an element of danger that appealed to the rascal, for, to give him his due, he was a man of courage, a man who faced odds willingly, and who found in difficulties and danger the stimulus that whetted his efforts and gave a zest to an undertaking.

"Well," he demanded impatiently, "you know me by now. Have I failed before? There was that affair at Nicholson's Cloof. Did I fail there? Then why now? As for you, who is to learn that you are mixed up in the affair? Go down to these people. Pass yourself off as a sportsman, and—leave the rest to me."

Carl stirred. He took the fat hand from his face and looked at his companion. "How much?" he asked curtly. "What will you do this for?"

The remainder of their conversation was carried on in low tones and with the greatest earnestness. These two rascals, for both were that, bargained eagerly, and it was quite an hour later before they parted. Then Mr. Carl Reitberg passed out of the house, roughly pushed aside a poor woman who begged alms of him, hailed a taxi, and drove away to his gorgeous mansion. He left Adolf Fruhmann richer than he had been for many a day, with the promise of abundance in the future and sufficient money with which to carry on the plot so craftily hatched in that back room in the grimy house off Whitechapel. The following day found the magnate down at Joe Gresson's wonderful hangar again. He was geniality itself. He had come to wish the crew and the ship a safe voyage and a rapid one, and to hope that nothing might happen to arrest their progress or to damage the airship.

"To my old friend, Mr. Andrew Provost," he said, "and to his wonderful nephew, Mr. Joseph Gresson. May they return triumphant!"

Lifting the glass of wine he had been sipping and standing up he solemnly drank the health of the party. Then, with a cordial grip of the hand all round, he left the ship under the pilotage of Sergeant Evans. His tongue was in his cheek as he stepped on to the gangway which led to the floor of the hangar. He turned to wave his adieus to the people above, distinguishable through the framework of the vessel. And then he regarded the Sergeant with a puzzled expression.

"Strange," he said. "I seem to know your face, to have met you before."

"The other day, sir," came the respectful and guarded answer; "I took your card up to Mr. Andrew."

"Yes, that must be the explanation," Carl told himself, and departed satisfied. He was more than satisfied, in fact, and hugged himself in the depths of his motor car. For the interview had gone off wonderfully. A reporter who, thanks to his own skilful arrangement, had been present, proceeded at once to write up a glowing account of the meeting, and that evening the world learned that Mr. Carl Reitberg had been aboard the airship, where he had generously wished all the utmost success, had drank to their health, and had shown in every way that he was a sportsman. More than that, he had intimated his intention of at once depositing one hundred thousand pounds at his bankers', so that, in the likely event, as he hoped, of the successful termination of the venture, Mr. Andrew Provost might claim it instantly. What could be fairer or more magnanimous? What could be better calculated to throw dust in the eyes of the public, and, more important than all, in the eyes of the crew of the airship? Carl Reitberg not only hugged himself as he sank back amid the luxurious cushions of his landaulette. He chuckled loudly. He rubbed his fat hands unctuously together and positively grinned. Yes, he had been wonderfully canny and successful. It remained now for the crafty Adolf Fruhmann to carry on the conspiracy and see it to a successful ending.

"Bah! Thought he'd seen me before. Didn't let on that it was out in South Africa," Sergeant Evans was murmuring as he entered the vessel again. "Now if I know Mr. Reitberg he ain't up to any good. He's a foxy fellow at any time, the chap who sits at home and does the gentleman, while those friends of his carry out the scheme that he's after. Well, I for one will keep an eye open."

The three days which passed after Mr. Midshipman Hamshaw added his important presence to the airship were decidedly busy ones. He himself had his kit to obtain and friends to say farewell to. And then there was the victualling of the ship, a matter of great importance. All day and night carts arrived at the hangar, and the crew of the ship, composed almost entirely of soldiers and sailors, were engaged in piling cases upon the lift and hoisting them into the interior of the vessel. Sufficient tinned goods were taken to last the party for five months. There was fuel to be considered, and one had to remember that a journey of the description contemplated demanded various weights of clothing, weapons, ammunition, in fact a hundred and one items. But at length, thanks to Joe Gresson's foresight and Andrew Provost's energy, they were gathered and stored in the huge storage rooms of the vessel. The hangar swung round easily with her head away from the wind, while the motors began to rumble. Stationed with Joe in the engine-room Alec and Dick watched the young inventor gently handle a lever, and looking backward saw the gigantic propeller reverse. The ship moved. Those wide lateral keels running upon rollers inserted in the wide slots on either side, which were part and parcel of the hangar, began to slide gently away from their holding. The ship backed slowly and surely out of her hangar till she was entirely clear. A bell sounded in the engine-room, while a voice was heard through the loud-speaking telephone. It was from Hurst, now trained to new duties, and at that moment stationed on the upper deck, right on the prow of the vessel.

"All clear, sir," he called. "She backed forty feet from the hangar. All clear."

Another bell sounded. "All clear aft," came from Hawkins, stationed near the propeller.

"Then we ascend. What's the time?" asked Joe.

"Eight thirty, sir," answered Dick promptly. "Eight thirty p.m."

"Precisely; and the day is Wednesday?"

"Yes, sir."

"Then in one hundred and twenty-four days, less three hours and thirty minutes from this moment, we are due to return. If we are here then, and our foreign office passport has been properly initialled, then we shall have won the challenge. We can let her go. Stand by there! I'm going to take her up quickly. Then London shall have a glimpse of their ship, and afterwards——"

"Yes, afterwards?" asked Commander Jackson, who had now joined them.

Joe shrugged his shoulders. "Who can say? I myself have confidence in the vessel. But accidents may happen. We might be delayed by the smallest and most unexpected circumstance. We can but make the attempt."

"And win or lose I shall be satisfied," chimed in Andrew. "Let her go."

The motors roared. Those elevator fans within the ship whirled at a giddy rate, and at once the gigantic framework shot upward till she was two thousand feet above the hangar. Then Joe touched another lever. The propeller in rear began to sing its own strange note. The ship moved forward and that adventurous voyage had begun.

"Starting's easier than returning," Mr. Carl Reitberg told himself with a chuckle when he read of the departure of the ship on the following morning and of her appearance over London. "Let 'em wait a bit. Adolf Fruhmann has yet a word or so to say in the matter."

CHAPTER VII

En Route for Adrianople

"And now, gentlemen, to discuss our route," said Mr. Andrew Provost once London was left behind, with its gaping and wildly-cheering crowds, amid which Carl Reitberg had a place, and the rascally Adolf Fruhmann also. "We are hovering at this moment over the Straits of Dover, and since, if our tour of the world is to be complete, we must waste no time, it will be as well if we map out a course without further delay."

In his practical manner he had provided himself with a huge globe, which now stood in the centre of the saloon table, with those who were to tour the world on the giant airship seated about it.

"Gentlemen," he went on, "the earth—or, rather, I should have said, the air— the air is before you and around you. Choose your path. To me and to my nephew the course we take is immaterial, with just this one reservation. We wish to take a path which will give us facilities for picking up both water and fuel. Now!"

Looking round the brightly-illuminated saloon he invited first the Commander, then Alec, and then Dick to give an opinion. But all in turn shook their heads.

"No, no," said the former eagerly. "To me it matters not a jot which course we take. Choose yourself. Or, if you merely ask for a suggestion, let us take the all-red route. Let us fly so as to pass over and call in upon as many British possessions as possible. There! That is a pleasant scheme. Why not?"

"Why not, indeed? Excellent!" cried Andrew. "Now, let us trace the route. But wait; there is one other to be consulted. I refer to Major Harvey, who came aboard just before we started. Perhaps he has some special wishes; let us consult him."

Sergeant Evans was at once sent to summon the latest guest aboard, and within a few minutes there entered the saloon a tall, well-set-up man of perhaps forty years of age, well groomed, spruce, and of active appearance, with features which might be described as prepossessing, while there was a firmness about the chin and a steadiness of the eyes which showed that the newcomer was possessed of courage. In short and in fact he was the beau ideal of a soldier, while his manner was easy and distinctly friendly. Nodding to all, for he had been introduced some three hours before, he sat himself down and looked across at Andrew.

"You sent for me," he said crisply, in a matter-of-fact way, even more businesslike than that of his host. "What is the question? Can I be of service?"

"Certainly, Major. There is a globe; you know already that we have been, as it were, challenged to tour the world, to make a complete circle of the globe. Well, then, choose a route for us. Commander Jackson suggests an all-red route, which shall take us over British possessions. If that meets with your approval, well and good. If not, then where shall we go—what course shall we steer?"

For answer the Major slowly rose from his seat, and, crossing to the table, carefully and critically examined the globe. Then he drew a packet of papers from his pocket, and, selecting one, handed it to Andrew.

"For me all courses are the same," he said with a smile; "but since I take it that from here to the centre of Europe is but a step for this magnificent vessel, I should be glad of the opportunity of visiting one part comparatively but a stone's throw from here. I speak of the Balkans. Please read that letter."

Andrew slowly opened the envelope, drew out the contents, and then donned his glasses. Adjusting them at the correct angle upon his nose, he held the letter up and read aloud.

"Adrianople, Thursday evening, 16 January, 1913."

"Adrianople!" cried the Commander. "That's the city now besieged for so long by the Bulgarian armies."

"Quite so; closely besieged," admitted the Major. "Very closely."

"Ahem!" Andrew cleared his throat. "You wish me to read it aloud?" he asked, waving the letter at the Major.

"Certainly."

"Then here it is. 'Dear Harvey, I write to inform you that I am held here in Adrianople, and should the siege continue much longer, the value of the information I have gained will be lost. But I cannot dispatch it in this letter. This must pass the scrutiny of both friends and enemies. Therefore it but announces my presence here, where I live as best I can. Please explain my continued absence to our mutual friends. Yours, Charlie.'"

Andrew took his glasses from his nose slowly, glanced sideways at the letter, and then direct at the Major. There was a puzzled look upon his face, a polite enquiry as much as to say, "Well, my dear sir, I don't understand. What has your friend Charlie to do with us? He's in Adrianople; so are scores of others. There's a British consul there, no doubt. Why should we go to this besieged city?"

Commander Jackson coughed; similar thoughts were passing through his quick brain also, though he gave his soldier friend credit for astuteness and common sense. "Must be something behind this letter," he said aloud.

"Certainly; Charlie knew that many eyes would see it before I received his hurried lines," said the Major. "But let me explain what it is that I gather by the reading of that letter. First, that Charlie is hemmed in in this besieged city. Next, that he has information which he cannot send through the post, or by means of a runner escaping from or permitted to leave the city. In fact and in short he has information of value, value to our mutual friends, who, I may further explain, happen to be the Government."

"Ah, I suspected something of the sort! What next?" asked Andrew.

"I will be frank," came the answer. "For the past three years Charlie and I have been engaged in some extremely delicate and important investigations in and around the Balkans. Pardon me if I am not more explicit on this matter. I left for London some two months ago, having lost all trace of Charlie. Now I know him to have obtained the information which we sought, information which, owing to the sudden onset of war and the siege of Adrianople, he is unable to impart. Well, Mr. Provost, that information is wanted by the Government at once. Delay is positively dangerous. I ask you in the name of this country to risk a visit to Adrianople and there attempt to pick up my friend and fellow investigator."

There was silence for perhaps two minutes, while the various people present in the saloon glanced at one another curiously, to see if possible what their fellows thought. Then Andrew spoke briskly and with marked decision.

"There will be guns about Adrianople?" he asked; "guns capable of sending shells high into the air? Mortars, in fact?"

"Precisely; there will be siege batteries. The Bulgars are wonderfully equipped. The Turks also, hemmed in in Adrianople, have some marvellous pieces."

"Any one of which, by exploding a shell within distance of us, could wreck the ship?"

The Major nodded. "True enough," he said coldly. "The risk would be great. If you are seen, a thousand rifles will be pointed at you. A hundred guns will be manœuvred so as to aim into the sky. The risk will be very great; I do not deny it."

"And the service will be equally great. You tell us that this matter is of urgent importance for England?"

Andrew asked his question sharply, as if he were cross-examining the Major. "You tell us that England has great need of this service? I ask for no details.

Anyone can see that we are discussing a delicate matter. I merely ask again as to its importance."

"And I reply that the service is of the greatest. More than that, I will explain that the War Office had appointed another officer to this ship, and only changed their selection at the last moment. I was given precise instructions to bring this request before you at the earliest instant. You ask me how great is the importance of this matter, and I reply without hesitation that, even if this wonderful ship and her crew were destroyed in the successful effort to gain this information, then great, overwhelming as the loss would undoubtedly be, it would be but a small price to pay for the news which Charlie has gathered. As for Charlie, that is but a *nom de plume*. The writer happens to be an officer high up in the British army."

The Major slowly surveyed his comrades, while he spoke deliberately. Then he drew a cigarette from his case, placed it between his lips and set a flaring match to it, with a nonchalance one had perforce to admire. For obviously enough Andrew's decision was of the utmost moment to him. Equally clearly it was borne upon the minds of those who listened that this mission, the barest details of which could be discussed, was of unusual importance. If Andrew and his nephew refused to jeopardize the safety of the airship by taking her into such a danger zone, then one could guess that particulars of the utmost moment would be lost entirely, or, what amounted to the same, their delivery would be so delayed that they would be useless.

"Well?" asked the Major, puffing out a cloud of smoke. "Your answer. I ask no favour. I have pointed out the risk."

"And I thank you heartily," cried Andrew. "Gentlemen, we will take the all-red route for this world tour, looking in at as many dependencies of the British crown as possible. And we will willingly take the risk of a visit to Adrianople. If there are any here who have no desire for this adventure, then we will set them down wherever they wish. Now, let us be moving."

It may be readily imagined that not one of those present in the brightly-lighted saloon had any qualms as to this projected visit, for to all of them was promised a novel situation. The Major and the Commander might hope, indeed, to witness a modern siege in actual operation, while no doubt the successful manœuvring of this fine vessel would be of sufficient interest to Joe and Andrew. For Dick and Alec there was, of course, a decided attraction in the suggestion.

"Who knows, there might be a rumpus of some sort," declared the former. "We might get to see a bit of the fighting. How'd you like that?"

"How'd you?" Alec grinned back at him. "You're the one to answer, for you're a man of war. You're in the Navy."

"I'll tell you. If there's just the merest chance of getting down into the city I mean to take it," said Dick. "Then there's no knowing what may happen. How is the Major going to find this fellow Charlie? That's what beats me, for Adrianople is a big city. And how is he to bring him or his news aboard without descending? I tell you this ship'll have to be steered right over the armies. She'll have to drop to easy distance of the city, and then—supposing a shell did happen to come our way—well——"

"You'd find yourself in the city precious quick, and so have your dearest wish fulfilled in a minute," laughed Alec. "We'd blow up, eh! There'd be a fine old crash on the roofs of Adrianople."

Joking apart, the danger was not likely to be small and the risk run by the crew of the airship was perhaps greater than had been anticipated. But Andrew and his nephew made light of any trouble, and indeed undertook this work with a keenness that did them credit. It followed, therefore, that within a dozen hours the airship floated high up above the besieged city. It was night-time, clouds floated thickly in the sky, while not a light showed aboard the vessel. Down below a few flickering lamps could be seen in the direction of the city, though the greater part was plunged in darkness. But away to the north and south, and on either hand, there were rows and rows of tiny blazing circles, the camp fires of the investors.

"Holding every outlet," said the Major. "Not a man can enter or leave the city. If they could, Charlie would have bade farewell to it long ago. But entrance from the air is another question altogether."

"And you propose to descend to the city?" asked Andrew.

"With your help, certainly. There is a huge mosque in the heart of Adrianople, and that is the place I shall aim for. There, or in the immediate neighbourhood, I shall find Charlie."

"And—and supposing anything should happen to prevent your returning, supposing you were apprehended by the Turks," suggested Andrew.

"Then the airship goes on her way again. It will be a misfortune, of course, but that is all. You have risked all to bring me here, and I shall not grumble if I am discovered."

In the darkness of the engine-room it was impossible to observe the Major's face, but at that moment it was stern and peculiarly determined. For without a shadow of doubt the descent into the city would be exceedingly dangerous. If he were seen by one of the besieged as likely as not he would be shot down on the instant. If not that, then he would be apprehended as a spy, perhaps; and short shrift was given, he knew well enough, to men of that description. But there was not so much as a tremor about him as, an hour later, he stepped upon the platform from which the lift ran, sat himself in the sling by which Commander Jackson had descended to the water on the occasion of Dick's misadventure, and whispered to his friends to let him go.

"Adieu!" he called gently. "Watch for a flare amongst the buildings to-morrow night. If you do not see one, then return again the following night. If still there is no sign, sail on and leave me. Adieu!"

The motor above hummed a low-pitched song, the sling at the end of the rope bearing this gallant officer upon it dropped from the platform and went shooting down under the airship.

"Good luck!" whispered Andrew. "Ah! There goes a very gallant fellow. Now, gently with that tackle. The barometer places us five hundred feet above the city. We shall have to lower very carefully when we have let out four hundred feet of the line."

In the inky darkness of the night the ship had slowly descended till she was suspended at the height mentioned above this besieged city. And now those aboard her slowly paid the rope out over the motor, letting it go foot by foot once they guessed that the burden they were lowering was nearing the ground. Perhaps ten minutes had passed before they found that the line hung slack. A pull upon it disclosed the fact that the Major must have left it.

"Haul in!" commanded Andrew. "Now, we will rise again, and sail right away from the city. Let us hope that our plucky friend will be successful."

The following morning found the ship hovering at a great height over a deserted stretch of country, where she lay inert in the air, as if resting after her long trip from England. But that night the motors hummed again, and presently she was back over Adrianople.

"Now, all hands set to work to watch for a flare," Andrew commanded. "We'll divide the city into various portions, and so make sure by giving a different part to each one of us that the Major's signal cannot go undetected."

But though the eyes turned upon the dark surroundings of the beleaguered city never left their object, there was no flare to attract their attention, and presently the first signs of dawn warned Andrew and his comrades that the time had come to depart. A loud detonation in the far distance, and a streaming flame of fire, hastened their decision, and they rose at once and headed away from the city followed by the noise of artillery in action. In fact, a fierce attack had begun upon Adrianople, and though the huge airship put many miles between her and the contending armies, the dull muffled roar of guns still reached them on occasion. But towards evening the battle slackened, and that night, when once more over the city, there was not a sound to disturb the silence; not a note came to the ears of the listeners above to tell them of the armies beneath them.

"Fine and clear, but dark enough for our purpose," said Joe, straining his head over the rail of the observation platform of the vessel. "Let us hope that we shall see the signal this evening, for I confess that I shall be glad to get away from those guns. Did you see the shells bursting as we left in the morning?"

"Guess I did," came Andrew's emphatic answer. "And a nice little mess they'd make of this ship if one hit us."

"Or came within a hundred yards of hitting us," said Joe decidedly. "If a shell were to burst within easy distance, the chances are that the concussion would break the framework and cause the gas to explode. So let's hope we shan't be long in such an unpleasant neighbourhood."

But the night passed again without so much as a flicker from the city. Major Harvey made no sign of his presence. Was he captured, or shot? or had he merely failed to discover Charlie?

"Captured or shot," said Andrew promptly, when they began to discuss the matter. "If he had merely failed to discover his friend he would have sent us a signal, and on returning to us would have made other plans to recover this information. There is no signal. That means that the Major cannot make it. In fact, he is dead, or he is a prisoner."

"While we are left helpless above the city," Joe added. "What's to be done? We'd never think of leaving the place till we are quite sure what has happened."

"Never," declared Andrew with energy. "Besides, there's another important matter to consider and to keep us here. The Major distinctly told us that Charlie possessed information of vital importance to the British Government. Then we have two reasons for remaining, one being the safety of our friend the Major, and the other being the need to discover Charlie. That seems to me to present unheard-of difficulties. For Charlie is merely a name. We haven't even a description of this officer incarcerated in Adrianople. Come, Commander, help us. This is a real difficulty."

It was more than that. It was a dilemma, for how could Andrew and Joe and his friends help the Major, seeing that they were high in the air? And how could they discover a man in the city of Adrianople of whose appearance they had no knowledge?

"Might be tall or short, broad or thin, dark or fair," said Dick. "It's a conundrum."

"Unless," began Alec.

"Unless what?" Dick snapped.

"Well, unless we were to investigate personally. For instance, this Charlie's an Englishman, eh?"

"Certainly!" cried Andrew.

"Then there aren't enough of our countrymen in the city to make it difficult to pick out our man. He's a soldier, that we know. It isn't so hard as a rule to tell when one looks at one of that profession. As for the Major, if he's alive, why, seeking might find him."

"But—but you forget. We're up here, a thousand feet in the air," cried Andrew testily.

"Quite so, sir," came the respectful answer. "But the Major descended. We could do the same."

"Bravo! It's the only course open," cried the Commander. "Mr. Provost, our duty is clearly before us. We must follow the Major, seek him out, and discover his friend Charlie. Come, I volunteer. It would never do for you or your nephew to make the attempt, for you have this tour to make, and you must be successful. For me it is different. I am in the service of my country; this is a question of duty."

"Hear, hear, sir!" chimed in Dick. "I'd like to come in support. May I?"

"While I suggested the movement and claim a place also," said Alec, with an eagerness foreign to him. "Why not, Mr. Provost?"

Why not? What one man could do, others could also. Besides, how could the crew of this vessel honourably retreat from this beleaguered city and leave a comrade in the lurch, to say nothing of losing something of a secret nature which they had been assured was of vital importance to their country? No— they must stay. They must go to the Major since he could not return to them.

"I agree," said Andrew, after some few moments' consideration. "You three shall be lowered, and to-morrow night we will return and look for your signal. But let me beg of you all to use the utmost discretion. One misfortune is enough without inviting others."

It was perhaps an hour later when three figures muffled in short, thick coats stepped upon the lift platform.

"Goodbye!" whispered Andrew and Joe. "A safe return!"

"*Au revoir!*" sang out Dick, in the seventh heaven of happiness. "Now, hold on, Alec! We don't want you to get tumbling over and so announcing our coming."

Hearty hand-grips were exchanged, and then the motor hummed its tune. The Commander and Dick and Alec sank out of sight and were at once swallowed up in the darkness.

CHAPTER VIII

The Besieged City

"Steady! Now, lower very slowly, for we are close to the houses."

Commander Jackson pressed the button of the electric indicator aboard the platform on which he and Dick Hamshaw and Alec Jardine were being lowered into the besieged city of Adrianople, and applied his lips to the loud-speaking telephone. He barely whispered into the receiver, but Dick and Alec knew well that his voice would be heard easily enough aloft.

"Stop! Move away to the right; we are directly above a very large building."

The platform of the lift jerked slightly as the motor above was arrested, and for the space of a minute perhaps, it and its human freight rose and fell as the long steel wire stretched and then contracted. Dick craned his head over the edge, for he was kneeling, just as he had been on that earlier occasion when the Commander came down to his rescue. Below, barely visible in the all-pervading gloom, he made out the dim, hazy details of a building, which stretched on either hand for some considerable distance. Then he turned on his elbow and stared upward, to find that nothing was visible. There was not even the barest outline of the great airship which he knew well enough was directly overhead, not a light, not a single sound, not even the gentle tune of that humming motor. But down below there were sounds. Hark! What was that?

"Men marching through the streets," whispered the Commander. "We shall have to be cautious, for it would never do to drop into the hands of the Turks. They would not understand our coming. We should be spies, as a matter of course. Hold on up there," his companions heard him whisper into the receiver of the telephone. "Hoist a little higher. Now, move ahead."

Somewhere in the distance a clock struck musically, the sound easily reaching the ears of the adventurous three descending to the city. One, two, three.

"Two hours more and we shall have the dawn," whispered the Commander. "Listen! Troops are on the move. There must be thousands marching beneath us. No doubt reinforcements are being taken to some part where a new and fierce attack is anticipated. Ah!"

Dick flushed as red as a beetroot in the darkness, and was thankful for the cloak it lent him. For who could help starting violently under the circumstances? A loud report had suddenly rung out away on their left, a detonation which set the air above the city reverberating. There was a flash in the distance, a streak of flame cutting into the darkness, and then, heard perhaps half a minute later, a hideous shriek, getting louder and more insistent.

"A messenger from the besiegers," said the Commander hoarsely. "Ah! It plumped into the house away over there to the right. Lucky we weren't directly over it."

It was fortunate for all three without a doubt, for that messenger from the lines of the Bulgarians or from those of the Servians, who were now aiding their comrades in this siege, was certainly not of the peaceful variety. That shriek, in fact, was followed by a clatter, by the crash of a hard, heavy body striking against masonry. Then there was a thunderous roar, a huge spot of flame and smoke and debris, and finally darkness and silence, silence made more intense by the occasional low moaning of some poor injured person. A second later another gun spoke from the distance, while the streak of flame from the muzzle was followed by a third detonation from a different direction, and later by half a dozen more. Suspended in midair Dick and his friends listened to the roar of the shells, to the clatter of tumbling masonry, and to the explosions that followed with feelings which can hardly be described as precisely comfortable.

"George! A near shave," whispered Dick. "Hear it, sir?"

"Hear it? Rather!" came gruffly from the Commander. "That shell went over our heads, and I reckon there cannot have been more than a dozen feet between it and us. Nasty, eh! if one were to hit the wire rope."

"Ugh! What's he want to talk like that for?" Alec grumbled beneath his breath. He peered over the edge of the platform and shivered. Not that he had not plenty of courage and spirit. But somehow the dangers of a bombardment seemed greater when suspended between earth and sky than when one has one's feet firmly planted upon Mother Earth. It seemed, too, that the jovial Commander felt the same also.

"It'd be nasty to get that rope cut, eh?" he asked again. "We'd fall heavily. Let's move on. Do either of you lads hear any more troops moving?"

A few minutes before there had been the muffled sound of a multitude of rough boots treading upon uneven cobbles. Sometimes one heard the clink of a sabre against the stones, or of one man's rifle against that of a comrade. And now and then voices had reached the three suspended overhead—sharp voices, as if officers were there issuing commands.

"Hear 'em?" asked the Commander.

"Moved on, sir, I think," responded Dick. "Now's the time for us to do the same."

"Listen! They've gone away to our left. You can hear their steps still," said Alec. "Ah! That ends all sounds from them. I suppose this is a general bombardment, sir?"

"Sounds like it," admitted the Commander. "Guns are directing shells upon the city now from every side. It's time, as you say, Dick, to get a move on. Ah! The ship has carried us away from that building. What's below us?"

They craned their necks over the edge of the platform and peered down into the darkness. "A garden, sir," suggested Dick.

"Clear ground in any case," came from Alec.

"Then lower away," the Commander whispered into the receiver. "Steady! Ah, she's bumped! Hop out, you fellows. All clear? Then hoist above there. We're safely in the city."

Did they hear a gentle hum from high up overhead? Dick fancied he could for one brief instant as the lift shot upward. But it may have been merely imagination. In any case there came quickly enough other sounds to drown any there may have been from the airship; for a monstrous gun spoke in the distance. The air above this devoted city shook and vibrated, while the steel monster launched into space howled and shrieked as it rushed to its destination.

"Down behind this wall," called the Commander, who had stood up to stare in the direction from which the shot had come. "Down, quick! That shell's coming straight for us."

Throwing themselves down upon the ground behind a low wall beside which the lift had dropped them, they waited breathlessly for the landing of that messenger. It shrieked a warning at them. It announced its coming in a manner there was no mistaking. Then suddenly it burst upon them. The shriek grew positively deafening, rising to such a blood-curdling pitch that it would have shaken the pluck even of a veteran. But it was muffled all in a second. There was a ponderous thud within a dozen yards of the adventurous trio, an uncanny silence, and then a detonation that threw them against the wall, and sent earth and stones and debris in every direction. And what a sight the wide-spreading flames of that explosion presented! Dick saw buildings all about him, buildings over which stones and clods of earth were hurtling. To his left, within two hundred yards perhaps, was an enormous erection, the actual size of which he could not hope to estimate. But the momentary flash of the explosion showed him towers and minarets, proof positive that here was a mosque, the mosque, no doubt, for which Major Harvey had aimed when descending into the city. That fleeting flash gave him in addition just one glimpse of a huge shape floating almost directly overhead, no doubt the gigantic outline of the airship.

"Lor! Supposing she felt the shock?" he groaned. "Supposing the airship has sustained some damage."

"Not she! As right as a trivet," came in somewhat shaking tones from close beside him, for unconsciously the young midshipman had spoken aloud. "But, jingo, what an explosion! I've been hanging on to my hair ever since. Hope we don't get another of those gentlemen within such close distance."

The hope was hardly expressed when a second shell announced its coming, and caused them once more to shelter close to the wall which had already given them protection. As for the giant airship, when Dick gazed aloft as this other messenger exploded, there was no longer a sign of her. No doubt Andrew and his nephew had set the elevators going, and were now high overhead, out of reach of danger.

"And so we've only ourselves to think about," said Dick. "What next, then? What are the orders, sir? I caught a sight of the great mosque for which Major Harvey said he would make. It's close to us. I suppose that's where we shall begin our search?"

Strangely enough there came no answer. Dick caught his breath, Alec gasped aloud. The midshipman could hear his breath coming fast and deep within two feet perhaps of where he was sitting.

"Wait," he whispered. "He was just to my right. I'll crawl that way and see where he has got to."

Getting to his knees, for till now he had been prone beside the friendly wall which had sheltered them from stones and splinters sent hurtling through the air by the shells which had fallen so close to them, Dick made his way along the edge of the wall in search of the Commander. And presently his fingers lit upon his figure. The officer was huddled up against the brickwork; and though Dick pulled his sleeve violently there came no response, not even when he kneeled above him, felt for his head, and spoke sharply into his ear.

"Come along and join me," he called gently to Alec. "The Commander's hit; yes, hit in the head. I'm sure of that, for I can feel that his hair is wet; and listen to his breathing."

Neither of those two young fellows had had up till then much acquaintance with wounds and injuries. But Dick had once seen a man lying severely stunned, and now he recognized one at least of the symptoms. For the unfortunate Commander was breathing stertorously—positively snoring—while he took not the smallest notice when his junior tugged at his clothing.

"Bend over him and strike a light," whispered Dick when Alec had joined him. "We'll have to chance being seen. Got any matches?"

75

Evidently Alec was well provided, for in a moment there came the tell-tale scrape of a lucifer being rubbed against the box. Then a tiny flame blazed out, a flame which Alec shielded with his hand, while he directed a portion of it on to the unconscious Commander.

"Yes; hit in the head. See, here's a big scalp wound," whispered Dick, making a rapid examination, and discovering blood welling from a nasty wound just above the Commander's forehead. "I'm not much used to this sort of thing, Alec, but I imagine that he's not very badly hurt. He's stunned, of course, and the thing is to know how to deal with him. First thing, anyway, is to tie a handkerchief round the wound. Get another match ready. Strike when I tell you to. Now. I've got his head lifted on to my knee and my handkerchief unfolded. Strike now."

With the help of that feeble glimmer, lasting perhaps for half a minute, they bound up the Commander's wound, and then, finding a raised piece of ground close to the wall, gently lowered his head upon it.

"Better than nothing. It'll act like a cushion," said Dick. "Now?"

"Ah—a dickens of a business! There's the Commander down and wounded, Major Harvey lost, perhaps dead for all we know, or only a prisoner; and this Charlie, whom we've never seen, and hardly heard of, somewhere in this awful city. What's to be done?"

"That's what I asked you," came quickly from Dick. "Let's see, we could make a flare with your box of matches I suppose, and so call the attention of Mr. Andrew. Pish! That's funking. Never! Besides, the airship's gone by now. Didn't it strike three as we were descending?"

"Three, yes; what's the time now?"

"At a guess four o'clock. Might be less; feels as though it were a heap more."

That, in fact, was the position. So much had happened since they set foot in this besieged city of Adrianople, that hours might have passed, and Dick really felt as if they had. And yet he knew well enough that that was not possible. But the mention of the hour made him recollect matters of greater moment.

"George!" he cried, "it will be light soon, and we shall be seen unless we manage to discover a hiding-place of sorts. Lor! This is the maddest kind of expedition I have ever been on, for here we are wanting a place in which to hide, and yet our job is to discover two individuals whom we can't possibly recognize unless we see 'em in broad daylight."

"While the airship has hooked it, eh?"

"Certain. It's getting a trifle lighter already, and she might be seen, which would be dangerous. Well now, it seems to me that we must do something pretty soon or we shall find ourselves in chokey. Look here, Alec, are you game to stand by the Commander while I go on a tour of inspection? The flash sent out by those two shells when they exploded gave me a rough idea of our surroundings. In any case I spotted a huge mosque away to our left, so I shall make over in that direction. I'll follow this wall, and when it comes to an end I'll take good care to get hold of something which will tell me I am on the right road when returning. Ah! Listen to that! Rifle fire, eh? Getting lighter outside the city and the pickets are having shots at one another. Or it is a real attack opening. Yes, there go the guns again."

This time the roar which came to their ears was, perhaps, not so loud, and it seemed probable that it emanated from the guns of the defenders. But whoever was responsible for the firing, the enemy ringing in the city lost no time in replying. For these were the days of strenuous fighting about the beleaguered city. The allies, consisting of the Bulgarians, the Servians, the Montenegrins, and the Greeks, had swept the Turks in all directions before them, till the former were within striking distance of Constantinople itself, while such important cities as Salonica had been captured. But Adrianople still held out beneath the command of Shukri Pasha, while Scutari also resisted the Montenegrins. It may be imagined therefore, that the presence of a strong force of Turks in Adrianople made it essential that the allies should detach an even stronger force to watch and hem in their enemy. For weeks the armies had, in fact, watched one another, passage out of the beleaguered city being impossible, while actual fighting was intermittent and confined to mere skirmishing. But now pour-parlers between the allies and the enemy had broken down. Terms for peace had been rejected by the Ottomans, and as a consequence the war had been resumed after an armistice of some weeks' duration. To force the Turks to accede to the terms demanded by the allies, Adrianople must be taken, even at a great cost, and it happened that the arrival of Andrew Provost and his friends had coincided with this period. Indeed, a furious bombardment of the city was to begin forthwith, shells were to pour into the streets and about the houses, while the encircling forts were to be rushed one by one, at huge cost to the allies and the Turks, and the siege pressed daily closer. Here, then, was an explanation of this beginning cannonade.

"Get down close to the wall," Dick called to his chum, as those answering guns opened and that same tell-tale shriek sounded in the distance. "Here come the shells. Hope they won't fall closer than formerly, for what has happened to the Commander may very well happen to us. Look out! Get down close. Wish to goodness there was a trench here in which we could shelter."

In spite of the fact that a huge shell had just whizzed overhead, Dick went scuttling along beside the wall on hands and knees in search of some shelter. And hardly three minutes had passed before he was back again close to Alec.

"There's a bit of a ditch close to the wall farther along there," he said hastily. "Let's carry the Commander there. Wait, though, till that beggar has passed us." That beggar happened to be a shell whose advance they could hear, and every instant they expected it to pitch in the ground somewhere beyond them. But this time it failed to carry to such a distance, and landing with a thud some few yards behind the wall beside which they lay, it exploded with violence, almost smothering them with dirt and debris and tipping stones from the wall upon them. At once Dick and Alec took the Commander by his legs and arms and carried his unconscious figure away from this danger zone till they reached the ditch of which the former had spoken.

"Better be in the open for a while than in one of the houses," said Dick, panting after such exertion, and bending over his officer. "I dare say we could manage to discover a house that's deserted, for there are sure to be numbers left untenanted at such a time. But the danger would be greater there. If a shell happened to strike the place, and one were not killed by it, one would stand the chance of being buried alive in the ruins. Now, you're game to stick here and wait for a while?"

Of course Alec was game. He was getting quite accustomed to those falling shells now, for more guns were speaking in the distance, and shots were raining into the city. All he feared really was discovery, and when he came to think of it the risk at present was not so very great. Indeed, while there was darkness no one was likely to stumble upon them, and less so just then when the enemy were battering the place, and people had their attention fully engaged in looking after their own security. It was when daylight came that the real danger would arise, so that it was urgent that one of them should at once seek out a place which would provide a haven.

"You hop off and leave the Commander to me, Dick," he said. "I ain't afraid. If any of these Turkish beggars interfere with me, I'll—well, I'll shoot 'em."

He felt for and handled the revolver with which Andrew had been careful to arm his young friends, and then slipped it back into his pocket.

"Right-o!" he said. "Off you go. But don't get lost and fail to find us again. Remember, too, that it's getting lighter; we ought to be hidden somewhere within an hour, eh?"

"And shall be," answered the midshipman optimistically. "Keep your hair on if people come near you, and lie low. This place seems to be out of the way, so I don't anticipate you'll have any trouble. So long! I'm going."

He rose swiftly to his feet and went off along the wall, the fingers of one hand trailing along the stones of which it was composed. Perhaps he went a hundred paces, more than that even, before the wall ended abruptly, the termination being jagged and broken. A few feet beyond was what appeared in the dim light to be a ruined house, while a few paces more brought him to a cobbled street, into which a shell fell as he entered. Stepping back into the shelter of a doorway, against which he happened to have arrived, Dick waited for the following explosion. Then he crossed the street, stepped on the narrow footway beyond and bumped heavily into an individual at that moment emerging from an opening in the house opposite. At once an angry shout burst from this stranger, while Dick distinctly heard the clatter of the end of a sword against the rough cobbles of the pathway. A moment later there was a glimmer of light, a hand shot out of the darkness and seized him by the collar, while the dark lantern, with its slide now drawn fully open, was turned upon him.

"Ah! Who goes racing about the streets thus at night when every soldier should be in the trenches, and every dog of a civilian in his house?"

The light was flashed full into his face. From the darkness behind the lamp a pair of fierce Turkish eyes glared at Dick Hamshaw, and in an instant the individual who had spoken shouted loudly.

"What! A European!" he cried. "In uniform too! How now? A spy!"

It may be imagined that poor Dick was dumbfounded. Not that he was ignorant of what had been said or shouted by this stranger, for Dick was quite a travelled individual and something of a linguist. But then he was the son of a sailor, and his father had for some considerable while been attached to the British Embassy at Constantinople. It happened, then, that Dick spent some five years in that cosmopolitan city, where he was surrounded by Ottomans, and forced to speak the language to some extent at least, simply because his father's servants were Turkish. There need be no surprise, therefore, that he at once took in the gist of what was shouted, while he blinked at the lantern held so close to his face. Then the hand gripping his collar seemed to stir him to action, that and the fact that it suddenly left his clothing, while there came a curious rasping sound telling him that this man had drawn his sword.

Things were looking decidedly unpleasant he decided. But what was he to do? Bolt! No, certainly not, for as the man swung to draw his weapon the lamp was turned partly upon his own person, and in a flash Dick saw that a revolver hung in his open holster. More than that, he saw that this was an officer. The very next second, before the sabre had quite left its scabbard, he had lunged forward desperately with one fist, into which he put all the force of which he was capable.

"Spy!" The officer was in the midst of the shout when the blow struck him on the forehead, for in the darkness Dick missed his aim and went a trifle high. But a lusty fist, wielded though it was by a youth not yet fully grown, and coming against the Turk's forehead so unexpectedly, had a startling effect upon that individual. His sword left his hand and went to the ground with a clatter, the man himself following swiftly and landed upon the cobbles with a thump. As for Dick, he turned to bolt for his life, guessing that other undesirable and inquisitive persons might be near at hand and have heard that shout. But he need have had little fear. If anyone had heard and were inclined to venture near, their inclination was subdued at once by the landing of a shell some thirty yards down this narrow street. Dick heard it crash against the cobbles and instantly threw himself flat, being only just in time to escape the succeeding explosion. A hot blast of flame and gas swept over his recumbent figure. For one brief second the street and the mean houses on either side were brilliantly illuminated, and then there was darkness and silence again, save for dimly-heard shrieks of terror from the distance and the moaning of a man nearer at hand. Dick scrambled to his feet, turned to go, and then swung his head round to look at the spot he had so recently vacated. There was a glimmer on the cobbles, and the faint outline of a lamp turned on its side.

"Why not?" he asked himself. "A lamp would be useful later on perhaps. That officer fellow is moaning. Wonder whether that's due to my blow or to the shell which just now exploded?"

As a matter of fact, his sudden blow had considerably startled the Turk, and had made him lose his balance with a vengeance. Then he had sat up giddily, only to be struck by a stone hurled in that direction by the explosion. Dick went hastily across to him, picked up the lamp, and closely inspected his late enemy.

"Captain of an infantry battalion," he told himself. "No, not a captain; merely a subaltern. Not so very old either. No hair on his face at any rate. Let's see how he's dressed. Greatcoat, belts and sabre, and revolver pouch. Nothing on his head at the moment but—ah, there's the fez! Why, it just fits me. Now I wonder if——"

It was hardly the place to stop and wonder, for without doubt a general bombardment had begun, and stray messages from the allies were falling about him. Dick took the lamp and went to the opening from which this officer had come. He pushed the door before him and found it opened easily. He knocked loudly, then entered without hesitation, and threw his light into the downstairs rooms. They were empty, as was also the upper part of the house.

"Just the sort of little crib we want," he told himself. "Sorry, of course, for the officer, but he shouldn't have been so inquisitive. Anyway, I'll have to borrow some of his belongings. But first I'll fetch Alec and the Commander."

Perhaps ten minutes later Commander Jackson was resting on a settee or divan in the house which Dick had selected, while Dick and Alec rapidly removed the Turk's greatcoat and fez as well as his weapons. Then they picked him up, and staggered away with his unconscious figure till they had gained a street some distance from the spot where he had accosted our hero.

"That'll do. He'll be picked up by his friends some time, and won't soon find his way back to the house. Jingo, ain't things humming!"

It was strange, as the morning light slowly stole upon the besieged city of Adrianople and penetrated the windows of that house borrowed by Dick and Alec, to see those two young hopefuls resting contentedly on the divan running the length of an upstairs room, eagerly discussing the food they had brought with them, as well as this curious situation. As to the Commander, he was no longer snoring so stertorously. He was conscious, and was gazing fixedly at his comrades.

"What next?" he was asking quite jovially in spite of his headache.

"That's it, sir," grinned Dick. "What next? That wants a heap of guessing."

CHAPTER IX

Dick Hamshaw Saves the Situation

There was pandemonium in the city of Adrianople as daylight stole coldly across the roofs of the houses and penetrated to mean streets and alleys, to the interior of houses large and small, and to the cloistered halls of the many mosques. Wailing could be heard on every side, the frightened cries of women, the piteous, hungry sobs of infants and children. For provisions had been short for a long time, while but seven ounces of bread formed the daily ration of each soldier, and civilians must fight for what they could see and live as best they could.

Shells rained into the place fitfully, ebbing and flowing as does the sea. They came in shoals like mackerel, then intermittently, crashing their way through roofs, thudding into the streets and open spaces, and bursting to right and left. And then, of a sudden, they would cease to fall. Comparative silence would reign in the city; while outside, in the neighbourhood of the forts, could be heard the rattle of musketry, incessant, rising and falling, overwhelmed every few seconds by some violent detonation as a cannon was discharged, and running in waves from one end of the defences to the other.

"Hard at it," said the Commander, listening to a great outburst. "You may depend upon it that the allies have decided to take the place whatever it may cost them. And if all the Turkish troops are like the poor objects one sees from this window, why, this business won't be long before it's ended. Meanwhile, if one may enquire, what are our prospects?"

He turned with smiling face to Dick and Alec, though the hands supporting his head on either side, and the anxious, drawn look about his eyes, told that he was suffering. Indeed he had a dreadful headache that morning, while the wound he had been unlucky enough to receive was extremely painful.

"If one may enquire?" he said again, with polite and jovial satire. "I am as a child in your hands, and, 'pon my word, you've done uncommonly well. What happened after I was knocked over? Tell me, do. I am still left gaping at the fact that a moment ago, as it seems to me, I was crouching beside a wall waiting for a shell to wreak its vengeance upon this unfortunate city. The very next, I appear to be in clover, reclining on a most comfortable divan, and—er—er—watching you two munching your rations. Now."

They told him all that had happened with a gusto there was no denying.

"And so you see, sir, here we are," added Dick, his mouth occupied with a hunch of bread and cheese which the thoughtful Sergeant Evans had provided.

"Precisely! Here we are. Afterwards, what? That's where I'm vastly interested. We appear to have got into a charming little pickle. How do we emerge from it?"

Neither Dick nor Alec could give him the smallest indication, for they themselves were nonplussed by the curious situation into which they had tumbled. Not that they had not given vast thought to the matter; for even then Dick had risen from the divan and was staring through the window, the noise of people moving down the cobbled street having attracted him. He swung round after a while, reseated himself, and took an enormous bite from the hunch of bread he was holding.

The Commander watched him as he ate it, watched him critically and with some amusement. "Come," he said after a while. "What's the manœuvre?"

Alec shook his head violently; Dick stood up, still munching, and once more stared through the window. He did not mean to be disrespectful to his senior, but, to be precise, his thoughts were so fully occupied at that particular moment that he hardly heard the sentence. Presently he turned again.

"I'm going out, sir," he said.

"Out! Impossible! You'd be spotted," cried the officer, his joviality gone instantly.

"Hardly, sir. You see, or perhaps I should say, you will see the reason. I can speak these fellows' lingo quite a little."

"Turkish?"

"Yes, sir. Father was quartered at Constantinople, at the British Embassy. I was there a good five years, and so learnt to know all about 'em. If I was disguised I could pass easily, and so I'm going in the gear of that officer."

"But—but why?" demanded the Commander.

"First, to find a more suitable crib for us, sir. That officer fellow may recover consciousness just as quickly as you have done, and then he may very well return to these quarters. That'd be bad for us. Next, there's Major Harvey and his friend to be thought of. We couldn't very well return aboard the airship without them."

"Certainly not. If they're to be found, then we find them," came from the officer. "But—look here, Dick, this idea means danger, don't it?"

"Risk, perhaps, sir. Nothing more."

"Supposing you were spotted?"

The Commander sat up quickly and looked anxiously at the midshipman.

"Then it would be unlucky for me, sir," came Dick's steady answer. "Of course, you and Alec would work hard to get back to the ship. But I haven't been spotted yet, and don't mean to be. Someone's got to go out, and I'm that someone, for I can understand these people. Now, Alec, give me a help with this gear. Say, how do I look? Fairly smart, eh? That fez always makes a fellow look fetching."

Dick made certainly quite a smart officer once he was dressed in the greatcoat, belts, and pouches of his late assailant, while the fez gave him quite an Oriental appearance. Indeed, the Commander was delighted.

"I don't half like letting you go, Dick," he said. "I'm the one who should be taking this sort of risk. But there—I couldn't stand steadily, and am therefore useless. Lad, shake hands. I'm glad you belong to us, and I must say that you two youngsters have done handsomely."

Dick coloured redly. Alec shuffled his feet and felt positively uncomfortable. And then the former gripped each of his companions in turn by the hand, saluted his officer, and turning, went out of the room. They heard the front door bang. They heard his steps on the cobbles, and looking out, Alec saw his chum strolling nonchalantly down the street. Then he turned into another, and in an instant was lost to view.

"Gone! Out of sight," he said, turning and speaking almost dismally to the Commander.

"And good luck go with him! A plucky lad, a very plucky fellow!" cried the officer. "But don't let's fret about him, for a midshipman's a midshipman all over the world and a wonder at getting into and out of scrapes. Now, let's see if we can get a fire going, for it's cold in this room and I'm positively shivering."

It may be wondered meanwhile what had happened to the gallant Major who had left the airship just two nights previous to Dick and his fellows. If they had but known the truth he had set foot in this beleaguered city within some fifty yards of the spot where they had landed. And then all his efforts had been concentrated on the task of finding that elusive individual known as Charlie. He groped his way around buildings and along streets; and for hours haunted the precincts of that huge mosque which the elusive Charlie had denoted as his probable location. The dawn was breaking indeed before he thought of his own personal safety and the need for some hiding-place. For the Major cut a conspicuous figure wherever he happened to be. He looked, in fact, precisely what he was, a soldier and a gentleman. Nor must the reader imagine for one moment that he and "Charlie", the high-placed officer of whom he had spoken, were merely spies engaged on some dangerous espionage. There is spying and spying. There is the patriot who for the sake of his country, not for mere filthy lucre or out of burning curiosity, will investigate matters of moment, such as guns and forts and equipment used by possible enemies of his country. And there are others who from the same patriotic motives will endeavour to fathom some new negotiations between Powers other than his own, some diplomatic move, some international conspiracy hatched in the secret recesses of foreign offices, perhaps never set down on paper, never signed and sealed, merely a secret compact, but still something of vital importance for his own people. We do not profess to guess what precisely was the business upon which the Major and his friend had been engaged. It was secret, it was of vital importance, and it was of the utmost delicacy. Let us, then, leave it there, merely remembering that the elusive Charlie had intimated to the Major that he had succeeded in his mission, while the authorities at home had thought so much of the matter and desired that information so greatly that they posted the Major to the great airship when on her world-wide tour, and urged Andrew and Joe Gresson to hazard a visit to Adrianople, even at the risk of wrecking a machine than which nothing would appear to be more valuable to Great Britain.

It was with an inner knowledge of this delicate affair that the Major strove to discover his friend, and for the moment we will leave him hastening through the streets of the city, gazing into the faces of passers-by as the dawn drew near, and risking discovery. In fact, he merely forestalled Dick, for the young midshipman was now engaged in a similar task with similar risks, seeking eagerly for those for whom he and his friends had descended from the airship.

"And it's like looking for the usual needle in the usual bundle of hay," he grumbled, as he dived into another street and strode down it. "A mighty small needle, by jingo! and an awfully big bundle of hay. But there's always the mosque. That must be the big one, and I don't go a step farther from it. My first job is to investigate every corner. So round we go. We'll do the outside first, and then dive in."

People hurried past him, civilians with wan, lean forms and faces. Half-starved soldiers dressed in rags, unshaven for weeks past, dragged their weary limbs past him. An officer, a dapper enough fellow at one time no doubt, stepped into the street before him, turned a hurried gaze upon him, and then retreated with haste.

"Funny, that. Spotted me, eh?" Dick asked himself. "Then why did he bolt as if he were afraid of me?"

It was a problem to which he gave his mind for some few minutes. He was still worrying it out when almost a similar thing took place. Two soldiers, under-officers without a doubt, tattered and dishevelled, emerged from a doorway and halted immediately outside to peer up and down the street. On seeing Dick's jaunty figure they bolted, positively bolted.

"This beats me hollow," that young gentleman grumbled. "What's the matter with me, or—er—with those jolly beggars? Surely it can't be that they're—jingo! it looks it. What did that officer say?"

His mind went back to the encounter he had some little time before and to the manner in which his assailant had accosted him. He recollected that Adrianople was then being fiercely assaulted. If he had been inclined to forget that fact there was the firing to tell him, that and the roar of shells raining round the city. Yes, he could hear the battle ebbing and flowing in the distance about the outlying forts which protected all approaches to Adrianople.

"Got it!" he cried. "What have the papers said? Let's see. Little enough, for correspondents have been barred and news sent by some of them at least has been secondhand information written up in a house perhaps a hundred miles from the fighting. But there's been awful disorganization amongst the Turkish battalions. Men have been anywhere at times except where they were wanted. Officers have lost their commands, while, what with hardship, fear of wounds or worse, and starvation, soldiers have strayed from their ranks or actually deserted. Jingo! That's it. The fellows who have been scared of me are shirkers. Lor! there seem to be a good many of 'em. That don't say much for the chances of the defenders."

In any case the discovery he had made was of little moment and gave him no help in his search. But it did put a little more dash and swagger into our hero.

"If they don't see anything wrong about me and get scared so easily, why, others'll be the same," Dick told himself with a grin. "I'll cut a dash next time I meet a soldier. A bit of bounce'll help to deceive 'em."

He carried the plan out in a manner which would have made Alec scream with laughing, for Dick was really too bold for anything. Meeting a squad of men some few minutes later escorting an ammunition cart along one of the streets he clanked his sword loudly, squared his shoulders, and took their salute without a falter.

"My word! That's better," he grinned. "I'll be ordering 'em about before I've done with this business. Hallo! A guard-house, eh? Yes, sentry posted outside. Jingo, call him a sentry! Of course, I know the poor beggar's been more than half starved for weeks past. But, what a figure!"

The wretchedly ragged fellow outside this guard house did indeed cut anything but a soldierly figure. He lolled against the post, his face drawn and thin and vacant, and innocent of soap and water for days past. And when, seeing an officer draw near, he shouldered his rifle, it was in an uncouth and distinctly unmilitary manner.

"Like to see one of our tars give a salute like that," said Dick bridling. "If the Turks are all like him, which I doubt, it ain't surprising that those jolly Bulgarians and their allies have made such a running. But let's get on. That's completed the round of the mosque. Now we enter and see what's doing."

Unabashed by the presence of a sentry at the door of the mosque, Dick marched boldly up to him and once more acknowledged a salute. Then he donned a pair of shoes lying in the doorway and entered without hesitation.

"It is empty," said the man over his shoulder. "I have orders to keep all people from entering, all save those who command."

Dick nodded curtly. He wondered whether he ought to make some reply; but fearing that the man would suspect him at once he went on without halting.

"Though I've got to chance it some time," he said. "I've got to ask questions so as to get information. Lor! why didn't I think of it before? I'll be a foreign officer serving with the Turks. It's said that there are something approaching a hundred German officers here in Adrianople. Right! I ain't over particular which sort of a country it is I come from. But I'm foreign. That's why I can't talk the lingo perfectly. Now we take a look round and then come back to gather information."

His tour of the mosque proved it to be much the same as others, except that this was huge and more brilliantly decorated than those Dick was accustomed to. It was deserted, without a doubt, not even a mullah being present.

"They are gone in fear lest shells should strike the building," explained the sentry at the door when Dick questioned him. "Pardon, your papers, please."

"Papers? Eh?" gasped Dick.

"All foreign officers carry papers to prove their identity. I took you for one of our own nationality at first, but now that you speak, though better than the majority, I see that you are foreign. Your papers, please."

It was an awkward moment, and perhaps few others would have escaped from it as did the light-hearted Dick. He gazed at the man in amazement. He stamped his feet with seeming rage and fumed and growled loudly.

"What! You ask for papers while shells fall into the city and there is fighting! You expect me to take such things into the trenches, then? What next! I keep such things in my quarters where you can see them if you come with me."

"Ah! Pardon, I did not think," the sentry answered abjectly. "Of course, it is not the time to make such a demand."

"As if one could enter or leave the city!" growled Dick, pretending to be only half appeased. "But there! let it pass. Tell me for what reason is there a guard-house yonder?"

"To house the patrols who police the streets. In times of peace the place is unoccupied."

"And now?" asked Dick curiously.

"There are a few men there. I myself shall be relieved by one of them."

"And prisoners?"

The sentry looked astonished. "Prisoners?" he asked, looking suspiciously at Dick.

"Yes, prisoners," declared that young fellow without a falter. The high hand he had played already had served his purpose wonderfully. Then why not continue? "Did I not say prisoners plainly?" he asked curtly, at which the man nodded abjectly. "Then why this surprise?"

"But—but pardon, sir, you asked as if it were not merely curiosity. It seemed as if you might be interested in some other way," said the sentry, emboldened for the moment and again surveying Dick in a manner which, if it did not show suspicion, at least told of his dislike of all foreigners. As for the midshipman, his interest was stimulated by the curious stubbornness of the man. Dick recollected that he was in search of Major Harvey, and that the latter had disappeared, had failed to signal to the airship, and was lost for the moment. Supposing there were prisoners yonder? Supposing this fellow and his mates placed in the guard-house to police the neighbourhoodof the mosque had seized upon the Major and were holding him a prisoner? Was it likely that they had reported their action? Hardly at such a time when the allies were pressing an attack, and if they had sent in a report a day before, no doubt in the hurry and bustle of hastening troops to meet that expected assault the matter had been forgotten. However, this was all guesswork. Dick had yet no certain information that prisoners were located in the guard-house, though he had his suspicions.

"And I'm pretty sure that this fellow is trying to throw dust in my eyes," he told himself. "It ain't difficult either to see why he's so stubborn and sly. I'm a foreign officer attached to the Turkish army. Half a mo'; I ain't. But that's what he takes me to be. Well, then, supposing he and his fellows had bagged the Major, they'd expect me to kick up a shindy and——"

In one instant he saw it all, and his suspicions were heightened.

"You have prisoners in the guard-house," he said severely. "Foreign prisoners. I will see them. Stay here, man; have a care what you do and say. Tell me, you reported the taking of these men?"

The sentry stood to attention, looking shamefaced and frightened.

"We could not," he excused himself. "No officer has visited us for two days now. There is heavy fighting."

"Ah!" Dick regarded him severely. "You dared to neglect to report," he cried angrily. "You took these men prisoner, careless whether they were friends of your army or not. There will be more said upon this matter, for learn this, idiot that you are. These men are wanted by His Highness Shukri Pasha himself. Yes, by the general in command of the defenders."

Dick positively blushed at his own assurance and cheek, while the unhappy sentry actually trembled. For this foreign officer was without doubt very angry and filled with indignation.

"I—we," he began in an effort to excuse himself.

"March down to the guard-house with me," commanded Dick. "You shall be relieved instantly, and shall yourself conduct me to these prisoners. A more disgraceful and high-handed proceeding I never experienced, and His Highness shall hear of it. To think that he is waiting for these men, these foreigners, while you, you fools, sitting here near the guard-house, hold them as prisoners."

Dick ought to have been an actor, for he stamped and raved at the unfortunate fellow, and altogether impressed him so much with the heinousness of the act he had committed that the sentry was ready to sink into the ground or do anything to repair his blunder. He was a very humble individual as he shambled down to the guard-house in front of Dick and surlily bade his comrade make for the mosque and there relieve him.

"Now, take me to these men," commanded Dick. "There are two?"

"No—three, sir," came the answer.

"Three!" Dick's hopes fell of a sudden. This statement that there were three prisoners took the wind entirely out of his sails and robbed him for the moment of his high-handed assurance. "Three!" he muttered. "I've been groping in the dark all this while, guessing wildly. But I've also been putting two and two together, and seeing that the Major was to make for the surroundings of the great mosque and expected to meet his friend there, why, when I gathered that this fellow and his comrades had made prisoners of foreigners I made sure there must be two. If it had been one that might still have been the Major taken prisoner before he had met this Charlie. But three! That's a stunner!"

For a little while he stood watching the shambling figure of the man going to take post at the door of the mosque. And then, roused by the detonation of a shell in an adjacent place, he turned sharply upon the fellow who stood before him.

"Three prisoners whom you have dared to hold without reporting!" he cried. "Lead on, man; this is monstrous. Take me to them."

Thoroughly scared now by the anger of the foreign officer, whom he imagined to be doing service with the Turkish army, and conscious that by making captures and failing to report he had been guilty of a serious offence, the man upon whom Dick, with his unblushing cheek and wonderful assurance and resource, had so completely turned the tables proceeded to obey his orders with a meekness which was apparent. In fact, he was obviously anxious to appease the anger of this officer, and so escape punishment for his remissness.

"Follow, sir," he said. "There are three prisoners as I have told you, and it may be that when you see how ready I am to act on your orders, you will forget the fact that I failed to send a report, remembering too, that the times are very unsettled."

They were that without a doubt, for all this while the distant rattle of musketry could be heard, rolling round the defences, now breaking out here with a severity which showed that an attack was probably being forced home, perhaps even at the point of the bayonet, and then dying down quite suddenly only to break out with virulence in another direction. And every now and again, sometimes very frequently, at others after quite a lull, heavy guns would open, shells would scream through the air, and rarely now one of the monsters would drop into the streets of the city or plunge amongst the houses, when the succeeding explosion would be followed by heartrending shrieks, by piercing cries, by the anguished calls of the helpless and defenceless.

Yes, the times were unsettled enough; Dick had his own troubles and could therefore sympathize. He bade the man hasten, and followed into the guard-house.

"And there was good reason for making these men prisoners," said the Turk, pushing his fez to the back of his head and turning to our hero, still with the hope that he might excuse his own breach of the standing orders of the army. "I will tell you. One, a big man———"

"Yes, a big man," said Dick eagerly. "The Major without a doubt," he told himself.

"A big man, and fat, very."

"Ah! Fat! Then that cannot be the Major. Get along with it," cried Dick peevishly, his hopes wrecked in a moment.

"Fat and big," went on the man. "We saw him in converse with some of the stragglers who had left the lines of trenches. He was inciting them to stay away."

"Or to return to their duty, which?" asked Dick curtly.

"The former, we thought," came the answer. "We arrested him. He was angry and shouted and threatened; but since he could speak only a few words of our language we could not understand the cause of his anger. Then there were two others, foreigners."

"Ah! Describe them," Dick almost shouted. It was hard indeed at this moment to restrain his eagerness.

"One, tall, and spare, and like a soldier."

"The Major," Dick told himself. "Hooray! Things are going to come right."

"And the other older, getting grey, also tall, and spare, and soldierly."

"Lead me to them at once," demanded Dick. "They are the men whom His Highness desires to interview. Come, lead quickly; there will be trouble about this matter."

That set the sentry shivering with apprehension, and made him still more eager to appease the officer who had accosted him. Leading the way towards the back of the guard-house, he took down a bunch of keys strung to a hook on the wall and with their help opened a cell. Dick looked in. An ill-kempt, unwieldy man dressed in the uniform of an officer was seated on a stone bench and scowled as the two appeared. And then, recognizing Dick as an officer he burst into a torrent of abuse, expressed in a language of which the midshipman was ignorant.

"Not my bird at any rate," he told himself. "My! Listen to the fellow. I'm sorry for him, awfully. But I can't get mixing myself up in his affairs. Now, let us see the others," he demanded of the Turk.

A minute later they were peering into an adjacent cell, in which Dick instantly recognized the Major. As for the latter, though he looked at our hero very hard and with suspicion, there was no recognition until Dick spoke.

"Major," he said. "Please be careful as I am disguised as a Turkish officer. I have come to demand your release."

"Demand my release! Turkish officer! Why, it's—it's Mr. Midshipman Hamshaw."

"Present, sir," grinned that young gentleman, saluting. "You see," he said, swinging round upon the soldier. "He recognizes me, and so does the other officer. Ah! There will be bad trouble over this, when Shukri Pasha gets to hear of it. Yes, trouble which——"

A groan escaped the wretched sentry. Ever since he had exchanged words with Dick, he had been conjuring up all sorts of pains and penalties as a consequence of his rashness. His knees positively knocked together as he besought this officer to spare him and forget the matter.

"Release them at once," cried Dick peremptorily. "Now, listen. If His Highness asks no questions, well and good. Perhaps we shall not be too late for this discussion even now, that is if you hasten. As to the third officer, hold him till you receive a written order, or till an hour has passed. Now, stand aside. Major, please follow."

"But—but you don't mean to tell me that you have obtained our release?" cried that astonished officer. "How? And where are we to go?"

"Please follow as if you had every right to be at liberty," answered Dick. "I'll tell you later how I've worked it. But come at once, for there is no saying when other soldiers may turn up, with perhaps an officer."

He stalked before them out of the guard-house and led the way into the streets of Adrianople, streets for the most part still untenanted. For civilians lay at home shivering beneath the cruel bombardment, and fearful of those dreadful shells. They were coming again into the city, and more than once Dick and the two who followed had to dodge behind some building to escape the bursting of a bomb.

"And now, perhaps, you'll tell us where we are going," said the Major, when they had gained a smaller street. "To the airship? Impossible. She would never dare to come here in daylight. Then where?"

"To join Commander Jackson and Alec," answered Dick. "We entered the city last night in search of you both. But—hush! Lookout! Let's hurry. If that isn't the very fellow I most wanted to avoid."

A figure had dived into the street immediately behind them, a figure strangely familiar. Dick eyed him suspiciously, and then recognized him with a start. For this man's head was swathed in bandages which left his face fully exposed, and that face was young, and smooth, and hairless. In fact, it was the very officer against whom he had collided on the previous night.

"Had he been back to his house and there discovered Alec and the Commander? Or was he now on his way?"

Dick asked himself those urgent questions, and then, spurred on by fear and dreadful foreboding hastened along the street, the Major and his friend close beside him, and the inquisitive officer in rear. Soon they turned into the street in which that house they sought was located, and for a moment the follower was out of sight.

"Run!" cried Dick, and took to his heels. "Now, into this house. Alec!" he called.

"Here," came back a jovial call. "And the Commander, both of us getting a bit anxious about you."

"Shut the door and bolt it," commanded Dick, careless of the presence of his seniors. "Now, peep through the windows. The owner of this house was following us a moment ago. If he tries to enter, keep perfectly quiet. I'm going to see how we can manage to get out of what may prove to be a trap."

If they had any doubts of that follower, these were cleared on the instant. There came the sound of steps on the cobbles, and then a heavy blow upon the door.

"Open—open in the name of the Sultan!"

Not one of those within answered. They stood back from the window waiting and watching. "Open!" they heard the command repeated, and then there followed a shrill whistle.

"Look, men are running across from a house almost opposite," whispered Major Harvey, peering through the window. "This begins to look ugly, and I'm not so sure that we should not be better off in our prison. Listen to them, and see that fellow carrying a huge hammer."

There came a crashing blow upon the door an instant later, a blow that almost shattered the lock. It was clear that within a few minutes the irate individual outside and his helpers would force an entrance. The Major turned in bewilderment to the Commander, for he could not quite understand this new situation. Then Dick burst in upon them.

"Come along," he said. "Let's sling it. There's a way out at the back, and I know a place that'll shelter us. Quick! Those chaps will be in in a moment."

They did not wait to argue or discuss the matter with him but followed at once. Stealthily departing by a door in rear of the building they dived into a narrow alley, and from that place heard a crash as the door of the house was beaten in. Then they turned and fled through the streets of Adrianople with a dozen Turks hotfoot after them.

CHAPTER X

A Thrilling Rescue

Perhaps no quainter or more exciting situation could be imagined than that which found Dick Hamshaw and his little party scuttling down the dark streets of Adrianople. For there he was, leading surely a strange following.

"Enough to make the people open their eyes and rub 'em hard," he told himself with a grin, for Dicky was not the one to be scared easily or disheartened. "Here we are, led by a Turkish officer, that's me; followed by a British naval officer, in uniform too, that's the Commander, and jolly groggy he seems to be after that wound of his. Then there's Alec—well, nothing out of the ordinary— while behind come the Major, almost a stranger, though we know all about him, and then 'Charlie', dear old Charlie."

"Where away? Where are you leading to?" suddenly came from the Major. "We've gained on those beggars. Hadn't we better stop a moment and discuss matters?"

Discuss matters when they were almost blown, and when the Turks were rushing pell-mell after them!

"Good idea," cried Dick cheerily. "In here! Come along. Now, bang the door. Jingo! Hope there ain't other people to kick up a rumpus."

Really his cheek and coolness were amazing, for hardly had the Major finished calling when Dick halted at a doorway leading into a small dwelling, threw it open, and beckoned them to enter. Then he banged the door to, and leaving his friends went off on a tour of inspection.

"All bright-o!" he whispered, reappearing. "Place empty. No one here for a long while and not a scrap of food. I squinted into what must be their larder."

"H—hush! There they are. Foiled for the moment," whispered the Major, peering through a narrow window. "Wait! They've halted and are looking about them. One of the men is pointing up the street, and let's hope they'll make off in that direction. Good! There they go as if the old gentleman himself were behind them. Now; what's the meaning of all this bother, and how comes it that you are masquerading in Turkish uniform? Dick, my boy, you've a heap to answer for. Seriously, though, I'm eternally obliged to you for liberating us from that prison. That reminds me. I haven't so far had an opportunity of making formal presentations. Commander Jackson, let me introduce Colonel Steven,

94

Intelligence Department, War Office, the 'Charlie' we've come after. Colonel, my excellent friends and comrades Mr. Midshipman Hamshaw and Alec Jardine. Now you all know one another."

Cordial hand-grips were exchanged all round, and here again one may say that seldom before was there such a curious meeting. As for "Charlie", the gallant Colonel Steven, Dick and his friends liked his looks immensely. He smiled at them all, not in the least ruffled by what had been passing.

"'Pon my word, gentlemen," he said, "but it needs an active man to keep touch with your movements. First I come most miraculously in contact with my friend, the Major, who descends actually and really from the sky. Then, when I am reclining comfortably in a prison where the circumstances of the bombardment, the breakdown of all discipline, and the natural hate of an Ottoman made it likely enough that I and the Major might have our throats slit, there appears upon the scene a Turkish officer, who is not a Turkish officer, but a midshipman from our own fleet, and who likewise has descended from the sky. Lastly, I am taken to a place of refuge which is no place of refuge, and from which I am bundled before even I have time to be formally acquainted with other gentlemen, birds of the same feather as my friend the Major. Really, this is almost enough for one long day."

Cool! Of course he was cool. His pleasant satire showed that, while his easy smile, his jaunty manner, the knowledge that he had been engaged on an important and doubtless dangerous enterprise made Dick and his friends take to the Colonel promptly. And naturally enough, though the midshipman was not easily abashed, he now waited for his seniors to give a lead. Not that the Commander was capable of doing so.

"I've a head that feels as big as a football and heavier than lead," he told them, sitting down of a sudden and looking faint. "Carry on without me; I'll be better in a twinkling."

"Then we turn to Dick. The Navy commands here," smiled Colonel Steven, while the Major nodded. "Have the goodness, Mr. Dick, to issue your orders. Really, though, lad, you have the situation at your finger tips. Do we stay here, or do we issue out again and seek some other residence?"

Dick removed his fez and scratched his head. It was not, perhaps, a very refined operation, but it seemed to help.

"You see," he began, "I'm thinking about the airship and how we are to rejoin her. Supposing we hide here and send up a flare to-night. Well, these johnnies may catch sight of the flame and rush us before we can board the lift. Awkward that, very."

"Then let us suppose that we change our quarters. Are we better off?" asked the Colonel.

"Perhaps. If we can find a crib, sir, that's easier to hold, more ungetatable as one might say."

"For instance," interjected the Major. "You've some such crib in your mind's eye, Dick."

"Well, there's the mosque. It's empty, save for a sentry at the door. There are four towers at least there, and I climbed up one of 'em this very morning. Now, a stairway could be held. There are no doors and windows in all sorts of directions. Besides, we'd be above the beggars who wanted to get us, and that'd be an advantage. We could hold out perhaps till the airship arrived to take us."

It was a likely enough suggestion, and the two soldiers thought well of it. But the Colonel soon put his finger on what appeared to be a weak spot.

"We're up in this tower, let's imagine," he said. "Then the ship comes. We're bottled in perhaps. How do we emerge? How reach the line which this ship throws out to us?"

"Wait. You haven't seen the airship yet," cried Alec. "Wait, sir, and you'll have an eye-opener. She can pick us up easily wherever we are, even on the top of a chimney, for her lift can be manœuvred with an ease and certainty that will astonish you. Oh yes, it don't matter where we happen to get to, Mr. Andrew and Joe can reach us."

There was pride in his voice. His words conveyed the impression that if anything in this world were a success it was the curious lift attached to the great airship, although, as a matter of course, that huge vessel was of even greater excellence. But it can be imagined that to one who had never seen the ship floating in the air, who had never even set foot upon her galleries, nor climbed to the height of her upper deck, it was hard to believe that what Alec described so glowingly could in fact be possible. Not that the gallant Colonel was a sceptic, or in the habit of decrying new inventions, or disbelieving in the possibility of things that he had never seen. On the contrary, he was very much awake and alive to the astonishing progress to be observed on every side, particularly progress appertaining to mechanics. For has not the latter end of the nineteenth century, and the beginning of the present seen an amazing advancement on every hand, an advancement beside which the progress of the so-called Victorian era pales almost to insignificance? Think of the conquest which the internal-explosion motor has accomplished, of the rapid road and sea locomotion it has made possible, of the trackless pathways of the air which it has thrown open to human beings. For the beginning and the end of man's first successful journeys at speed through the air, upon machines heavier than the atmosphere which supports them, is attributable almost solely to the petrol motor, that internal-explosion engine which less than twenty years ago was but the crudest of inventions.

Colonel Steven had kept in close touch with the whole movement, and had, during the hours he lay in prison with the Major, listened to his description of the wonderful airship which Joe Gresson and his uncle had constructed. He was burning to board the vessel, to ferret out its secrets, to understand its construction; and he may be forgiven if he failed to comprehend quite how the ship could manage to remove himself and his friends even from the tower of a mosque, should the party happen to find themselves in such a position. However, the discussion as to their movements was cut short at the moment. Cries were heard from the street, and the Major soon made an important announcement.

"That fellow again!" he cried, in low tones. "He and his followers had run out of sight, and I was in hopes that we had thrown them off the scent. But they are coming back, yes, and numbers have joined them. All the ragtag and bobtail of this terrible city have joined in the search."

Dick dived towards the window there to join him, and stood peering out into the street. It was true enough that the man who led these searchers was returning, and true too that others had joined his following. Indeed, some fifty ragged fellows were trailing after that young Turkish officer, whose head was swathed in bandages, and amongst them, immediately in rear of the officer, was no less a person than the sentry whom Dick had accosted at the door of the mosque, and whom he had duped so cleverly.

"Jingo!" he cried, turning with a somewhat scared expression upon the company. "They've got to the bottom of the whole business. The chap in advance is the beggar I collided with last night, and I suppose he's anxious to get back these clothes I was compelled to borrow. Then there's the man who was at the guard-house, and who helped to put the Major and the Colonel in prison. Jingo! They're entering the houses on either side and searching them."

There was a blank look upon the faces of the forlorn little party. Not that they were frightened, or were likely to submit themselves as prisoners without a struggle. But the outlook was black without a doubt. This mob of Turkish soldiers, dressed in their ragged khaki uniforms, unkempt, undisciplined, capable of any violence now that the only authority over them was represented by a single youthful officer, were searching every corner, and when they came to the house in which Dick and his friends had sheltered they would find the party, would drag them out and then, perhaps, shoot them.

"Nasty place," admitted the Colonel. "Regular troops might be trusted to make prisoners of us, to treat us decently, and wait for their officers to investigate the matter. Now——" he shrugged his shoulders. "Well," he said, "we might find ourselves placed against a wall and shot down deliberately. Adrianople is in a condition of disorder, which one may imagine will get worse rather than better. Who is to prevent violence just now, when every soldier who can be controlled is in the firing line? That officer? No."

"Not he!" Dick cried. "He was furious last night. He'll be more angry this morning. Besides, all these fellows are wasters, men who ought to be in the forts but who have slunk to the rear. I ain't going to wait to be torn to pieces, or shot out of hand. They've rifles with them, sir."

"While we have revolvers," said the Major coolly. "Now, Dick, you're leader still. What happens? Do we wait for these gentlemen, or—what?"

"We pick the Commander up, carry him out at the back of the house, and slink off to the great mosque," came the instant answer. "It's not more than three hundred yards from us, and if we can only get within easy distance we can keep this mob off with our weapons. Shall I lead the way out of the back door, sir?"

"At once," came promptly from the Colonel. "See, I am a strong man, and as hard as nails. I will shoulder the Commander. Come, Jackson," he said, turning to the naval officer who had meanwhile struggled to get to his feet, and had sunk back almost fainting. "Now, up you go. That's the way. Cling with your arms round my neck. I've a good grip of your legs, and can manage to use my revolver. Ready, Dick."

"Then off we go," cried the Major. "First Dick, then the Colonel, then Alec. I bring up the rear, and Alec can help me if there's any bother. Come, don't let us delay any longer; those ruffians are already getting far too close for our safety."

Silently opening the rickety back door of the house that had sheltered them, Dick peered out and issued into the open.

"Come," he called gently. "There's a garden here, and a door at the end. It ought to take us into another street and so away from those beggars. Listen to 'em. They're kicking up more row than those fellows away in the trenches."

To speak the truth, this mob of unattached individuals in search of our friends were by now infuriated at their want of success, for it began to look as if they had been completely hoodwinked. Some fifty of them were dashing into and out of the houses, breaking doors open with the stocks of their rifles without the smallest ceremony, and venting upon cupboards and beds and woodwork, where they imagined someone might be hiding, all the ferocity they might have been expected to display had they been directly engaged with the Bulgarians.

98

Many had their bayonets fixed, and drove them deep into recesses, into dark corners, and through the very heart of the gigantic mattresses on some of the beds. They bellowed at one another. Some even slipped cartridges into the breeches of their rifles and fired into the cellars and through the windows of the houses. Altogether there was pandemonium in that part of the city, pandemonium made worse by the rattle of musketry in the distance, by those bursting shells which still clattered amidst houses and streets, and by the shrill cries of terror, by the sobs and execrations of the civil population now subjected to this added trouble.

"Ah! See! We have found their last lair. Look!"

The sentry whom Dick had accosted at the mosque came rushing from the door of the tenement which our hero had but just vacated and waved an object aloft. It was a cap, the same which the Colonel had been wearing, and which the effort to lift the Commander to his back had dislodged from his head. In an instant the Turk had pounced upon it, and there he was now in the street, calling the officer and his ragged following towards him, gesticulating and shouting.

"See! I remember this cap. It was upon the head of one of our prisoners, one of the foreign spies sent in here by the Bulgarians."

"And the men themselves. You saw them also?" asked the officer, snatching the cap from him.

"The house is empty. They are gone. That cap proves that they were there lately."

"Fool! Did you not look for them? Did you not attempt to discover whence they had gone?" was shouted at him, while the furious officer looked as if he were capable of shooting him down in his anger. "Into the house," he bellowed. "Empty! Nothing here to keep us. Then out at the back. Look. The ground is soft after the melting of the snow. Here are fresh footmarks. Follow! Follow!"

Led by the officer the mob went tearing down the tiny garden of the humble tenement, and burst their way through the gate at the bottom. Indeed, in their eagerness and fury at having been so duped, and in their knowledge that order was done with in Adrianople for the moment, they tore the gate from its hinges, trampled upon a couple of harmless civilians walking in the road to which the gate gave entrance, and then seized and beat them unmercifully.

"Release their throats so that they may speak!" commanded the brutal young officer who led this riotous following. "Now, we seek some foreigners who but lately escaped along this road. You saw them? What! You shake your heads. Shoot them!"

It was a sample of the justice and treatment which Dick and his friends might encounter if they fell into the hands of these rascals. At such a time it seemed that friend and foe were alike to these men, skulkers for the most part. Furious at the thought that the two unfortunate people they had come upon could not help them they hurried them to the house opposite, and perhaps would even have gone to the length of shooting them had not one of the poor wretches shouted at the top of his voice:

"We can help you," he called. "Give us but the opportunity, and I swear by the Koran that we can speak. But you have beaten the breath from our bodies."

"Then release them. Speak!" commanded the officer. "We seek some foreigners."

"Five men passed us but a few minutes ago, one of whom was injured and was borne by a comrade. They were hurrying towards the great mosque, and a Turkish officer led them."

"The same—the ones we seek! They went this way?" demanded the officer.

Hardly had the route been indicated when the whole mob was in motion again, racing off along the street in pursuit of our hero. Nor was it long before these wretches came in sight of the forlorn little party. A shriek of glee escaped them immediately. Men levelled their rifles as they ran and pulled their triggers, careless where the bullets went, while the ruffianly officer drew his revolver and sent shot after shot at Dick and his fellows.

"Keep straight on, Dick," the Major sang out. "Those fellows couldn't hit a haystack at the pace they're going, so we've only fluke shots to chance. That's the mosque, ain't it?"

"Yes, sir," Dick called out over his shoulder. "Two minutes'll do it. Then we cross the floor of the hall, reach the foot of one of the towers, and then, by jingo, the business begins with a vengeance."

"Then on we go. When we reach the tower, let Alec help the Colonel carry our wounded friend to safety. You and I, Dick, 'll do our best to teach these rascals a lesson. Ah! That's a sentry."

Well, it was a sentry at the moment the Major was speaking, for a ragged Turk emerged from the entrance to the mosque and stared in amazement at the scene before him. It filled him with perplexity to observe a Turkish officer racing in his direction, followed by a strange quartet, one of whom was carried on the shoulders of a comrade, while in rear, and getting rapidly closer came a mob of his own fellows, led again by an officer whose head was swathed in soiled bandages. However, he was as sharp as others of his country and smelling a rat immediately swung his rifle up to his shoulder and covered the dashing Dick. But his finger never quite reached the sights. Indeed, as we have intimated, he was a sentry at the moment the Major called to our hero. The next he was merely a bundled-up and extremely astonished human object. For Dick planted a seaman's blow on the end of his prominent nose, a blow that brought a thousand stars to the eyes of this sluggish Turk, and toppled him backward in masterly fashion.

"One for his boko!" shouted the incorrigible Dick. "Number two does for his rifle. Ah! The pouch of cartridges might be useful. Here we are. I've got 'em both. Now, we make for the tower—quite close and handy."

It was a little more than ten yards across the floor of the hall, and long before the followers had reached the door of the mosque the Colonel had entered the narrow door that led to the steep steps ascending to the summit of the tower. Alec followed instantly, and together the two bore the now almost unconscious Commander upward. Dick slung his borrowed rifle over his shoulder, strapped the cartridge belt about him and leaned against the wall mopping his forehead. As for the Major, he blew his nose loudly, brushed some dust from his boots with an impatient movement, and then turned smiling towards his companion.

"Congratulations once more," he said in the complimentary tones he would have used in a drawing-room. "And next, please?"

Dick flushed a rosy red, and then spoke out promptly.

"Still to lead, sir?" he asked.

"Of course, lad! Why not? Haven't you done well for us? Besides, this is entirely a naval expedition, while for the moment I am merely a civilian."

"Then, now that we've given Alec and the Colonel a little start we had better retire up the steps. Those fellows could rush us here. But higher up it wouldn't be so easy. That right, sir?"

"Certainly; up we go—ah! The steps curl round and round a central pillar. That's really excellent. You go ahead, Dick; I'll follow. The higher we can get the better, I think, for then we string these men out so that the front of the line is a good distance from those who follow. Listen!"

They stood still for one brief moment, and listened to the mob of Turks enter the mosque. Scurrying steps could be heard on the hard pavement, while for the most part the men themselves were silent. A minute later, however, while Dick and his friend were still ascending, a shout came rolling up the narrow, curling stairway.

"This way, comrades," they heard. "This way! The sentry at the door tells us that they rushed across to this tower and entered. Now, friends, we have them safely. Let us consider our movements."

There came the confused sound of men discussing some matter volubly. Occasionally one of the Turks would raise his voice above the others, then there was silence.

"Wait! Don't move for a moment," said the Major. "Now, what's happening?" He placed his ear to the central column which bore this curling flight of steps and stood motionless for some few seconds.

"Coming up to us as quietly as they can," he said softly. "The time for giving them that lesson or for going under is coming. Do we stay here, or climb higher?"

"Higher, sir, I think. It's too dark to see easily here, but there's a window up above us. If we get a little higher than that, we shall be in the dusk and see these beggars nicely. I'll call to them when they come in sight and warn 'em."

It was not a time for words nor for a discussion, and promptly the two climbed higher, halting when they were some six feet above a small, unglazed opening, which admitted light and air to the stairs. Here they were joined a moment later by the Colonel.

"Came back to join in this little picnic," he whispered. "We left the Commander on a wide balcony up there, from which one gets a really magnificent view of this awful city, and even of the lines of the besiegers and the Turkish forts and trenches surrounding the place. The minaret runs up a great deal higher, and there is a stairway. But the balcony is good enough for us, and if we are driven there we can hold the entrance to it. Well, now, how does the matter go?"

He was as cheery and as cool as if he were at home in his own rooms in London. That is, he was calm and by no means ruffled at the thought of the danger with which the little party was confronted. But as to being actually cool, one could hardly expect that after his recent exertions. The perspiration was streaming from his forehead, though he mopped his brow time and again, and still panted heavily.

"Hard work clambering two hundred steps with a heavy man on your back," he laughed. "And these naval johnnies are heavy, I can tell you. Well? How do we stand?"

The Major lifted a warning finger to his lips. "Gently does it, Steven," he said. "They're coming. Dick here will call to them and give the rascals a warning when the first gets in sight. But I don't fancy that'll stop 'em. Let's be ready for a turn up."

"S-sh! There's the leader."

The Colonel hardly whispered the words. He was pointing down the curling stairway, and there, some ten feet below the open window, coming into the flood of light which poured in through that aperture, was a crafty, crawling figure, a man clambering up the stairs on hands and knees, a young man gripping a revolver in one of his hands and causing the barrel of the weapon to clink on the stones each time he put that particular hand down.

"Now," whispered the Major.

"Halt!" called Dick, sternly, in the Turkish tongue. "You who follow us, halt now, or take the consequences, and listen well to these words. We are not spies. We are Englishmen, friends of the Turkish nation."

For some few seconds there was silence, a deathly silence, broken, however, by the deep breathing of the Colonel, and by the deeper gasps for breath of many of the mob clambering upward. Then came the clink of that revolver barrel, a hoarse oath from the Turkish officer bearing it, for the young officer with whom Dick had collided still led this band of ragamuffins, and later a swelling shout of rage from the stairway, pouring from the throats of furious men perched at various elevations. An instant later the officer stood upright, his weapon flashed, while a bullet struck the curving wall just beside the Colonel, and went ricochetting off it till it thudded and stopped against one of the steps.

"Good! That at any rate tells us what to expect," said the Major grimly.

"Stand back, Colonel, and you too, Dick. No use all three of us chancing a bullet. It's lucky, too, that this stairway curves always to the right, for that lets one shoot without peering round. A right-handed man coming up will be bothered. Yes, I thought so."

Peering round the curving central pillar which bore the steps he caught sight of the officer's head, for he and Dick and the Colonel had started backwards after that first shot. The man's body then came into full view, and lastly his right arm, with his weapon pointed upward. Instantly the Major's weapon cracked, while the Turk dropped his revolver with a howl.

"Very nice shooting," reflected the Colonel. "Back of the hand, I think, Major. It'll make him more cautious."

Or more furious. The latter seemed to be the case, for that howl of pain was followed by a bellow and by a hoarse roar of anger and excitement from below. A hundred feet then shuffled on the various steps, while the officer, his eyes blazing with anger, launched himself upward. But the revolver was no longer in his wounded hand, a fact which the Major noticed with wonderful sharpness. Indeed, his own movements showed within the minute that he was fully awake, and ready for an emergency. They saw him step hastily downward and throw his shoulders backward. And then out shot one of his fists, repeating the blow which Dick had delivered to this pugnacious individual on the previous night. And now, as before, it was equally effective, for the officer shot backward as if struck by a hammer, and, cannoning into the man behind, upset him also. In fact, half a dozen of the mob were thrown down by the Major's sudden action, their cries and shouts deafening Dick and the others. The noise which followed was positively terrifying, for fifty furious Turks shouted and screamed their loudest, while not a few let off their weapons careless of the consequences. As for the head of this attacking force, relieved now of its leading spirit—for the officer lay stunned upon the stairway, and would have rolled downward but for the press about him—it showed wonderful dash and determination. Fanaticism and hate had stirred these men to fury, and without a pause they rushed up the stairs, some with bayonets thrusting forwards, others heralding their approach with rifle bullets. It was clear, in fact, that they would quickly smash their way through all obstacles, and though the Major and Dick and the Colonel in turn brought down a man with their weapons, thus delaying the others, and for some few minutes faced the attackers, discretion bade them retire towards the gallery.

"There's a door there that we can shut and bolt and bar outside," cried the Colonel. "It'll be the last stage in this business, but safer and better than stairs fighting. Now, up you go."

"After you, sir," said Dick, touching his cap in nautical fashion.

"Eh? After me, why?" began the Colonel. Then he laughed and smacked the midshipman gaily on the shoulder. "Sinking ship, eh?" he grinned. "Never! But the skipper leaves last, that's it, my lad. Like your grit immensely, that I do. Well, Major, do you or do I lead the retreat?"

A sharp crack came from that officer's weapon. He jerked his head quickly, leaned forward, and again pulled his trigger. "You," he said at length. "I'm busy; in a moment I'll follow. Dick, look out for these beggars, and run up immediately after me."

"Right, sir! Certainly, sir!" came from the youthful Dicky.

"Then off we go." The Colonel left his friends guarding the stairs and ran up three at a time. Then the Major followed, while Dick waited coolly to convey to a charging Turkish fanatic the fact that there was danger above, and then went scampering after the others.

"Here he is. In you come, my boy. Now, bang the door; that's got it!"

The Colonel threw the massive door at the top of the steps against its supporting frame and leaned against it, while the Major slipped the bolts into position. Then, gasping after their exertions, they turned to observe Alec and the Commander. Imagine their amazement at seeing the former stripped to his vest, and frantically waving his shirt over the stone balustrade of the gallery. His face was purple with excitement, his eyes were blazing, while he shouted as if he had suddenly gone crazy. And then, while the two more sedate officers watched him in amazement. Dick began of a sudden to copy his antics. He danced across the gallery; he shouted and waved his hands and threw his cap upward.

"Mad! Gone suddenly crazy! What on earth has happened to them?" demanded the Major anxiously.

Then Dick swung round upon him and the Colonel, subdued his own excitement with a violent effort, and, drawing himself upright, saluted briskly.

"Airship in sight, sir," he said. "Alec reports that he's called 'em up with his signals, and—and they'll be here in a jiffy."

CHAPTER XI

Some Facts and Figures

How strange to be upon the transparent galleries of the great airship again, to tread those flimsy-looking but undoubtedly stout floors, and to look upward at the giant framework, all transparent, faintly outlined for the most part, appearing to be filled with emptiness, and yet enclosing the life of this enormous vessel! Yes, it was strange indeed! The relief was so great that it positively set the gallant Major dancing, while the Colonel, though he had stepped from the lift fifteen minutes earlier, still mopped his brow and blew heavily, as if recovering from some extraordinary sensation.

"'Pon my word," he spluttered time and again. "'Pon my word, that experience was really terrifying. I felt positively scared, frightened, almost paralysed by the enormity of the danger."

Once more he mopped his forehead, while the genial Andrew regarded him with friendly interest.

"Quite so, quite so, Colonel," he ventured. "Narrow shave; very. I'd have been scared, too, dreadfully, I do assure you. How many of the rascals were there?"

"Rascals! What! You don't think?" began the gallant officer, still mopping his forehead, and regarding Andrew with every sign of indignation. And then he smiled, the first time since he had set foot on the airship. "Really, Mr. Provost, I think? Yes, Mr. Provost, you do not think that I was referring to those rascals from whom we so recently escaped? I, er—don't you know—I am not in the habit of being scared when in the execution of my duty, and escape from those Turkish ruffians was distinctly a duty. I was referring to the manner in which I was plucked from the terrace of that minaret and whisked upward. 'Pon my word, my scalp feels sore after such an experience. Forgive me if I say it, but wonderful though that experience was, it was also terrifying."

It well might be, and indeed Dick and those fine tars, Hawkins and Hurst, and the others had felt the same sort of terror. For think of the nerve-racking journey which the Colonel had taken. Alec's frantic waving, and Mr. Midshipman Hamshaw's equally mad behaviour had heralded the advent of Joe Gresson's marvellous airship. As that forlorn little party stood upon the gallery of the minaret attached to that great mosque in Adrianople, with those fanatical Turks howling within but a few feet of them, and kept at bay merely by the thickness of a door, a huge, transparent shape had dropped towards them. At one moment, when Alec first sighted it, it presented but a speck in the sky. And then it had positively fallen towards the minaret till one could see the figures on her main gallery. Instantly that familiar lift had swung downward, turning and twisting giddily upon its single strand of steel wire, till the dangling platform was actually resting on the gallery which supported Dick and his friends.

"All aboard!" that worthy called out cheerfully.

"First lift the Commander in. Now, Colonel."

"Get on that frail craft! Be whisked aloft!"

Who can wonder if the gallant Colonel did demur for the moment? For a fresh breeze caught that thin steel rope and swayed it from side to side, causing it to drag and pluck at the platform.

"After you. Now, I'm ready."

It was characteristic of the Colonel that he hesitated no longer. But still one cannot blame him if he clutched one of the four steel ropes which ran from the corners of this flimsy, transparent platform to the ring above, to which the single cable was attached, and clenched his teeth tightly. Indeed, we will think none the worse of this gallant man for the fact that he actually blanched as the lift started upward, Dick having spoken into the telephone. As for that incorrigible young fellow, he was now not entirely a novice in matters appertaining to the airship, and, satisfied of the security of the strange lift upon which he stood, he leaned over the edge as the motor above whisked them upward and waved his cap at the Turks from whom they had so fortunately escaped. Indeed, hardly had the lift started upward when the door at the top of that long, curling stairway was broken open, and a crew of furious ruffians launched themselves on to the gallery.

"*Au revoir!*" called Dick. "Sorry not to be able to stop to entertain you. Call on us aloft; do, there's good fellows!"

A bullet whizzing past his head put a summary end to his taunts, while the buzzing motor whisked the rescued party out of sight of the maddened and astounded Turks within a minute. And here they were on board, safe and secure.

"And as hungry as hunters," cried Alec.

At that very moment a gong sounded, while Sergeant Evans put in an appearance.

"Luncheon ready, gentlemen," he said with the utmost suavity, as if there had been no such thing as an exciting rescue, and as if he had had nothing else to think about. "Commander Jackson's compliments, and he feels wonderfully better."

"Then we will go to the saloon," said Andrew. "Joe seems as clever with a patient as with airships. Come, Colonel, we can leave the Commander to my nephew while we eat. Welcome aboard the airship!"

"And now tell us how it happened that you turned up at such a fortunate and exciting moment," asked the Major, when lunch was finished and the friends were seated smoking about the table. "Remember, you were to return during the night. Adrianople is hardly a safe place for an airship at this moment. Think of the result of a shell bursting close to this vessel."

"Precisely! Think also of the members of our party stranded in the city," smiled Andrew. "Joe and I discussed the matter."

"And decided that we would risk everything," said that latter. "After all, it gave one the opportunity of conducting a valuable test. This ship is supposed to be transparent."

"Extraordinary!" declared the Colonel. "Why, 'pon my word! but really, one can see right through her. There's a man patrolling the deck high overhead, a sailor by the look of him. Surely he's yards above us—almost, it seems, suspended on air. And yet one sees that there are beams and girders all about us. You mean to tell me, sir," and he addressed his question to Joe in particular, "you mean to say that those girders are of solid, strong material, and enclose a space filled with hydrogen? In fact, a space which supports this huge vessel?"

"Yes and no. For the most part, certainly yes," declared the young inventor, blushing with pride. "But the gas happens to be merely coal gas. You see, I chose it with an object. On a long trip such as this, that is to say a voyage which is to circle the globe, one must expect to lose gas from the compartments which go to fill the bulk of this huge vessel. In the case of Zeppelins and allied vessels the loss is appreciable. Here, thanks to celludine, which happens not to be porous, the loss is, in fact, negligible. Still, accident may give rise to leakage. It may become necessary to refill the whole vessel."

"Then you descend?" asked the Colonel, obviously interested in this explanation.

"We should already have been forced to descend," Joe corrected him.

"Precisely; and call at some gasworks?" the Colonel interjected.

"No; we carry a gas producer. We have coal in abundance; the rest is easy."

It might or might not be. To the Colonel it was wonderful; in fact, so interesting that, what with the excellent meal of which he had partaken and this discussion, he quite forgot that experience when being swung upward to safety. Indeed, he must needs go off at once with Joe on a tour of investigation, while Andrew chatted with the Major.

"And so you determined to risk it," said the latter.

"Certainly! You couldn't expect us to leave the greater part of our number in the heart of that city!"

Andrew sauntered across to one of the wide-open windows of the saloon and pointed downward. Yes, there was Adrianople, a mere blotch beneath them, its outline dim and blurred, its streets and houses merged into one another; its trenches, its forts, its struggling defenders utterly obliterated. A black line, with dark clumps here and there, showed merely the presence of the attackers, while tiny and ridiculously dim points of fire betrayed the guns which even then were speaking.

"Listen! Yes," reflected Andrew, "we heard the guns from a distance, and, risking all, made our way back towards the city. And there we lay, almost at this elevation, while the sun slowly rose and flooded the place. Then we gradually dropped nearer and nearer to the houses."

"And no one saw you?" asked the Major.

"None, I believe. All were too engaged with the fighting. It was Alec, I suppose, who first caught sight of us, and Hawkins who saw his signal. After that, you know what happened. And now, Major, what becomes of 'Charlie'? You have been lucky enough to discover him, and one presumes that he has come aboard with his secret. Bear in mind that I hold this vessel at your disposal. If necessary we will return to England. Or we can set the Colonel down wherever he may think most convenient. But if time is of importance, and his destination is England, then I suggest that we make use of the aeroplane which we carry. Come and inspect it."

They tossed their cigar stumps out of the window, took one more look downward at the forlorn city, and then ascended to the wide deck carried on the top of the airship. Overhead, as they trudged along it, fluttered the long aerials suspended to the thin masts erected for wireless telegraphic purposes, while far down below, almost in the centre of the main gangway, a man could be seen bending over transmitter and receiver.

"You see, we are well equipped," said Andrew. "Of course, if it so happened that the Colonel could send his information by wireless, then it would be a great pleasure to have him with us. In any case, let us inspect Joe's aeroplane. Here it is; now, take close stock of it."

That was a privilege which Dick also enjoyed, for his inspection so soon after his first arrival on board had been hurried. Now he approached the machine in question burning with curiosity. For Dick was one of the adventurous fellows who are so frequently to be found in the two services.

"Flying or submarine work's in my line," he had told his fellow middies. "But flying in particular."

And here was something upon which, for all he knew, he might learn his first lessons. In the sunk hangar located on the wide upper deck of the airship lay a machine which might well have attracted the attention of some of our expert flyers. For Joe Gresson was no ordinary inventor. As we have endeavoured to convey to the reader, the silent Joe was indeed a genius, a young man thoroughly well trained in the principles of engineering, and gifted with a brain of unusual capacity. Hence his great airship. Hence also this adjunct to it. Dick and his friends looked upon a machine differing only in form and size and engine from those common at the moment. The principle was precisely the same, and yet the perfection of engineering and design incorporated in the machine in question made of it an article of astonishing efficiency.

"Same as many others at first sight, but different," observed the Major, while Dick had his head thrust almost into the very heart of the machinery. "Why, there's the Colonel. Well, Steven, what do you think of the vessel which brought us out to Adrianople just in time to snatch you from that extremely uncomfortable city?"

There was a glow on the bronzed, if somewhat pinched, face of the one addressed; for, as we have said, Colonel Steven was an enthusiast where modern advancement was in question, while the science and art of the flyer was as attractive to him as to any.

"Think, my dear Major!" he observed. "What can one think? One is absolutely and positively astounded. I can now scarcely believe that I am really on the top of an enormous airship, bigger even than a Zeppelin, and suspended some hundreds of feet in the air."

"Pardon—thousands, Colonel," said Joe's quiet voice. "Here is the exact reading—ten thousand two hundred and eighty-five feet." He stepped across to one of the posts that supported the rail running round the deck and consulted an instrument affixed to it.

"Ten thousand feet! But——" gasped the Colonel, "you'll explode."

"Bust, in other words," Dick whispered to Alec. "Call a spade a spade, my boy. That's the worst of getting senior in any service, for you have to choose and pick your words, which is a bit of a nuisance. 'Bust' here is the correct and proper description."

"A Zeppelin would," added the Colonel, failing to hear Dick's grinning aside.

"Pardon once more: a Zeppelin would be incapable of ascending much above six thousand feet. At least, that is their record so far, and it is for that reason that, though a menace to all nations who have none, supposing Germany were to declare war, and such nations were within the six hundred miles radius, the Zeppelin is still not entirely mistress of the air. There is always the speedy, powerful aeroplane, capable with ease of ascending infinitely higher, far out of range of her deck guns, for Zeppelins carry weapons above just as you see here, and from that point dropping bombs upon her."

"Ugh! Disagreeable sort of game that," laughed the Major, shrugging his shoulders and staring upward. "Nasty thing to receive a bomb when slung even six thousand feet in the air. You'd come an awful crasher."

"As to exploding," continued Joe serenely, "of course one no longer experiences at these high altitudes the normal fourteen pounds per square inch one is accustomed to on terra firma. The atmosphere is rarer, it weighs considerably less, and exerts decidedly less pressure. Hence, as you rightly assume, the envelope of a Zeppelin tends to tear. But, my dear sir, permit me to hand you a sample of sheet celludine. See, it is transparent, flexible, and extremely light. Please tear it, using as much force as you wish, and thereby prove that it is neither tough nor unstretchable."

The inventor held out a single sheet of his wonderful yet simple material, while Dick craned his neck forward to get a closer view. As for Alec and Andrew, they were already versed in the characteristics of the stuff, but none the less interested. At once the Major complied with Joe's wishes.

"Light, transparent, flexible," he said. "Yes, admitted. You agree, Colonel. Now tough and non-extensible; that is, won't stretch."

"Like rubber," interjected Dick.

"Quite so. Hang on—no, you're too light yet. Who ever heard of a midshipman having weight? The Colonel will suit my purpose. Now, Steven, pull with all your might."

As was only to be expected the experiment proved the value of celludine conclusively.

"I've been through the same sort of game," laughed Andrew. "I've tugged and pulled and stamped on the stuff till I was hot. Then, gentlemen, I put my money into this ship. I had had a practical demonstration."

"But we were talking of exploding," said Joe. "Of course, each one of the gas compartments has a safety valve, so that if at any time the pressure from without should lessen to a dangerous degree, then the valves open and gas escapes. But you were looking at the aeroplane. I propose to make use of it presently; for our friend, the French airman whom Dick was sent to rescue, is now recovered and wishes to be landed."

A close inspection of the heavier-than-air machine designed by Joe Gresson proved of absorbing interest, for here again celludine entered into the greater part of its construction. Possessed of two planes, these were supported by girders passing to right and left, and braced together in a manner which made

111

them peculiarly rigid, while the lower and upper planes were supported on the girders holding those positions respectively, some three feet only separating them. Immediately beneath, forming, in fact, the foundation for the girders, was a long, boat-shaped body, with sharpened prow, no visible keel, and a flat bottom tapering from stem to stern. The latter extended a considerable distance, and supported at its end two small elevating planes and a big vertical rudder. Finally, two struts on either side had spring wheels attached to them, while the steel stampings, to which they were bolted themselves, had a form of spring attachment which one could realize would provide against severe shocks when landing.

"Then she can come down on water or on land?" asked the Colonel, adjusting an eyeglass which he had just produced. "Most interesting. And how, pray, does she return to her parent ship, this gigantic air vessel?"

"How? By merely circling above and dropping on this deck. I will show you," said Joe, his face flushed with pride. "But first allow me to describe the method by which the pilot controls the machine, and how lateral and fore-and-aft stability are assured. See, there are the same movements as on other machines for controlling height, for turning, or 'banking', to use the technical expression. One merely sits in the cab placed towards the stem of the boat body where the levers are located. Come, Colonel, and you too, Major, and Dick. Try a spin. I can assure you that there is no risk in the matter."

"But—but set off when ten thousand feet from the land, when one can distinguish no single object," cried the former, aghast at such a suggestion. "Yes, I'll come," he said a moment later, deliberately screwing his monocle a little tighter into position and looking at the inventor. "You tell me there is no great risk, and hearing that, I accept the invitation. After all, you must not blame me if I show some little trepidation. My dear sir, I am not a bird, and this is the first occasion on which I have ever ascended from native earth."

As for the Major, he too nodded his willingness, though he also felt not a little trepidation. As for Dick, one may say that the happy-go-lucky fellow hardly ever counted risks, such is the record of midshipmen. But even so, a glance through the transparent material beneath him towards the brown blur far, far below caused him an undoubted tremor. But he had grit. He had proved it, and now leaped into the boat without further hesitation. The Colonel and his brother officer were already there, while Joe stepped in behind them.

"Take your seats, gentlemen," he said, with a smile which went far to reassure them. "Now, we are ready, save for the fact that our engine is not yet running, while the doors of this sunken hangar are not open. But I pull this cord hanging overhead. See! An electric motor raises the whole shed and opens it. Then we press this little pedal—more electricity, my friends—a six-volt battery feeds a small motor aboard here and turns the engine round. Now air is forced through my paraffin carburettor and the vapour resulting is fed to that gasometer in the bows of the boat. Yes, it's a gasometer, just as you see on land, though much smaller. Thence the gas passes to the engine, where it receives more air and—ah! she's off. Listen to her humming, and for one moment notice the position of the engine. It is centrally placed, immediately beneath the planes, and is suspended from a single point. Thus it is free to swing both backward and forward and from side to side. There lies the secret of automatic stability. Say we are coasting along and a gust cants us to the right. The heavy engine still keeps in the same vertical position, while this whole machine turns as it were on that single point. You can readily follow that certain levers attached to engine and machine will be altered in position, and as a direct result the wing tips are warped in a prearranged manner, the back planes rotate upward or downward, or the rudder itself is operated. That is for coasting, for use when on a long, straight flight, when one wishes to take note of one's surroundings, to eat, or even to sleep."

"Sleep!" gasped the Major.

"Why not?" came Joe's cool answer.

"But up in the air, thousands of feet up!"

"As well there as within a hundred feet. The action I have been describing is automatic. There is no question of human error in its behaviour. So long as the planes have room for manœuvring, and the engine does not stop, there is no need to interfere in the slightest. Set your course, lock your tiller, and go to sleep. But you shall see; for the moment I will trust to my own skill in manœuvring. In fact, by pulling this small lever I secure the engine. In effect it is now suspended not only from a single point, but fixed rigidly to the framework of the whole machine. Then if I wish to bank, no automatic action can disturb my calculations. We are ready, I think. Look! flexible tubes above the engine carry the water from the force pumps to the motors on the hubs of the two propellers. There you see precisely the same hydraulic system of conveying power as is used elsewhere in this airship. No need, therefore, to have a dozen men holding the machine down, for the propellers are motionless, the bypass being full open. But I close it now—watch them twirl. I shut it almost completely——"

"Hi! Hold on!" shouted Dick at that instant, while the Colonel gripped the sides of the cab and actually dropped his monocle.

"We're off!" bellowed the Major, jamming his hat down on his head and clenching his teeth tightly.

"Away she goes!" called Joe, his face set, his eyes glued on the deck before him.

Those two propellers hissed and roared as they rotated, the biplane resting so tranquilly a moment earlier beneath the transparent roof of her shed leaped into the open, her wheels already engaged with the rails placed there to guide them. In a moment or two she was speeding along them at forty miles an hour, so fast, indeed, that Dick could feel her lifting already. He sat down hard, bit his lip, and tried to look as if the trip before him was of little moment. But the gallant Dick's heart was fluttering in the most uncomfortable manner. Indeed, we must report the fact that Mr. Midshipman Hamshaw was almost reduced to the condition of abject funk. For the machine lifted of a sudden. The deck of the airship, that deck which only a few hours before had seemed to the midshipman so insecure, so frail, so wanting in stability, and now—so curious is the change of opinion brought by altered circumstances—which offered such a firm standing, that deck flashed from beneath the biplane. One second there was the familiar, transparent mass of the airship beneath them; the next they were perhaps a hundred feet from her, out in the open, suspended on thin air, supported by the atmosphere upon a machine which relied on no gas to sustain it, but merely upon the upward push of the ether into which she had rushed. No wonder that the usually dashing Dick clutched firmly to the side of the cab and uttered a breathless "Jingo!"

CHAPTER XII

Carl Aboard the Biplane

There is a very old and no doubt true saying that everything comes to those who wait, and Mr. Carl Reitberg may be said to have been one of these fortunate individuals. For all that he desired seemed to be about to be consummated.

"At last! A brilliant inspiration, really," he was telling himself almost at the identical moment when Joe Gresson set out from the great airship with the Major, the Colonel, and Dick, and swooped into space upon his wonderful biplane. "A really brilliant inspiration. Here have I been thinking and bothering and cudgelling my brains for a means to—to—er—well, to put a stop to what might well be an astounding triumph for that Andrew Provost and his conceited nephew, when a sudden thought strikes me, all difficulties are cleared away, and the future becomes rosy."

The stout, roundabout figure of this little man who spoke English with an accent, who loved the freedom, the customs, and the institutions of Great Britain, and who had waxed rich and prosperous because of the protection and many opportunities which the country or her possessions had given him, rolled round in the deep armchair in which he was seated, while his hand groped for a cut-glass tumbler standing on an adjacent table. The deep-set, cunning eyes saw none of the surrounding magnificence which the walls of his smoking-room displayed; for Mr. Carl Reitberg was deeply immersed, lost in thought, carried away by the brilliance of his inspiration.

"Yes," he reflected again, "a brilliant inspiration. Here was I in London—or rather, to put it correctly, here am I in London—hearing on every side tales of the airship, of her strength, of her swiftness, of her original design, capacity, and extraordinary power; and yet there is no way of moving, no means of arresting the world tour of the air vessel, no method of—er—er causing an unfortunate accident Then, when all seems to have gone badly for me, when, owing to my own stupid impulse, my desire to be applauded as a sportsman, the bank holds one hundred thousand pounds which I have deposited, without power of withdrawal, against the day when the ship returns, then, I say, difficulties suddenly fly. It is strange how a man's brain at last hits upon a solution."

In his delight he had begun to speak aloud, addressing his words to the four walls of the room, to the costly pictures attached to them, to the velvet curtains, the cigar cabinets, the table loaded with bric-à-brac, and to curios and valuables in general. In any case he had not included the only other occupant of the room, had never once turned his eyes in his direction, had seemed to have forgotten him utterly. But the man there, lounging placidly in a deep and luxurious armchair, smiling sardonically, and nursing a damaged arm which he wore in a sling, was listening intently. Once he scowled and growled something beneath his breath. And now that Carl Reitberg seemed to have finished he stole a look at him, and leaned over and coolly helped himself to a cigar which, by the breadth of the gilded band about it, might have cost a small fortune.

"A brilliant inspiration, eh?" he asked languidly, settling himself back in his chair when he had set his cigar going. "What?"

The words brought his host back to Mother Earth with a start. To speak the truth there was no love lost between Carl Reitberg and Adolf Fruhmann, for that rascal was the other inmate of this room. The pompous little owner of this magnificent establishment would have ignored his one-time accomplice had he not need of him. Now he put up with his presence as best he could. Not that Adolf Fruhmann was of much value at the moment; for an accident in the streets had left him with a broken arm, much to Carl's annoyance.

"That's what I was telling you," he answered savagely. "Here are you fool enough to get an arm broken, thereby rendering yourself helpless when it was a matter of arrangement between us that you were to act——"

"One moment; not so fast," came from the other. "You speak as if I'd asked that taxi driver to run me down, as if I enjoyed the suffering that's followed. Besides, if I'm helpless for the moment, and you've been fool enough to plant a hundred thousand pounds into a bank in such a way that you can't finger it till this challenge is settled, why, it's for you to move, you to risk your own skin, I'm thinking."

Certainly there was no love lost between them, and if Carl imagined that Adolf would cringe and whine when in his presence, the events of the past few days had entirely undeceived him. For Adolf had become a leech, a detestable fellow who clung to the man who desired to employ him. From that squalid tenement dwelling down by Whitechapel, he had removed himself to Carl Reitberg's luxurious mansion, and protest on that indignant gentleman's part had no effect.

"We've just got to sink or swim together," observed Adolf, with a scornful smile when his would-be benefactor flared out at him and bade him depart. "We're old chums, don't forget that, old partners, and—and there's a few who would like very much—very much indeed—to meet us."

It was a significant statement, and Adolf took no trouble to rob his words of the sinister threat which underlay them. From the meek, half-starved, down-at-heels ruffian, he had of a sudden, once he had been discovered by Carl, become a sleek, sardonic individual, sleeker perhaps for the fact that the best of London tailoring had turned him out in the latest of fashions. Indeed, in the well-dressed, or rather, somewhat over-dressed individual lolling in the deep armchair in Carl's room, it was hard to recognize the unkempt, unwashed rascal of but a few days earlier.

And his benefactor was helpless. As Carl lay back watching his accomplice through half-closed lids, he was bound to admit that here was one item in which his scheme of attacking Andrew Provost had miscarried. Adolf Fruhmann had got disgracefully out of hand, and was almost unmanageable. He had picked him out of the gutter merely for a purpose, and knowing that for gold this rascal would do almost anything. And now he was actually afraid of the man, dared not order him away, was fearful that a word from him might jeopardize his, Carl Reitberg's own position.

"Well, I suppose I shall have to put up with the nuisance," he reflected, as he scowled at his companion. "After all, it will not be for long, and later, when I have made use of him, why there are ways of ridding oneself of a nuisance. Now," he said aloud, "you were asking about this brilliant inspiration."

"I am incredulous. Carl Reitberg with an inspiration worth hearing of!"

The man was positively offensive, and caused the fat and pompous Carl to squirm, while the ferrety little eyes, sunk behind their lashes, positively glared at the rascal who had spoken.

"Well, let us hear it," said Adolf flippantly, flicking his cigar ash with one finger, and inspecting the glowing end with every sign of approval. "Carl Reitberg has an inspiration; his friends long to hear all about it."

"It is about the airship," began Carl, ignoring the man's words, though his cheeks were purple.

"It always is," came the retort. "You dream of the thing; you think of it by day and night. That hundred thousand pounds weighs as heavily as a ton of lead."

"And rightly so," Carl answered sharply. "I was deluded, I say. I had no idea that this Joe Gresson could succeed in his undertaking, I——"

"Exactly," came the dry answer. "If you had been fully awake you'd never have issued that challenge. You were too cocksure, Carl. You put down that money feeling that it was safe. Now you're doubtful. So am I. You'll lose it if all that the papers report is correct. Just fancy! the ship sails across to Adrianople quicker than an aeroplane could take you. She hovers over the city. She rises and falls and disappears at will. Then she heads back for England, while her wireless tells *The Daily Flier* all the news. If that hundred thousand pounds were mine—and some of it will be according to our agreement—why, I'd begin to get fidgety. I'd begin to dream and seek for inspirations. Well, what's yours?"

"I use the wireless also. I call up the ship. I follow the idea of behaving as a sportsman."

"Ah!" Adolf smiled satirically. "That cost a heap!" he said. "Well?"

"I ask to be taken aboard for this world trip. Can they refuse me?"

It was his companion's turn to show some irritation. If Carl Reitberg had the intention of accompanying the great airship on her voyage, then it could be with one object, for there were no secrets between these two rascals. He desired to gain access to the ship with the sole idea of wrecking or damaging it. Very good, that! Crafty! Quite commendable.

"But there's myself to be considered. If he succeeds, what do I get? Where is the reward promised?"

The ruffian eyed Carl with undisguised contempt, and yet half fearfully.

"Clever idea, very," he said aloud. "You go aboard for the trip. There is, perhaps, an accident. Unfortunate, of course, but—er—necessary. You are as sorry as the others. You express a thousand regrets—but all the while you are laughing in your sleeve. You are really thinking of something far harder to give than regrets; you are thinking of your one hundred thousand pounds, eh, my friend? That is, I think, the beginning and end of the inspiration."

It was so obvious that Adolf admired the craftiness of the scheme that Carl almost forgave him. But the next few seconds undeceived him, and reminded the magnate of the fact that he had others to consider.

"Of course," said Adolf slowly, "our bargain holds good. If—if there is an unfortunate accident, and the voyage of the airship is arrested, you return and pay me the sum promised."

"But——" cried Carl indignantly, his fat cheeks swelling.

"There are no buts in the matter. I am paid, or I blab. I have a long memory, and there are other things I can mention. No, friend Carl, we swim or sink together, as I have said. You leave England. Good! I look after your house, your servants, and your interests during your absence. Supposing you fail—supposing this—er—accident doesn't happen, then you fall back on your dear friend. I seek for an inspiration. I attempt another accident. In either case, if you are successful, or if the honour falls to me, our bargain holds, I am paid what was promised."

It was a sordid business; but no doubt there are other rascals of the same kidney haggling over even less unsavoury schemes in the great city of London. But this was evident, Carl was in a corner, hoist as it were by the very rascal he had hoped to use merely as a tool, and then to throw away when no longer useful. It was a bitter blow, but to be endured, and he must not allow it to prevent his following the line of action he had suddenly decided on. He gulped down the contents of his tumbler, scowled at his companion, and then stretched out for the telephone receiver. A moment later he was dictating a telegram to be dispatched by wireless to the great airship.

"Mr. Carl Reitberg presents his warmest congratulations to Mr. Andrew Provost and his clever nephew, and asks to be allowed to accompany the party aboard the airship during some part of their world trip. Wire place at which ship could call."

Down in the depths of the airship, in the Marconi operator's cabin, the operator was busily employed some few minutes later, while the aerials above flashed in the sun and clicked in their own extraordinary fashion. Then a paper was thrust into Andrew's hand as he paced the deck arm in arm with the Commander.

"Umph!" he said, handing it to the naval officer. "Rather spoil the fun of the party. I ain't too fond of Mr. Carl Reitberg."

"But it's sporting of him, eh?" reflected the officer, now rapidly recovering.

"Sporting? Er—yes—that's what he aims at particularly. Sad if he were to spoil also the ship's chances."

"But surely that's impossible—one man spoil the chances of the ship's success!"

"Well, perhaps I'm unduly suspicious. Carton, wire back that we shall be pleased to receive him, and that Joe Gresson will call for him in London. Then call up Joe. He's well within range of the ship's wireless, and repeat the message."

And thus it followed that while Joe, with the Major and Colonel and the derelict Frenchman on board, were coasting towards England, having once demonstrated to our friends the security of the biplane, the aerials aboard that wonderful machine clicked, while the receiver told out its message. An hour later, perhaps, while Carl Reitberg was snoring in his luxurious chair, the telephone summoned him from slumber.

"Be ready to start to-morrow morning early. Joe Gresson will call for you. Warm welcome awaits you aboard the great airship."

Carl simpered. His pig-like eyes lit up wonderfully, and for one brief moment he wore the appearance he had borne when Joe first met him aboard the Hamburg-Amerika liner. He was positively genial, and any old lady of a credulous disposition happening to observe him at that moment would have set him down definitely as a most engaging, kind-hearted, and simple gentleman. And so he could have been, had he not at heart been a scheming rascal. For Carl Reitberg was that. If he had been a patriot, if he had belonged to some

119

other country than England, and for her sake had decided to destroy the airship with her crew, we would have recorded the fact plainly. But Carl had no country, not even that of England, which had fostered him, protected him, even innocently aided him in some of his rascally schemes. His scheme was merely for personal objects, to save his pocket, to win a challenge, to defeat Andrew Provost and Joe Gresson, and all the while appear in the public eye as a sportsman, something understood by the people and sure to make him wonderfully popular.

The hours that followed were busy ones indeed for Carl, and Adolf Fruhmann aided him wonderfully in spite of a damaged arm. They retreated to a garret in a street off Soho, where they remained till day was almost dawning. Nor did they present themselves at the place as Carl Reitberg and Adolf Fruhmann respectively. No; they went disguised, using false names also. What passed in that garret we need not enquire into; but this is certain: when the two rogues finally left and drove away in a taxi, there was a suspicious square box beside them.

"Gently, gently! You carry it," suggested Carl, as they stepped out of the cab and walked away.

"Very well; I'm not afraid if you are. The things are safe till you begin to tamper with them. Then——"

Adolf raised his eyes expressively and sniggered. "Then there's an end to you and—and the airship," he giggled.

"H-hush, man! Are you a fool? Here! Step into this cab. We can drive straight home now, I think."

They had dived into a side street for a moment, where they had rapidly removed the beards which had disguised them. Now they hailed a taxi, entered, and boldly told the man to drive to Carl's address. The following morning found the chief of these two rascals dressed for an outing. An immaculate knickerbocker suit clad his rotund proportions, while the monocle he—like the gallant Colonel—affected transformed him into an object such as one sees at St. Moritz, one of the band of heroes who go to look on at somewhat hazardous winter sports and continue always to look on only.

Buzz! The telephone called him. They were speaking from his office in the city, to which all telegrams were sent. "What's that?" demanded Carl incredulously, when he had listened to the message. "Eh! I am to drive out to Hendon, where Mr. Gresson will pick me up? Where's the airship?"

"Somewhere above Italy," came the answer. "Mr. Gresson arrived yesterday evening in an aeroplane."

"An aeroplane! But—but—surely he doesn't expect me to—to travel in such a thing with him!" cried Carl tremulously, much to Adolfs amusement and ill-concealed contempt.

"Why not?" he asked. "You've asked to go on a flying trip. Where's the difference between a ship and plane? Pooh! You're a sportsman, aren't you? Then you've got to show spirit."

But that was just precisely the virtue of which Carl was most deficient. He could ape the sportsman, providing no physical display of courage were wanted. He could even venture a trip in the airship, knowing now from excited reports from all quarters that she was the last word in such matters; and when the time came, and the moment were opportune, he told himself he had the nerve to place that curious box he had just procured in the most advantageous position, set its contents going, and then decamp. Oh, yes, he would decamp, quickly too, to be sure! Why not? That would merely be discretion.

"Supposing there was an accident?" he suddenly blurted out, his face fallen, his features as long as a fiddle. "Supposing the box were overturned! Besides, I've never been in an aeroplane. Hundreds of men have lost their lives when flying."

"A noble end for a sportsman, truly," grinned Adolf. "Let me go, then? A broken arm will not prevent my acting."

"No; I'll take train to Turin. I could be there as soon as this aeroplane," he said, almost tearfully. "Are you there? Why don't you stay at the telephone? Is Mr. Joe Gresson at the office?"

It was that young inventor himself who answered.

"Good morning!" he said curtly enough. "Glad you are coming. We leave in two hours' time."

"But—but I am detained," cried Carl desperately. "I cannot leave then. I will catch the midday continental express and go to Turin. I shall be there to-morrow evening."

"While we shall be beyond that city this afternoon," came the curt answer. "We must not delay longer, for though I calculate that the airship could circle the twenty-five thousand and odd miles which a trip round the world comprises in some seventeen to twenty days, yet there may be breakdowns——"

"Ah, yes, certainly! I hope not," said Carl swiftly.

"That's nice of you. But there may be, while we may desire to deviate a little. Indeed our trip will not take us along a straight line. We propose to take an oblique course, and therefore must make the most of every day that remains to us. Therefore we leave Hendon almost immediately."

"And pass Turin before the evening!" cried Carl aghast. Such rapid travel spelled catastrophy to him. "I—I—do you expect an accident?"

"An accident?"

"Yes; to your machine. Aeroplanes are notoriously dangerous. I—I—really think that I'll not——"

"Sorry, Mr. Reitberg," came Joe's curt answer. "But we must push ahead. If you wish to join us at all you must come now, and on the biplane."

The pompous city magnate put the telephone down with something approaching a groan. Indeed, his features were positively haggard, his fat cheeks hung flaccid, his mouth drooped, his eyes were bloodshot. He might, indeed, have been a condemned criminal. And then Adolf's sneering laughter stung him to some show of courage, or perhaps it was desperation.

"It is the only, the last chance," he said. "I'll go. I'll risk travel in this abominable machine. Herman!"

He tugged at the bell and shouted for his butler.

"Call the car round," he ordered magnificently. "Put my baggage on board, and—er—please be careful of this box. It's very valuable."

"In fact, there is glass inside, old curios," added Adolf, guffawing as the man shut the door behind him. "Curios for dear Andrew Provost. A present from London city to the great airship! A token of love and esteem from Carl Reitberg."

The ruffian was a humorous fellow at times, and his cynical mind often perceived a vein of fun where others saw nothing. His confederate's nervousness, the dilemma into which he had managed to introduce himself in his efforts to get aboard the airship provided Adolf with a vast amount of amusement, and he was sniggering still when his friend marched ponderously out of the establishment.

"*Bon voyage!*" called Adolf after him, as he stood on the steps of the gorgeous mansion, his undamaged arm tucked beneath his coat tails, a cigar of Carl's most expensive brand between his teeth, and a smile wrinkling his somewhat sardonic features. "*Bon voyage!*Have no fears. I'll look after things in your absence."

But oh that voyage! Oh the terror before starting! Carl Reitberg, sportsman, cut but a sorry figure as he shook Joe's honest hand and clambered into the cab of the biplane.

"But—but you'll never venture to rise above the ground in this?" he cried aghast. "It's not even made of steel or wood. It's transparent stuff, and looks frightfully fragile."

"Try it," grinned Dick, who was one of the party. "Ask Alec to jump on the wings, or—oh, I know, Mr. Reitberg, try a ride on one yourself! It'd be a ripping sensation to lie out there on one of the planes while she was soaring."

"Brat! Conceited young midshipman! Wants kicking!" Carl thought angrily. "But if they've come all the way from the neighbourhood of Adrianople, why, I suppose the machine is strong enough. Horrible it seems to me! But I must screw up my courage. Ah! He's started his engine. Why couldn't he wait a little longer till I'd settled down. Stay still there, young man. We're moving, and if you get too much to one side the thing will capsize once we're off the ground."

Alec regarded the trembling magnate with a pitying smile, though quite politely. "Oh, that's with ordinary aeroplanes, sir," he said loftily. "You can't upset this. You ask Joe. We'll try, just to impress you."

"Try to upset the machine when in the air! Madness!" Carl positively scowled at Alec, and then at Dick, catching him grinning. Then his attention was called elsewhere. Joe shut down his bypass valve abruptly. The propellers roared. The biplane shot forward and mounted into the air as if eager for a struggle. They were up a hundred yards before their passenger had had time to fasten his grip quite to his own liking on the edge of the cab. Then Joe banked her.

"Put me down!" roared Carl, scared out of his senses, for the machine had tilted, and from his own position he could look direct to the ground beneath. He felt the machine slipping bodily sideways.

"Got in an air hole," observed Joe calmly. "Skidding a trifle. But she can't go far. The cross sections between the planes hold her up nicely. Up we go again, turning all the time. Hold on for a moment."

It was truly a terrifying experience for Carl, and he never quite became accustomed to this new form of locomotion. Even when Joe, having elevated the machine to the height of ten thousand feet, set the automatic gear in motion, and, lighting a cigarette in the shelter of the cab, went to chat with the Major, the magnate felt far from happy.

"But—but," he quavered, "leave the steering gear! Who, then, controls this machine? What is to prevent us being dashed to pieces?"

"Atoms, rather," suggested Dick, always ready with something likely to improve the occasion.

"Eh?" asked Carl.

"You said pieces," grinned the midshipman. "We're ten thousand feet up. We wouldn't make jelly even if we fell. We'd be smashed to atoms."

"Horrible! Loathsome young fool!" thought Carl, groaning at the mere mention of such an ending. "Anything will be more pleasant than this. When will this awful trip be over?"

Flying steadily at over one hundred miles an hour it can be reckoned that the biplane soon swallowed up distance. In fact, late that afternoon she was over Italy, while an hour afterwards she swooped out over the Adriatic Sea, where she sighted the airship. Not that the latter was easily visible. But a practised eye could make her out.

"See—the airship," said the Major, pointing towards her for Carl's benefit.

"Ah! Yes. Then we sink to the water?"

"No—we swoop towards her and land on her deck."

"In midair! Is it—is it really safe?" asked this nervous passenger.

"As houses," interjected Dick. "Hold on, sir! Don't speak to Joe, or he might make an error and drop us over the edge."

It was a huge, if unkind, joke to watch the twitching face of the magnate, and, as is often enough the way of youth, Dick and Alec enjoyed Carl's discomfiture immensely. But they were near the ship now. Joe sent his biplane higher, till she was two thousand feet above the air vessel. Then he banked, banked till the machine looked as if she would turn turtle. But there was a master man at the controls, and at once the biplane dived downward, curling spirally, with her engine stopped, till she looked as if she would drop through the heart of the ship below her. Then the engine hummed, the propellers revolved, the biplane righted, dived swiftly, rose a yard or two, and then dropped without a quiver on the broad back waiting to receive her.

"Welcome!" said Mr. Andrew Provost, accosting the party, and helping Carl Reitberg to alight. "Welcome to the ship which by your own challenge you yourself helped to erect."

He led him to the lift, escorted him down to the gallery below, and showed him his cabin. In fact, Andrew did all that a host who is a gentleman could do for a guest. He didn't like Mr. Reitberg; he made no pretence of doing so. He was polite as a matter of course, and because it was good manners. But whatever he thought of this stout little magnate, indeed, whether he suspected the true depths of his sporting instincts, Andrew never imagined that he had just welcomed a crafty ruffian, a schemer, a mean-hearted man who, now that he was safely aboard, would leave no stone unturned till he had wrecked the vessel. As for Carl, he sat himself down by that precious box of his and mopped his forehead.

"I've put up with a heap," he said. "Now my time's coming."

CHAPTER XIII

To the North-west Frontier

It would be difficult to find anywhere an individual who settles down to new surroundings, to luxury, or to privation so quickly, so easily, and with so little discussion as does your British Tommy or Jack Tar. Given a piece of good cake tobacco, a jack knife, and a pipe, he will, so long as he has a few boon companions, soon have the air humming with his yarns or his songs. In fact, both of these estimable beings are right good fellows. Let us descend, therefore, to the men's quarters aboard the great airship. Lined with sleeping bunks on either side, with huge windows which made it possible to provide the best of ventilation, furnished with electric radiators for use in cold latitudes, or when flying at a great altitude, the part assigned to the men was a paradise compared with the quarters they might have expected. And on the evening after the return of Joe and his party with the stout and nervous magnate, Hurst and Hawkins and their cronies were gathered together, smoking like chimneys and chattering like a cageful of monkeys. As might well be expected also, their superiors in the saloon came in for some discussion.

"I was a talkin' of 'im," reiterated Hawkins, licking his lips, for he had removed his pipe for that particular reason; "of Mr. Alec Jardine; and I says as 'e's the boy fer a sailor. 'E's like Dicky, so 'e is, and Dicky's the properest sailor as ever I set eyes on."

"To which I agrees," exclaimed Private Larkin, Jim Larkin as he was known, no less a person than Major Harvey's soldier servant. "'E's a sailor, 'e is. And p'raps 'ed make a soldier too, fer all I knows. But this here Alec, why, he's got the cut of a soldier, 'e 'as. Don't you deny it."

He was almost ferocious as he addressed himself to Hawkins, and we must admit that one unaccustomed to those in the men's quarters might have even been alarmed. For Private Larkin was not blessed with the most attractive of countenances. To begin with, his head was remarkably big, too big for his body, and most of the head seemed to be composed of a pair of fat, bulging cheeks, above which were a couple of equally bulging eyes which had a most disagreeable habit of fixing upon people, staring them out of countenance, and then of squinting. They were at it now. Hawkins blew fiercely into his pipe.

"Stow that 'ere squintin', shipmate," he growled. "A man ain't never sure what you're lookin' at. Fust it's 'is face. Then it's 'is boots, then it's—it's what not. Now, you nor I ain't likely to agree on that 'ere youngster. You says he'd make a soldier. I says as 'es fair cut out fer a sailor. Let's leave it at that in case we gets to quarrelling. Let's jaw about this here fat little feller, him as the papers called a sportsman."

"Sportsman!" chimed in Hurst in his most scornful tones. "I like that. Sportsmen don't funk when it's a question of flying."

"Then you ain't one," came Hawkins's laughing answer. "Nor you nor me was so precious merry when we were hoisted aboard this here ship; and I stakes my davy neither of us are so eager to go aboard that aeroplane. It ain't every sportsman that has the nerve to fly, so jest you mark it. And every sportsman ain't like this here Mr. Reitberg, him as has an accent jammed up with his words every time he opens his mouth."

"But 'Sportsman''s what the papers called him," said Larkin, scenting here another theme for fierce argument For this merry soldier loved to bandy words, to discuss matters threadbare, while the very meeting with a member of the allied service was sufficient to make him disputatious. If Hawkins said that the visitor who had recently arrived on board was a sportsman, Larkin declared with decision that he was no such thing. His little red, pointed moustache seemed to erect itself towards his eyes, while the latter turned upon Hawkins and Hurst in succession, and then upon the other tars a stare which was positively threatening. "Sportsman! Ho, yes! That's what they called 'im. And what does Sergeant Evans say? What's 'e say, I ask?"

There was no response, for the simple reason that none knew. The worthy Sergeant was, indeed, given to keeping his own counsels. None the less Larkin professed to be aware of his opinions.

"Of course, none of you knows," he told them triumphantly. "You wouldn't, for the Sergeant's always kind of suspicious of seafaring folks. Not that I agrees with him there," he added, by way of apology, while Hawkins and Hurst bridled and drew heavily on their pipes. "But it's his way. He keeps quiet when the Navy's round about. Still I know, and I'll tell you. 'E says 'watch 'im'. That's what Sergeant Evans says."

"Ah! Watch 'im?" repeated Hurst thoughtfully. "And why?"

"'Cos 'e's a sportsman. 'Cos it's this here Mr. Reitberg that challenged Mr. Provost to build the airship and sail her round the world; and—what's a sight more than all—'cos he's been and gone and put one hundred thousand pounds—one hundred thousand golden, shining sovereigns—under lock and key, and given the key into someone else's keeping against the day when the ship's cruised round the world and safely returned to England. It was that that caused the papers to describe this here Mr. Reitberg as a sportsman. And it's that very thing that's going to prove as he ain't nothing of the sort. 'Im a sportsman!—with an accent you could cut with a knife, clipping the king's English! 'Watch 'im,' says Sergeant Evans, and that's what I'm doing."

Thereat Jim Larkin stared pugnaciously at his companions, each in turn coming in for a broadside from those prominent, squinting eyes of his, while every feature of his face seemed to be working so as to let the company in general know that Jim had a grievance. Then his pipe went to his mouth, a pair of thick lips opened, tilting his fierce red moustache, while the stem was thrust between an uneven row of exceedingly black teeth. It was only when he had contrived to make the pipe draw, and had puffed out a billow of smoke, that Jim's features relaxed. He actually smiled at Hawkins. "And don't you go and get nervous like," he told the tar, in a protecting tone of voice, "'cos there's me aboard, and the Sergeant, to say nothing of that there Alec Jardine, what's fit ter be a soldier. Mind, I ain't sayin' as 'e ain't cut out fer a sailor too. But if a youngster's that, it don't always say as he'd do for a soldier. No. Don't you think it, and as regards that sportsman, don't you and your mate get nervous. As I've said jest now, there's——"

"Stow it," growled Hurst, roused to anger by such patronage. "Why, if I couldn't with this one hand manage that Mr. Reitberg, why——"

He stopped abruptly, his vocabulary being insufficient to express his meaning, while Hawkins, Pierson, Peters, and the others nodded their approval. Nor did they resent less than he the uppishness of Private Larkin. There were covert threats to "show him what". Big, brawny hands doubled up into formidable fists, while the eyes of the tars sought those of the soldier, returning his previous broadsides in a manner there was no denying. Then a broad smile disarmed them. It was only Jim's fun. The crafty fellow had been merely joking.

"Lor!" he grinned. "It do make a chap smile to pull the legs of you sailors, and it's a treat to meet some of ye and get chatting. But you jest remember what I've said. There's a sportsman aboard. You watch 'im."

As far as they were able the crew of the airship did indeed keep a very watchful eye upon the portly frame of Mr. Carl Reitberg. He never left his cabin to pace the deck but some bare-footed sailor followed, or met him by accident as it were, or made pretence to be on watch, and paced the deck within easy distance. Down below, too, there was the Sergeant. As we have narrated, he claimed an old acquaintance with the magnate, though he was careful to keep that fact to himself, merely repeating his warning to his employers. He even went so far as to inspect Carl Reitberg's baggage, a task of no great difficulty since he acted as valet as well as mess sergeant.

"Any particular wishes, sir?" he asked politely, soon after Carl's arrival on board. "If you will kindly hand me your keys I will unpack and stow your things in the wardrobe."

The lordly magnate handed them over instantly, with a curt nod of approval. He was even pleased to hand the Sergeant a golden coin on his return to the cabin. For his trunk was unpacked and removed to the baggage apartment, while his clothes were laid out in the drawers of the wardrobe.

"Keys, sir," said the Sergeant, handing them to him. "What about this box, sir," and he pointed to the one which had accompanied Carl, and of which he had been so careful. "Shall I take it to the baggage room?"

"Certainly not! Er—no, thank you," exclaimed the magnate promptly, and with some acerbity. "Er—leave it there. It's full of—er—valuables, things I wish to show to Mr. Provost. I had it sealed, and would have brought the things in a safe but for the fact that it would have been so heavy, too heavy for this vessel."

"She'll carry tons and tons, sir," came the respectful answer. "A dozen safes wouldn't make any difference. So I'm to leave the box, sir?"

"Decidedly! Ah! I see that the seals are unbroken. That's satisfactory."

It may have been satisfactory to Mr. Reitberg, but it was anything but that to Sergeant Evans.

"Don't I know his foxy ways, too," he told himself, when ensconced in the privacy of his pantry diligently cleaning silver. "I haven't served with the military police in South Africa without learning something, and there's things I remember. For instance, this Carl Reitberg was someone else out there, and not half so fine and mighty. I.D.B. they called him, which means illicit diamond buyer. And there were other things he was suspected to be, things that people forget when they see him dressed so fine and know that he's as wealthy as they make 'em. I know—foxy! That's him—I'm watching!"

So here was another following the very same plan adopted by the men forward, while, had he but known it, even the redoubtable Dick with his chum Alec had embarked on the same service.

"Of course, Andrew and the others don't believe he's here for anything but a tour," said the former very abruptly, within two days of Carl's arrival. "Perhaps he is, perhaps he isn't. I'm not going to trust to luck, eh, Alec?"

"Certainly not; he's a fishy beggar. We'll take it in turns to dog him."

128

It followed, therefore, that Mr. Carl Reitberg was a very astonished individual. He had already noticed the close proximity of sailors whenever he trudged the upper deck, a promenade of which he soon became exceedingly fond, for a magnificent view of the country over which the ship was steering could always be obtained. But that proximity he put down to the fact that the men had their orders, and that this being a ship it was only proper that watches should be kept.

"Makes one feel secure and safe when high up," he told himself. "'Pon my word this flying through space is magnificent. I never dreamed I could do more than endure it. As for the aeroplane it is an abominable invention. Never again do I set foot in the machine. Ah, Mr. Dick, I think! Midshipman, I hear. Always up to mischief."

It was part of the magnate's scheme to make himself agreeable to all and sundry, and now, as Mr. Midshipman Dick joined him, he greeted that promising young officer with effusion.

"Sea dog, eh?" he quizzed. "Budding Nelson."

"Budding Nelson be blowed!" was Dick's disrespectful answer, only it was *sotto voce*. "Sea dog! Listen to the fellow. Makes a chap feel ill. Morning, Mr. Reitberg!" he said aloud. "Having a constitutional?"

"Regular custom," the fat little gentleman told him. "Travelled a lot, don't you know, and have learned how to keep healthy. Come, tell me all about the vessel."

Yes, it tickled the vanity of the magnate immensely to find himself so popular. The guineas which he had distributed amongst the crew caused him to be saluted constantly, a fact on which he preened himself. And now even the youngsters had taken a fancy to him. If Dick were not at his elbow, Alec was there, listening respectfully to his words, pointing out details, laughing uproariously at his stories. But Carl Reitberg did not know that one and all were watching. He never suspected *that*, never suspected that there were those on board by whom he himself was suspected.

"Fine," he told himself in the privacy of his cabin. "Fine—couldn't be better. I'm getting bosom pal all round. Wait till I open that box and show the contents to 'em."

He went across to it and inspected the seals. Yes, they were intact, a huge blob of wax at both ends indented deeply with the vulgar seal which hung upon his own massive frame, from a chain capable almost of holding the airship.

Meanwhile the great airship ploughed her easy path through the limitless leagues of the atmosphere, hardly even trembling as her powerful screw pushed her forward, never wavering in her course, save when the master hand of her inventor or the hand of the watchful steersman willed that she should swerve to one side or the other. There were times, too, when Dick or Alec would take post in the engine-room, and there stand at the levers which controlled the movements of this giant vessel. Never once did the gallant midshipman lose his admiration for this work of art, this massive ship, so huge, so stable, and so strong, and yet so extremely frail in appearance. Never did he cease to wonder at that magnificent vista of almost transparent girders and beams and rods ranging overhead, whenever he cared to crane his neck and stare upward. Nor yet had he ceased to grin and find abundant amusement in the figures of his fellow passengers.

"It's like a peepshow all the time," he told Alec one day with an expansive grin. "One looks upward, as if through a window, and there are the people we know, walking overhead, strutting backwards and forwards for all the world as if they were flies. And one gets to know 'em by the size of their boots, and—er—by other signs. For instance——"

"There's Mr. Andrew," said Alec.

"Sure enough—number one size boots, dapper, very."

"Military walk, smart and alert. White moustache to be seen also, but coloured yellow by the celludine through which one sees him. Then there's the Major."

"All there; walks quickly backwards and forwards. You can tell he's a soldier."

"Then there's Hawkins and Hurst and the rest of the men rolling as is the custom with tars. Say, Dicky, why do sailors roll? Is it side only?"

That brought a flush of wrath to the cheeks of the indignant Dicky.

"Side!" he gasped. "Side! You ever saw a sailor suffering from swelled head? Look here, my son, I'll punch yours if you ain't more careful."

But it was all fun. They grimaced at one another and then grinned widely as another figure appeared in the peculiar perspective of men tramping overhead. It was the magnate, the high and mighty Mr. Reitberg, the sportsman who pronounced his words with a very peculiar accent, and who was fond of describing himself as English to the backbone.

"Tell him a mile off," sniffed Dick. "Big, flat feet, rest all corporation. Can't get a glimpse of his ugly phiz for the size of his tummy."

What a joy it was to these two bosom friends to send the ship bounding forward! To stir up the motor gently purring beside them, to rouse it as it were to a gentle fury, for that was one of the points of Joe's handiwork and genius. This paraffin-fired motor of his ran as smoothly as any turbine. You might accelerate it as much as you could, and still it purred, though at its highest speeds the purr had become angry and assertive. Yes, it was a joy to shut close, to bang and bar as it were, the throttle and set the hydraulic pumps into full action. And how the ship responded. She leaped forward, and there had been times when the speedometer mounted in the engine-room told that the vessel was thrusting herself through the air at the incredible speed of two hundred miles an hour. Impossible! we hear some sceptical reader exclaim. Why? But five years ago aeroplanes were spoken of derisively, while their speed seldom exceeded forty miles an hour. To-day they can shoot through the air at a hundred, and the day is fast approaching, thanks to Joe Gresson and others of his kidney, when that speed will be as nothing. Why, then, should this great airship not be able to attain to even double the greatest known speed of an aeroplane? Why, indeed? Her design was all in her favour. There was hardly a projection about her to cause wind friction and delay her passage, while the smooth celludine with which she was coated slid through the atmosphere with an ease that had never been approached before. Add to these points, which all make for speed, engines of the highest efficiency, a transmission of the latest design and purely hydraulic. As carried out on the airship this means of conveying power from the engines to the propeller guaranteed but the merest fractional loss. In fact, what loss there was was negligible. And the propeller itself was one for which aviators would willingly have given a small fortune. But enough of such explanations. We live in a world of marvellous and incredible invention. The armchair sceptic and unbeliever of to-day has his views and scepticism shattered almost before he was finished speaking. The marvels of the Zeppelin, acknowledged to be the last word in airship construction, were now overshadowed and belittled by the wonders of Joe Gresson's invention. The world was raving about the ship. Scientists and inventors in every country were longing to be made familiar with its intricacies. Steering over the placid surface of the Mediterranean Joe Gresson and his friends hovered over the port of Alexandria, and thence sailed for Cairo. Shrill cries greeted her from the sandy desert about the ancient pyramids, while a motley crowd waved to her from their summits. But there was no time to halt. With one long look at the placid, cruel, yet gentle face of the sphinx the ship's head was swung towards the east. An hour later a long ribbon of blue, shimmering in the sun, and hedged on either side by an unbroken expanse of yellow, told of the great Suez Canal.

"We'll follow it through its length," said Joe, now at the helm. "See! We are seven thousand feet up, and one can perceive a huge portion of the canal, severed here and there by the bitter lakes through which it runs. Ah! There's a ship. Let's drop down close to her."

The vessel plunged. One who was ignorant of her powers would have imagined that she was about to crash to the ground. But she was merely descending at her fastest pace, and plunging brought her within hailing distance of the ship then passing through the canal, even before Mr. Reitberg had quite recovered his nerve or his equilibrium.

"*Himmel!*" he shrieked, as the vessel headed downward and shot toward the sand. "Hold her! She is falling! We shall all be killed."

He formed the mad resolution of rushing to the engine-room, and stepped in that direction. But, as we have said, the inclination of the decks considerably upset his equilibrium. The magnate indeed took a header, slithered along the smooth platform beneath the gas chambers, and landed up against one of the partitions with a bang which shook his eyeglass from its holding. By then the vessel was within a hundred feet of the canal, sailing along directly over it, and just ahead of the ship ploughing her way through the water.

What cheers there were! How the passengers on that eastward-bound vessel crowded the decks and shouted! And then the liner hoisted her Union Jack, and dipped it formally. At once the watchful Hawkins responded from the deck above, while again cheers came to the ears of Dick and his friends.

"And just contrast the two ships," said Alec, when they had progressed in this fashion for perhaps an hour. "Look! You can see the airship's reflection in the water, and, my! ain't she a whopper!"

Yes, she was huge, vast, incredibly enormous. And yet how smoothly she sailed along, and with what little effort! It was a fascinating picture to behold. Dick found himself following the giant outline, picking out the various points till then invisible from the deck above, or from the platforms below. For instance, four huge attachments puzzled him immensely, for they hung from the framework and seemed without purpose.

"All the same they're meant for business," Joe told him, with that quiet, half-cynical smile for which he was notorious. "Oh yes, Dicky, we don't have useless attachments on this ship, unless—ahem! it's amongst the crew. I ain't, of course, referring to midshipmen."

But he was. He was teasing the gallant Mr. Midshipman Hamshaw, and had he been Alec there would have been a rumpus.

"Seriously, though," he went on when he had had his laugh, "they're for landing. You see, it don't do to bump a ship of this description. We want to reach terra firma gently. Now, if you were to jump from a height you'd land on your toes if possible, come down on to your heels, and then bend your knees, all by stages as it were, quickly enough you understand, but offering such graduated resistance that there would be no shock at all. That's what happens with those attachments. Each one is thirty feet in length, and hinged inside the frame of the airship at its upper and forward end. Now, watch us. We'll bump to the ground. How's that?"

It really was remarkable, and so thought the people on board the liner. For Joe's practised hand arrested the engines. The ship came to a standstill. Then she fell as if she were a dead weight, was arrested within twenty feet of the ground merely by touching a single lever, and then descended sharply. But there was no shock. Those four antennæ hinged upward beneath the weight, gradually met it, and then held her firmly suspended. Even the glassware on the saloon table was not shaken.

"And now for a trip on terra firma if only to stretch our legs," cried Joe. "We'll take it by turns, half at a time."

It was singular how everyone fell in with the views of the young inventor; and, in fact, it was to be observed aboard the airship that though there was no recognized captain, no officers, and no regular crew, yet the work aboard progressed with a smoothness which was remarkable. There were rules, naturally enough, and all aboard had been assigned duties. But the simplicity of the whole contrivance, and above all, the efficiency of the engines, called for the smallest attention.

"Merely see that the lubricators are working, and that the fuel feed is right, and things go along merrily," said Andrew, who was becoming quite an engineer.

This opportunity of a trip ashore was seized upon by all in turn, and long walks over the sandhills were indulged in. Then the airship picked up passengers and crew once more, and rising from the sand steered a course east and north, swooping over the deserts of Arabia. All the following night she sped on without a halt, and when the lively Dick again trod the deck he looked down upon the Arabian Sea. But it was merely a corner of that vast ocean, for within a few hours the vessel was sweeping over Persia.

"A sparsely inhabited country, and therefore one where we may venture to halt for a while without fear of interruption," said Joe. "Our water supply is running short, and if we are to continue our regular baths every morning we must fill our tanks again."

Whoever heard of an airship carrying baths and water tanks of big capacity? But this one did, and bore the weight as if it were nothing. And the completeness of her equipment was again demonstrated, for, having sighted a huge lake in the heart of Persia, and made sure that there was not a town or a village in sight, Joe dropped the ship directly on the water, setting her elevators to work so gently that they held the giant framework but six feet above the surface.

"Now we drop our pumps, set the motors going, and in a jiffy fill the tanks," he said. "Watch the whole performance."

But there was little to see, though Dick and Alec, ever the most curious of those aboard, strained their necks to watch all that was passing. Two snake-like, flexible metal pipes were passed from the engine-room through apertures specially constructed for the purpose. Then the motor hummed a little louder, while one of the pump attachments was set going; the gurgle of water splashing into the tanks was the only indication that the operation was being performed with success. An hour, indeed, sufficed to replenish their supplies, when the ship shot upward once more till some six thousand feet of pure, sun-lit air lay beneath her.

"And now for the north-west frontier of India, where our soldiers are ever on the watch," said Joe. "Come, Major, you feel no nervousness? You have no fears, I hope, lest our gas should run short and land us in the arms of some of those gentry who look upon an Englishman as a dog, to be slaughtered on any and every occasion?"

"You may take me where you will, in chains if you wish," was the smiling response. "After the things that I have seen I have the utmost confidence in both the leader of this expedition and on the ship his hands have constructed. There! I cannot say more."

It may be stated that only one person aboard the airship had a doubt as to her capacity and his own security, and, as may be guessed, that individual was Carl Reitberg. But then he was always nervous for his own skin.

"The north-west!" he gasped, when Joe told him of their immediate destination. "But—but that's where there are always little wars and skirmishes."

"Precisely," observed the Major, with cutting abruptness. "Our best soldiers are bred there. I've had a dose of the north-west myself. Keeps you alive, sir. And if you aren't lively, why——"

"Ahem!" lisped Dick. "You're dead, dead as a herring."

"And you go there?" stuttered the magnate, his face paling, his fat cheeks trembling.

"Certainly!" declared Joe.

"But supposing something happened, supposing——"

"It won't, I hope," came the answer.

"But it might," chimed in Dick, grinning. "Then there'd be a ruction. Say, Mr. Andrew, ain't they fond of torturing folks first?"

It was too bad to tease the wretched and craven Mr. Reitberg. But there was no suppressing Dicky or his boon companion Alec. While in their secret heart of hearts the Major and perhaps Joe and Mr. Andrew were not altogether sorry. Nor did they say much to comfort the unhappy magnate. Indeed, that stout and crafty gentleman was thrown into a violent flutter two days later. For the wireless apparatus aboard suddenly picked up a message.

"Someone calling, sir," reported the operator. "Calling with an apparatus of low power. I can't quite tap the message, though it has been getting stronger."

"Then we're moving towards it; we'll send her ahead. Wonder what it is?" said Joe. "There are few wireless instruments in this part of the world, and those there are belong to the British forces. Report again when you can read the message."

At once the ship was sent ahead at her fastest pace, while the wireless operator returned to his instruments. Nor was it long when he appeared with a report.

"A force of Gurkha soldiers held up in the hills, sir," he told Joe. "Calling for help, but not yet in touch with the instruments of their main party. Urgently require relief. Ammunition almost run out. I told them to expect us."

"Certainly!" cried Joe. "We'll do our utmost to relieve them. Major, kindly see that arms are served to the men. Sergeant Evans has the keys of the magazines."

"But—you will never venture to attack whoever is hemming in these British soldiers," cried Mr. Reitberg, aghast.

"Then you'd let 'em be shot down, eh?" asked Andrew angrily.

"Er—well, how can we help it? It is their own business. Why should we rush into danger?"

The magnate was positively shaking. He could scarcely stand, so violently were his knees knocking. As for Joe, he turned on his heel and went straightway to the engine-room, while the Major hurried off to issue weapons to the men. Andrew regarded his guest grimly, and with difficulty smothered his rising anger.

"Sir," he said with dignity, "those men are British soldiers. This ship is British also. If there is a call for help we take it, whatever the risk. Remember that you yourself owe to our country a debt which a service such as this is will only partially help you to repay. There, sir, if you are nervous retire to your cabin."

But Mr. Reitberg's anxiety would not allow him to do that. He paced the broad deck of the ship a prey to terrible forebodings. Then, driven from the open by the fierce rush of air there, he slid off to his cabin.

"Shall I, now?" he asked himself, as he handled that box with its seals still adhering. "Shall I set the clockwork going and so put a stop to the course these fools are taking? Ah! No! That would not do here. But later. Yes, later I will punish them for incurring this danger."

Love for his own security forbade his taking the rash step he had for the moment contemplated, for the consequences, he reflected, would be disastrous to himself as well as to his fellows. But later; yes, he would open that box; that is, if he were still living. For the ship was plunging furiously onward, and every few minutes the wireless operator telephoned his news of an impending British disaster. There were a thousand dusky natives hemming in but fifty Gurkha soldiers and one British officer. Their ammunition was almost spent. The enemy were within charging distance of them.

"Tell 'em we're coming fast," was Joe's curt answer. "And, Major, just make all ready for action."

CHAPTER XIV

A Brush with Pathans

"There! At last! Listen!"

The Major held up a hand for silence while he hung out of the window of the gallery running beneath the huge framework of the airship.

"Look! You can see the flashes from the guns of the Pathans," he called. "A circle of them, getting very close too. What's the latest message?"

"Officer hit, sir," reported the wireless operator. "Several men hurt since we were first called up. Ammunition gone completely. They expect to be rushed at any instant, and in any case once night has completely fallen."

"In fact a dangerous if not desperate situation," said Andrew, his voice anxious. "Now, what do we do? I am prepared to make any sacrifice that may be necessary. But wait; could we not direct our searchlights on the enemy and so scare them away? They are sure to be ignorant savages, and a beam from above might very well throw them into a panic."

But Major Harvey shook his head decidedly, though one could not see the movement, for all lights aboard the ship had been switched off. Outside there was darkness, getting more intense every minute, while, as the Major had informed them, one could detect flashes spurting from a hundred points in a circle, while the rattle of musketry came faintly to the ear. The position of the dusky enemy was, in fact, clearly outlined by those flashes, and looking downward Dick could imagine the position of the gallant little band of Gurkhas stationed somewhere in the centre awaiting the rush of the enemy.

"With bayonets ready fixed," he told himself. "But it'd be short work in the darkness. Those Pathans would creep in—are creeping in even now—and outnumber our fellows by twenty to one. Yes, this is a tough little business."

It was obvious that the Major viewed it in a similar light, while he was emphatic in his reply to Andrew.

"Might scare 'em a trifle at first with your lights," he told him shortly. "But, bless you, these Pathans aren't so uneducated as you imagine. They've lived so long within call of the British that they keep in touch with big movements. The many friends they send down into the plains to loot rifles return with tales of what they've seen, with news of what they've heard in the bazaars and hovels they've frequented. So they've seen motor cars for a certainty, and possibly a solitary aeroplane. In any case they know the sahib can rise into the air and stay there. That's why their astonishment won't easily be turned to alarm. But if there were daylight the size of this ship alone might send 'em skeedadling. No, Mr. Andrew, we've got to do something active."

"At your service. In what way, Major? Mention it and you will have our support."

"Then ammunition's wanted; so's an officer."

"And you suggest——?"

"With your approval I propose to descend to our troops, taking ammunition with me. You have service rifles aboard and have an abundant store of cartridges. Then lower a few cases as rapidly as you are able."

Andrew was not the one at such a time to stand chattering, while had he been one of undecided mind Joe would have given an order promptly. Fortunately both uncle and nephew were alike in that respect, and at once assented to the Major's proposal. A low call, indeed, brought Hawkins and Hurst and a few of the others hurrying forward, with Sergeant Evans and Private Larkin in close attendance.

"I've roused half a dozen cases of ammunition already, sir," reported the Sergeant. "They're being carried at this moment toward the lift."

"Good!" cried the Major. "Then there need be no delay. Now, Mr. Andrew, if your nephew will kindly locate our friends below, so that I may be dropped directly toward them, we will soon bring a change to this situation. And once I have landed, a searchlight turned upon the enemy will be of great advantage. I need not ask you to be cautious not to turn the beams on the little party I hope to have the honour of commanding within a few minutes."

Brisk and abrupt as became a soldier about to undertake a hazardous expedition, the Major at once stepped toward the lift. Joe himself made for the engine room, and within a minute a dazzling beam was flooding the landscape below, not the ordinary beam that one would have expected, but a cunning circle of rays controlled by a lamp of Joe's own invention. In fact he had merely taken the precaution to place a black disk in the centre of the enormous reflector of the lamp, so that the central beams were almost entirely occluded. Staring down from the airship, her crew and passengers found that they were above a mountainous district. Huge rocks and pinnacles cropped up from a plateau which was barren and strewn with boulders, while the general trend of the ground was steeply downward, from the point immediately beneath the vessel. It was there, gathered in a circle surrounded by rocks, that the feeble central rays, the few which had managed to escape the obliterating disk, fell upon some sprawling figures.

"The Gurkhas," cried Dick. "Look at 'em waving. And see the enemy!"

The latter were easily visible, and it made Dick catch his breath when he observed that some were within two hundred yards perhaps of that little central group. Creeping forms were half hidden behind rocks. Others were worming a way across open ground, while, as the beams played upon them, not a few of the dusky enemy stood upright and waved their arms and shouted. Indeed, some turned tail and ran. Then loud commands recalled them, while one figure erected itself, a figure swathed in flowing garments, arms were tossed overhead, and those in the airship could hear a stentorian voice haranguing the men.

"Listen!" cried the Major. "Ah! 'My brethren,' he calls to them, 'my brethren, be not fearful of the white light which shines from the sky. It is not magic. It is merely the lamp from the balloon of the infidel. What harm may a lamp do then to the faithful? How can it come between us and these Gurkha dogs whom we have been seeking this many a day? Then cease to take note of it. Fear not, but push forward, for their ammunition is exhausted. Now, I myself will lead the rush.'

"What's our height?" asked the Major abruptly.

"A thousand feet," suggested Dick.

"No, six hundred," Joe corrected him from the entrance to the engine-room.

"Then lower me to our fellows, then ascend out of range of shot. Many of those Pathans are armed with modern rifles and could riddle the ship. Now, sir, I am ready."

"So am I," cried Dick, taking his place on the platform of the lift, where the ammunition cases had already been placed.

"And I also," chimed in Alec, joining him.

"But——" began Andrew.

"Let 'em come," said the Major. "It'll be a fine experience for them. But you know the risks, lads."

Dick grinned. He had a way of doing that when excited. Alec merely slung his rifle across his shoulders and gripped the supporting cable.

"Lower away then," cried Andrew. "Now!"

The motor hummed that cheerful refrain to which all had now become accustomed. The platform sank from the gallery gently at first, and then fell rapidly. And as it went, the rays of the lamp were shut off completely. But a few moments later, when the telephone bell sounded and the Major's voice was heard, the beams again swamped the underlying landscape, showing the lift but a few feet above the group of Gurkhas. "Lower," they heard from the Major.

"Grounded, and as gently as possible," said Joe. "Ah! They've taken the cases off. Now, up she comes. Send the ship upward; and, Hawkins."

"Sir," that worthy responded, saluting in nautical fashion.

"Put the men at the windows of the gallery and let 'em fire down upon the enemy. Sergeant Evans, you'll see that there's ammunition."

There was at once brisk movement aboard the ship, while down below the patter of rifle shots had already come from the central group of soldiers. Indeed, those ammunition cases were already opened, and within a minute of the Major's arrival the Gurkhas had all received a supply of cartridges.

"I'll post myself in the centre," the Major told Dick and Alec swiftly. "You, Dick, take command of the men on the upper face. That's the point from which the rush is likely to come, for that's where their chief is stationed. Alec, take the lower slope, and look out for crawling rascals. Ah! They've opened from the ship, and some of the Pathans are replying."

Bullets indeed were hissing upward, and twice Joe flinched as a missile hit the celludine sides of his pet airship.

"It'll—it'll bring us down, won't it?" gasped Andrew, though he showed no signs of terror.

"Not it," came the reassuring answer. "We shall lose a little gas perhaps, for those bullets make but the smallest opening. It would require a shell to do great damage. Even then, don't forget that there are quite a number of compartments. Wish to goodness I had brought bombs aboard the ship. A few dropped on the heads of the enemy would send 'em scuttling."

The need for such inventions was beneath the ship without a doubt, for the circling beam of light showed that the Marconi operator had made no error when he reported that there were a thousand Pathans hemming in the Gurkha soldiers. Indeed, every little rock seemed to shelter a recumbent figure, while rifles could be seen protruding from a hundred crevices. Moreover, the arrival of the ship had stirred the enemy to greater exertions, while the fact that ammunition had now reached the defenders of the central position roused them to fury. The loud crackle of musketry from the ship also helped not a little to force the Pathans to complete their task at once or slink away into the darkness.

"Massing up above me, sir," Dick reported coolly, when the Major crept across to the post he had taken some few minutes later. "I've seen that chief of theirs twice and tried to pot him. But he's artful. He and his men are closer. They'd have been here by now but for the light which shows their positions. The Gurkhas ain't wasting many shots either."

In the half-light playing over the defenders it was possible to see the short, sturdy forms of the native soldiers, those hillmen who have fought so often side by side with their white comrades. They lay in a circle, each man behind cover, with magazines crammed in preparation for the moment when the enemy would charge. Slowly and deliberately they were shooting cartridges from their pouches into the breeches of their weapons, and every half-second there was a sharp report, and often enough an answering shriek from the enemy.

Ah! Suddenly that tall figure clad in flowing raiment stood erect, while the chief waved a rifle over his head. Instantly a dozen weapons held by the Gurkhas covered him, and Dick himself swung his own rifle to his shoulder. But the figure dropped out of sight promptly, only to appear a minute later some fifteen feet to the right. It was a broad-bladed tulwar which the beams from above them showed him to be waving. A loud shout escaped him, and instantly, as if it were a signal, as undoubtedly it was, the Pathans became silent. Not one drew trigger. Then the clear, ringing voice of the chief was heard once more.

"Telling 'em to make ready," said the Major crisply. "Listen! This is what he says. I know their lingo and so can translate. 'Brethren, the hour has come to end this little matter. If we delay, then the infidel will prove too strong for us. Drop, then, your rifles and firearms. Take to your knives, and when I shout once more rush in upon the accursed infidel.'"

"Got him!" declared Dick a second later. "Hate shooting a fellow in the open, but then, it's he or us. Eh, sir?"

"Quite right! A good shot and a plucky one," cried the Major. "You risked getting a bullet from the enemy. That shot of yours will quieten them for a few moments. But it won't stop the rush. Every man in a tribe such as this is capable of leading his fellows. Yes; watch closely, and you, men," he went on, turning to the Gurkhas, and speaking in their own language, "obey the officer here. The enemy will rush at any moment. As they come, pour volleys into them, then stand shoulder to shoulder and give them the bayonet."

A hoarse cheer came from the sturdy Gurkhas, a cheer answered by Hawkins and Hurst and his fellows overhead.

"There's me and Larkin and few more of the boys as would give summat to be down there a waitin' for them 'eathen," said the former, growling the words into Joe's ear. "Me and some of my mates 'd give a heap to be alongside of them 'ere Gurkha fellers, a standin' with bayonets fixed. Lor, sir, see them Pathan villains! If they ain't all crawling and crawling towards one corner."

From the gallery of the airship it was possible to see everything, and with a twinge of apprehension Joe discerned perhaps five hundred figures now. They were leaving hollows and cover from all directions, and were creeping and worming their way towards one quarter, the point from which their chief had called to them.

"Very serious," he told himself. "They're massing for a charge. I'll drop the ship closer and chance more of their bullets, though for the last few minutes they have left us alone. Ah! Sergeant Evans, what do you advise?"

"Send the ship a trifle closer, sir," came the prompt answer. "Get directly over those varmint. Then—then leave 'em to me. I've prepared something for 'em, something that'll blow a few of 'em back into their own passes."

"A bomb?" asked Joe, dumbfounded, for as he had said, he had brought nothing of the sort aboard with him. Indeed, firearms and weapons of offence generally were not of great interest to him. His was the subtle mind which gripped larger affairs, affairs such as this airship, and her simple yet extremely efficient equipment. But if he were ignorant of weapons, cartridges, and bombs, Sergeant Evans had at least some acquaintance with such matters.

"Thought we'd likely enough want something of the sort, sir," he said. "So I've got 'em ready. Move the ship directly over 'em, sir. Quick, too, or they'll be starting to rush, and then nothing will hold them. There! See them Gurkhas! The Major's drawing them all close together, so it's clear that he's seen what's passing."

The unusual opportunities that the light playing upon the surroundings of the Gurkhas gave offered opportunities to the gallant Major which otherwise would have been missing. Indeed, the paucity of numbers of the little British force was in a measure compensated for by the darkness which hung over them, and by the brilliant light surrounding their enemy. Had there been no cover there, save in the centre, no doubt that spreading light would have enabled the Major quickly to send the Pathans scuttling. But the ground was strewn with rocks, rocks which offered first-class cover, and even gave protection against bullets fired from the airship. Not that Hawkins and his comrades missed their chances. Many a crawling enemy did they locate, and many a Pathan did they cause to bite the dust. But they could not stop that concentrating movement no more than could the Gurkhas; and presently, peeping from behind the rock which sheltered him, Dick made out a mass of human beings to his front, every rock and crevice seeming to hold a figure.

Suddenly a man stood to his full height, careless of the weapons wielded by the Gurkhas. Two arms waved frantically above his head, while there was the gleam of steel flashing in the rays of the electric light pouring down upon them. "The hour is here; Allah bids us advance. To those who fall, there is happiness and glory in the long future. Charge!"

He was a brave man, and at any other time Dick would willingly have seen him spared. But he was a leader, and, as such, of danger to this little party. It was, therefore, with a sigh of relief that he saw the man's figure suddenly straighten. The chief leaned backward, his arms widespread, his tulwar dangling from one wrist Then, with a shriek, he leaped forward, crumpled up in midair, and fell heavily upon a boulder.

"But another will take his place," whispered the Major. "Dick, this is even hotter than I had anticipated. I was rash to let you and Alec come. For me, it is merely a matter of duty, for an officer was wanted badly. For you, it is a different matter, and if anything happens——"

"It'll be duty for me too, sir," answered the midshipman coolly. "I'm an officer too, sir, don't forget that. Besides, we ain't dead yet. A long way from it."

That was Mr. Dicky Hamshaw all over. His cheerful optimism was catching. It was just the thing for which his tars adored him.

"If that ain't Mr. Dicky there a-standin' out in the open!" shouted Hurst at that very moment, catching sight of the familiar figure of the young sailor as the lamp above swayed and swept a few scattered beams over the Gurkhas. "He's a-shakin' 'is fist at the 'eathen, and he's a-standin' in the open. Get under cover there, sir," he bawled loudly through the window of the gallery, while Hawkins and the others stared anxiously down at their middy.

"And there's Mister Alec, 'im as is too good for a sailor," chimed in Private Larkin, though the effort at humour at that moment cost him something. "Blest if he ain't a-standing alongside of that 'ere Dicky, a-talkin' to him as cool as a gineral."

"Stop talking, men, please," came from Joe, in anxious tones. "Now is the time to pepper the enemy, for I fear that they are about to charge. Yes. Look! Another rascal has risen to lead them."

The crackle of musketry from the grouped figures of the Gurkhas told plainly enough that the time for trial was upon them, while if Joe and the crew of the airship had a doubt, the lamp soon convinced them. That slow, careful movement of concentration was now completed. Perhaps five hundred of the enemy were gathered in one quarter, and but two hundred yards separated them from the Major and his command. And a third leader had suddenly put in an appearance. The Gurkhas could not see him, though Joe and Andrew could. For he was behind an enormous piece of rock, where he was busily haranguing his fellows.

"And a-callin' of 'em to 'ack Mr. Dicky Hamshaw to pieces," growled Hawkins, adjusting his sights on the figure. "This 'ere's for an 'eathen—a black-'earted 'eathen!"

His weapon snapped, there was a loud thud as the bullet struck the rock behind which the chief was standing, and then a shout from Mr. Andrew.

"They're off! They're charging!" he cried.

"Make way! Now, drop her a trifle, sir," called Sergeant Evans, who had posted himself at one of the windows. "That will do. Stop her. Now watch."

He tossed something from the airship and craned his head as far as was possible. As for Hawkins and the rest of the crew, they fired madly down upon the enemy. For those five hundred figures, partly hidden some few seconds earlier, were now in the open. They were rushing together across the two hundred yards of barren ground which alone separated them from the forlorn Gurkhas. In half-dozens, in clusters of ten and more, in ones and twos and threes, with streaming banners, with waving arms and whirling knives and tulwars, they were descending upon Dick and his gallant comrades as a whirlwind, a human avalanche which would overwhelm them. It made Andrew positively ill with fear of the consequences. He shut his eyes tightly and gripped the frame of the window. As for Joe, he darted towards the engine-room, with the mad, half-formed idea of sending the ship plunging downward, charging that charging host, in fact. Even Hawkins forgot to use his weapon any longer. Sergeant Evans alone retained perfect coolness.

"Another second," he shouted to them, "one little second, and then——" The answer came before he had finished speaking. The head of that charging column was suddenly enveloped in a blinding flash, a flash the brilliance of which dimmed the rays from the ship's lamp. Those whirling Pathans melted, as it were, were swept aside, were blown out of sight by a terrific explosion. Even those in the airship above felt a portion of the concussion, while the vast ship itself trembled and swayed ominously.

"What is that? We are hit with a shell! We are falling!"

The stout figure of Carl Reitberg appeared at his cabin door, clutching at it convulsively. But not one took the smallest notice of him, save Andrew, who turned and bade him curtly to be silent.

"A few feet ahead, sir," called Sergeant Evans. "Now, that'll stop 'em."

Once more he leaned from the window of the gallery and tossed something into space. And again there were some seconds' anxious waiting. Then there came a mighty explosion, more forcible than the first—a concussion and blast of flame and gas which shot the ship upward. Down below it brought havoc to the Pathans, for it fell almost in the centre of that still-charging host, sweeping perhaps a hundred out of existence. Howls resounded on every side, while the rays streaming down upon this battlefield showed dusky figures scuttling away in all directions. And then came cheers, hoarse cheers of relief from the

Gurkhas, while Hawkins and his comrades made the night hideous with their shouting. Indeed, for perhaps five minutes the noise continued, while occasionally a shot rang out as a Gurkha sighted some crawling figure. Then Joe manœuvred the ship over the spot which the Major had been holding, and let her settle gently.

"Now for food for the men and more ammunition, beside help for the wounded," he said. "Let's bustle."

The following morning found their work completed; while, as the ship rose once more, she sighted a relieving column within a mile of the little force to whose aid they had come on the previous evening. It was clear, in fact, that there was no longer need for delay, and therefore the airship was headed eastward. Nor had Joe Gresson been idle in the meanwhile. He had repaired the few holes in the envelope of the vessel, and had set his gas producer in action, thereby replenishing losses. And now he steered for the heart of India, for Delhi, in fact, where he proposed to restock his larders. Two days later found the party hovering over that ancient and historic city, while that same evening the huge airship lay resting tranquilly outside the fortifications, within sight of the famous ridge of Delhi, a vast multitude gazing on her.

Doors in that long gallery were thrown open, officers and high officials, both British and native, thronged the ship, while even ladies partook of Andrew's hospitality. Indeed there was a merry party in the saloon, while Dicky Hamshaw was conducting an admiring party over the vessel. Only one individual was missing. It was Mr. Carl Reitberg, at that moment skulking in his cabin.

"At last," he was chuckling, as he rubbed his hands together, and gently prised open that curious box of his. "At last the time has come to teach these people a lesson. A little caution, a little watching, and then the ship flies in pieces. Of course, it'll be sad for the men. I've no grudge against 'em. But then, how can I help killing a few? The destruction of the ship is all-important. Yes, a little cunning and I shall lay the bombs, set the clockwork in motion, and go. Who is to say that it was not due to a dreadful accident?"

The man's face was positively hideous in its cunning. Those aboard the airship were indeed face to face with a crisis.

CHAPTER XV

The Great Attempt

A motley crowd thronged the narrow streets of the old city of Delhi, that city to which for so many years the eyes of the natives of India had ever been turned, the same quaint, battlemented stronghold which had seen those mutineers arrive flushed with the success of their first massacres of sahibs and mem-sahibs and children, had witnessed the struggle of sepoys to overthrow the British Raj.

A noisy crowd of gesticulating people, as dusky almost as ebony, some resplendent in many-coloured robes and turbans, others, the coolies, clad in but the lightest raiment, bargained at the numerous booths, or sat on their haunches in the sun, basking in the heat, smoking their hubble-bubbles. Now and again a sowar passed, mounted on his wiry animal, as fine a soldier as this jewel in England's glorious crown could well produce. Then came a Gurkha maybe, though very few were to be found in the neighbourhood of Delhi; a tall Sikh followed, his dark eyes glowing beneath his huge and picturesque turban. In short, a motley crowd, a crowd of surpassing interest, wended its way hither and thither, some about their ordinary business, some on shopping bent, others merely idling, trusting to meet chance acquaintances when they could forgather in some quiet corner and chatter about the huge airship.

"Ripping!" declared Alec, when he and Dick had looked on at the throng for perhaps an hour, and had strolled through a number of streets. "It's quite the most interesting thing I have ever seen. Look! There are English people mixed up with the natives."

There was every nationality one could imagine almost. Slim, sly men from the hills, in the neighbourhood of the North-West, a couple of Afghan merchants but recently arrived by way of the Khyber Pass, a Parsee banker, a native clerk, a postman of dusky colour. Then a group of chattering women, a bevy of girls from the nearest school, clad in garments very similar to those worn by their European sisters. And later a gorgeously-caparisoned elephant, with some native prince in the howdah. A band sounded in the distance, and presently a British regiment swung by, the natives on either side salaaming to the colours, which Dick saluted in naval style. Nor were our two young friends the least interesting of the people bustling about the streets of Delhi. A couple of clean, jolly, well-set-up young Englishmen they looked, their white drill suits and topees suiting them admirably. But there were others of interest also. Three sailors swung by, barging through the crowd with that curious roll so common to men of the sea. Need we say that they were Hawkins, Hurst, and Pierson, with the cantankerous and unlovely Private Larkin in close attendance? And didn't they take good care to salute our two young friends!

"It's him!" growled Hawkins fiercely in Private Larkin's ear when he caught sight of Dick and Alec. "Now then, all together, and mind there ain't no skulking."

"'Oo's a skulking, I'd like to know?" came in grumbling tones from the soldier even in the midst of a fierce salute. "One would think as you naval chaps was the only ones as could do a job of this sort nice and handy! 'Sides, I'm salutin' Mr. Alec, 'im as is fit ter be a soldier, and will be. I ain't no doubt as he'll pass the Navy. It ain't in his line, yer see. Too much red tape and pipeclay for 'is liking."

It was another effort on the part of this pleasant individual to get up a fierce argument, and had the men been gathered in their quarters aboard the airship no doubt Hawkins would have obliged him. But there was too much to be seen on every hand, and therefore, with a growling "Come along, you," he led the way past our heroes and down the bazaar.

"Hallo! Mr. Carl Reitberg of all people! Thought he was abed, quite done up after that little affair of ours on the north-west frontier," exclaimed Dick, some few minutes later. "The high and mighty Carl Reitberg seated in a gharri careering about the streets of Delhi. Look at him shouting because the crowd don't move aside soon enough for his majesty. And where is he going?"

"Which reminds me that we haven't kept up that watch since we came to Delhi," said Alec. "Think he's up to any games?"

How could one answer that question? No doubt the magnate had his own business to transact, and indeed, halted at a bank and entered. When he emerged Dick saw that he was tucking a well-filled purse into his pocket. He struggled into his cab, mopped his forehead with a handkerchief of brilliant hue, and then gave directions to the driver.

"Vote we follow," cried Dick. "I don't like our guest's face, to be quite frank with you. What's he drawing money for? Where's he going?"

"Might just as well expect other folks to be asking the same question about us. But we'll follow. Here, out of the way, you son of a gun. Hi! Gharri!"

Alec displaced the dusky individual who barred his path, and waved frantically to a cabman. A minute later the two were seated in the gharri, which at once set out in pursuit of the one that Carl Reitberg had taken.

"Booking office of the railway," said Dick, ten minutes later, seeing Carl descend and enter an office so labelled. "Had enough of the airship it seems, and will make the trip to the coast by train. But that's queer, ain't it?"

"What's queer? Why? How?" asked Alec in a breath.

"Don't be a donkey! Carl Reitberg's queer."

"Ill? He don't look it. Seems to be he's very much alive-o!"

Dick turned an indignant, not to say angry glance upon his companion.

"You are thick!" he said bluntly. "I wasn't referring to the health of our estimable friend. I was referring to his actions. They're queer, ain't they?"

"No—why? Why shouldn't he return by train and steamer if he wishes to do so?"

"Because at breakfast this morning he told us all how he was enjoying the trip. Pretended even to have been charmed with our little brush with those Pathans. Said nothing would induce him to part with the airship till she had landed him in England."

"My! Yes. Greasy beggar," reflected Alec. "What's it mean? Playing double. But perhaps he ain't booking. Look here, I'll hop in and listen to what's passing."

Mr. Carl Reitberg was without a doubt booking a seat for Bombay. Alec squeezed himself through the throng of Europeans in the booking office, and managed to reach a spot just behind the magnate. There he heard him enquiring for the next ship sailing from Bombay, and watched as he booked a cabin.

"You're right; it's mighty queer," he told Dick on returning. "What does it mean?"

"Everything, perhaps; perhaps nothing. He's foxy, and means to clear out, that's plain. But it don't say that he means us or the ship a mischief. Not that I'd trust him. Sergeant Evans is full of dark hints, and could tell us a yarn, I'm sure, if we encouraged him. I'm going to set a watch on Mr. Reitberg."

"Those beggarly brats," reflected the magnate, ten minutes later, when he emerged from the office and saw a gharri passing with our two young friends aboard. "Sight-seeing, I suppose. Well, they've not seen me buying my ticket. No one has. I've thrown dust in their eyes nicely. Now I can return to the ship, wait my chance, and then——"

It made him chuckle. He sat back in the gharri smiling and perspiring, mopping his forehead from time to time. And it was with a wonderfully elastic step that he strode from the gharri to the airship, roughly pushing aside the throng of natives and entered the gallery.

"It'll be a big affair," he told himself with a grim smile. "Of course, as I've said before, I'm sorry about the crew. But that's their lookout. A hundred or more of these natives blown to pieces will make not the smallest difference. Dinner-time to-night'll suit admirably. Then we're all aboard. The men'll be in their quarters, with perhaps one patrolling on the deck above, and two outside, to keep the curious natives at a distance. I'll be late for dinner; yes, that's the card to play. I send my compliments to Mr. Andrew, and beg to be excused as the heat has upset me. Excellent! A splendid excuse. Then, when all's quiet, I set the bombs in position, creep out of the ship, and while Delhi is lamenting the terrible catastrophe, and thousands are chattering, I simply board the train and take the road for England."

He sat down in his cabin to mop his forehead again, and then took off his coat and waistcoat. "Come in," he cried testily, to a knock at the door.

It was Sergeant Evans, respectful and polite as ever. "Dinner half an hour later this evening, sir," he said. "I'll put your things out now, so as not to disturb you later."

"Terribly hot," gasped Carl. "Hardly feel as if I could eat anything. Shouldn't wonder if I didn't turn up for dinner, Sergeant."

Like the well-trained, polite fellow he was the Sergeant expressed no surprise. He merely touched the button which controlled the electric fan and set it going.

"Hot in here, sir," he said. "That'll make things cooler. Hope you'll feel better presently. Half-past six now, sir. Perhaps a little sleep would put you right, and make you ready for dinner."

"Perhaps," agreed Carl laconically, mopping his forehead again. "I'll try. But don't disturb me. If I don't turn up after the gong has gone, leave me to myself. I'll be sleeping."

The face of the Sergeant was inscrutable as he left the cabin. If it said anything at all, it expressed commiseration for this somewhat stout and unwieldy sportsman, and the hope that he would soon feel more himself. But if his features meant that, his immediately following actions contrasted curiously with them. For the worthy Sergeant passed into his own quarters, and from thence into his pantry. And by a curious freak of fortune that pantry happened to be immediately next to the cabin occupied by the worthy Carl Reitberg.

"Don't I know him? Oh no! Certainly not!" observed the Sergeant beneath his breath. "Mr. Carl Reitberg, yes, that's his name now; I.D.B. back in South Africa in the old days. He's feeling queer, and he don't expect he'll come along to dinner. Well, we'll hope he will. But we'll see what's happening in the meanwhile."

So straightway he crept to the wall of the pantry, and slid aside a tiny panel, some two inches long, and of half that height. It was quite a simple contrivance, and had merely required a sharp knife and a slip of sheet celludine. A hot iron

149

had cemented the runners of this slide to the wall, while anyone entering either the pantry or the adjacent cabin would have found it difficult to detect this opening. An inch-square aperture gave a wide view of the quarters allotted to the magnate, and of that individual himself.

"Felt ill, did he? Poor chap!" observed the Sergeant. "Thought he'd follow my advice and have a sleep. Looks like trying, don't he?"

The fat form of the magnate was engaged at that precise moment in anything but an attempt to fall asleep. He was leaning over that precious box which he had brought aboard with him, and which he would have others believe contained valuables of great interest. The seals were broken already, and half a dozen of the screws with which the lid was secured were already drawn. The magnate was puffing heavily in his efforts to loosen one which was strangely tight and refractory. At length, however, after a fierce struggle, he succeeded, and some ten minutes later had the box open.

"And here's where the fun begins," said the watching Sergeant. "I'm as keen as possible to see what he's got in that box, and what he'll do with 'em. Ah! Two nicely rolled parcels, Mr. Carl, fresh and clean from the hands that wrapped 'em in Old England. Valuables, to be sure! Priceless; deserved a safe if only this ship would have carried one."

There was a grim smile on his lips as he closely watched the movements of the scoundrel bending over the box. For here indeed was a conspirator. If there had been any doubt, the man's own movements would have betrayed his uneasiness, his guilty thoughts, for Carl was decidedly uneasy. Never a man of courage, rather the reverse, as he had abundantly proved, the doing of this miserable and wicked deed he contemplated shook him severely. Though he imagined he had braced up his shaky nerves for the adventure, and though he encouraged himself by the thought that there was no personal danger in the matter, no fear of discovery, and no difficulty in getting clear away, yet he was frightened, frightened of his own image. It caused the Sergeant to smile, indeed, when Carl, suddenly catching sight of his own reflection in the mirror opposite him, blanched and gripped the table.

"Gave me quite a turn," he gasped, his strong accent more noticeable than ever. "*Himmel!* But this deed requires more force than I had imagined. But there is no danger. Can be none while I have my ticket for the train and boat in my pocket. As for the bombs, they cannot explode till the clockwork is wound. Then I merely set the hands to the hour at which I desire the explosion, and— leave."

"Very simple," smiled the Sergeant. "And I wonder where he'll put his bombs and how this ship's going to suffer. Of all the rascals I ever set eyes on, it's him. Sportsman! Tish!"

He had seen enough, and went off to the saloon to lay his table and make ready for dinner. There was a thoughtful look upon his face, an expectant smile which boded little goodwill for Mr. Reitberg. As for Dick and Alec, they were nonplussed by the disappearance of the one they had determined to watch. He had gone to ground in his cabin and was resting there.

"Having a sleep, sir," the Sergeant told them naïvely. "Finds it precious hot. Don't fancy he'll turn up for dinner."

"Then I'm going straight to Joe and Mr. Andrew," Dick whispered to Alec. "We've found out that this sportsman's going to hook it. Then what's he up to?"

"Something, perhaps; nothing, perhaps. Let's hang on a bit and watch when the others are at dinner. Carl can't slip out of his cabin by the window, now can he?"

Dick admitted the fact briskly.

"Then he has to come by way of the gallery. Good! We watch at either end. We nab him if he tries hanky-panky."

"And if he don't. Supposing he just clears off for the station?"

The question was somewhat of a facer, for how could Dick and Alec then interfere? Carl had as much right to leave the ship as they had. Then, supposing he went by the ordinary route, through the gallery and so into the open, who could arrest him? It would be an outrage, a breach of good manners; worse, in fact.

"Oh, let's leave that question to later," said Dick airily. "He ain't going by the window, that's certain. Then we watch at each end of the gallery, and if he gets up to monkey tricks, why, we bowl him over."

Little did the magnate imagine that three at least of his fellow passengers were waiting for his appearance. Not that the worthy Sergeant showed much concern. Now and again, on his numerous visits to the pantry, he slid that panel aside and squinted into the cabin. But he went on with his duties, prepared the table, set the chairs, and finally rang the gong briskly. As he did so the clock in the saloon chimed eight. It was precisely half an hour after Mr. Andrew's usual hour for dinner, and with soldier-like exactness the Sergeant announced the meal at the very moment for which it had been ordered. He escorted Joe and his uncle, the Commander and the Major, to their places, announced that Mr. Reitberg wished to be excused, and murmured in Joe's ear the fact that Dick and Alec had returned to the ship and had then departed again.

"Then we won't wait," said Andrew brusquely. "Let us go on with the meal."

"Certainly, sir," replied the Sergeant.

At once he served the soup, with the help of an assistant. Then he took his stand behind Andrew, waiting and watching the diners as becomes a well-trained attendant. But had he forgotten the rascal in that adjacent cabin? Had he allowed the matter to escape his mind? It would seem so, indeed, though there was no excuse, for but a matter of ten minutes earlier he had watched the crafty Carl set the hands of his two clocks to eight-fifteen and wind the springs. Why, he must be mad, crazy, for at that very moment Carl Reitberg was preparing to emerge from his cabin. But Sergeant Evans went on with his waiting methodically. He removed the empty soup plates and the tureen, and having placed clean, hot plates before the diners handed the fish to each in turn. There was no hurry about his movements, no sign of anxiety about his face. He did not even bother to observe the clock. Instead, he offered sherry to each of the gentlemen present, put the decanter back upon the sideboard, and motioned to his assistant to hasten to the kitchen for the next course. It was ten minutes after the hour. In five minutes those bombs with which the dastardly Carl hoped to wreck the vessel would explode. In five short minutes——Hark! What was that? Joe turned slowly in his chair. Andrew glanced across at the Major.

"Dick and Alec larking again," observed the Commander dryly. "A little more shipboard discipline is what our Mr. Dicky Hamshaw requires. What a noise the brats are making."

There was indeed quite an uproar in the gallery outside. The voices of Hawkins, Hurst, and Larkin were heard in succession. And then the door of the saloon was burst unceremoniously open, figures appeared outside, and a moment later Carl Reitberg was thrust into the chamber, Hawkins and Larkin gripping his shoulders, while Dick and Alec followed immediately behind them.

"Caught him in the act, sir!" shouted Dick, excitedly, addressing Andrew. "Watched him place two bombs in position along the gallery. Here they are. At least we guess they're bombs, though they're wrapped in paper."

That saloon had never before witnessed such a curious gathering, nor such excitement if one describes the matter fully. Not that Joe and his fellow diners betrayed great concern. Their stern faces merely showed disgust, loathing for this Carl Reitberg, while the well-trained Sergeant looked on with polite indifference, showing just a trace of annoyance, as if he objected to the dinner being so unceremoniously disturbed. But there coolness ceased altogether. Dick and Alec were dishevelled, red-hot with excitement, trembling with the importance of their discovery. Hawkins's broad face showed a righteous anger which was on the point of boiling over, while Private Larkin's fierce face gave one the idea that he was within an ace of exploding. In the centre, pinioned by the arms, pale and wabbling, was the magnate, speechless with fright, his pig-like eyes rolling with terror.

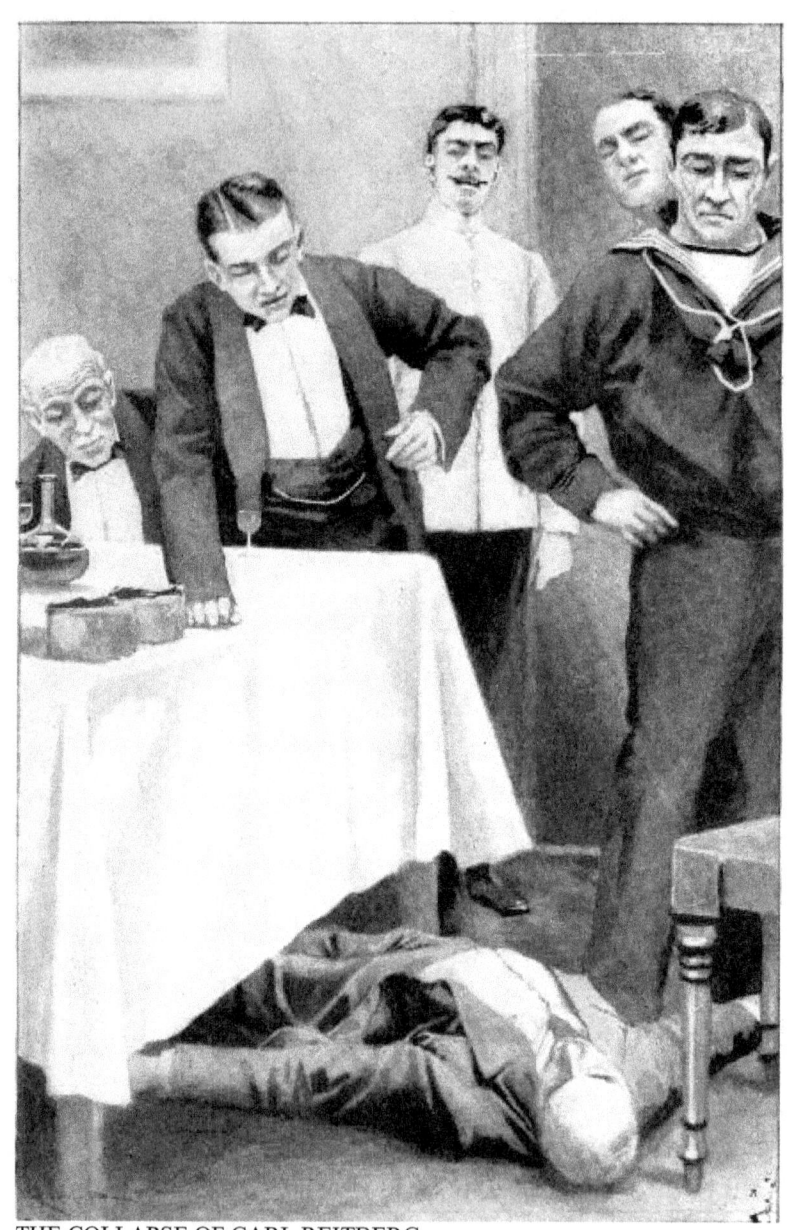

THE COLLAPSE OF CARL REITBERG

It was one of those unexpected situations when one would have felt surprise if the dinner were not abandoned, the crew of the ship aroused, and a huge commotion set going. But Andrew Provost had already given abundant proof of his coolness. Joe, too, was not so easily frightened, while a calm demeanour on the part of the Commander and the Major was to be expected. But no one would quite have anticipated the line of action which Andrew adopted.

"And so you have discovered this Mr. Reitberg, our guest aboard, in the midst of an attempt to wreck the vessel!" he said softly. "Well, well, you may be mistaken."

"Impossible, sir," cried Alec. "We watched him first. He's a ruffian."

"But—but still there may be some little error," Andrew asserted. "We will give our guest the benefit of the doubt for the moment and investigate the matter. Place a chair there for him, Sergeant."

"But—but these beastly things are set to go off in four minutes," shouted Dick suddenly. "Look, sir. I've stripped the paper from the bombs. There's a clock attached to the outside of each. It's ticking, and the hands are set at eight-fifteen. They'll explode then and blow the place to pieces."

"Four minutes, you said. I make it but three," Joe exclaimed of a sudden, taking the bombs. "That's too bad. Dick, you must give it up as hopeless. You couldn't possibly get these bombs away to a safe distance in that short space of time. Eh, Major?"

"Hopeless. Let 'em cut and run, Dick and Alec and the others. I'm too old to make the attempt. Put the bombs on the table."

Was everyone mad? Had these diners gone completely crazy? Dick looked round in bewilderment, and went scarlet with anger. For the Major was actually sipping his sherry, while Joe was thrusting a morsel of fish into his mouth. As for the Sergeant, he placed a chair for the magnate between Joe and Andrew, plumped that perspiring and shaking individual into it, and having taken the two bombs from Dick put them on the table within a foot of Carl Reitberg. We make no excuse for Hawkins and his friend. They turned at Andrew's nod and bolted.

"Not for me, thanks," said Dick desperately. "Sherry, please, Sergeant."

"Ditto," gasped Alec, seating himself.

"In fact, we swim or sink together. Or shall we say, we stand shoulder to shoulder awaiting the last great flight of this giant vessel?"

There was a quizzing tone in the Major's voice, and he was actually winking. Winking! And so was the Sergeant.

"Sherry, sir. Yes, sir," he observed, in his ordinary, matter-of-fact tones, placing a glass before our two young heroes. "And don't you expect nothing," he whispered. "Them things is O.K. You'll yet eat a dinner."

Meanwhile things were hardly going comfortably for Mr. Reitberg. The rascal sat far back in his chair, tilting it backward, his two hands gripping the table, and his bulging eyes fixed on the hands of the two clocks attached to his infernal machines. He was livid with fear. A cold, clammy perspiration covered his forehead. His fat cheeks shook and wobbled in an ugly manner, and what little hair he had positively bristled. His breath came in choking grunts, wheezing from his lungs, while his lips were dry and parted.

"One minute more; only one minute," he gasped at last, staring at the clock faces. "Only one minute."

"Pardon—rather more. Perhaps two or three seconds," observed the Major icily. "Then, Mr. Reitberg——"

"Take me away. Let me leave the place. Throw those bombs out of the window—I say, throw them away. They'll explode; they'll kill me. They'll tear me to pieces."

The wretch foamed at the mouth, his attention concentrated all the while on those two clock faces. His eyes were bloodshot now, his nails digging like talons into the table.

"Then they are really bombs? You actually meant to wreck the vessel?" asked Andrew.

But the rascal cowering in a frenzy of terror at the table hardly seemed to hear his words, much less to heed them. He was bending lower now, ducking his head, and yet looking upward from beneath his brows at the hands on those two dials. They were near the quarter. In ten seconds they would reach the point at which he had set the trigger. And then——

"Take me away!" he screamed, foaming at the mouth, and looking hideous in his terror. "Kill me now. Shoot me. Don't let me be blown to pieces by these bombs. Ah! I will kill myself."

He made a desperate effort to seize a knife from the table, and no doubt would have done himself some severe injury. But the Commander seized his arm.

"No," he said sternly. "This is your trial, a trial of your own making. Learn now what it is to set bombs to slaughter other people. Endure to the full the torment that others were to suffer."

The strain was too great for the magnate. A gurgling cry escaped him, and a moment later he was stretched full length on the carpet.

"Call in the others," commanded Joe curtly. "Let us go on with our dinner. And by the way, Sergeant, tell Mr. Dick and his friend that there's no danger."

"No danger!" shouted the midshipman. "None! Why, I've been hanging on to my chair hard expecting to be blown to pieces."

"Like Mr. Reitberg, only different," smiled Andrew. "Lads, you've shown splendid pluck. Now, let's eat. As for the bombs, they happen to be empty."

CHAPTER XVI

Record High Flying

It required quite an amount of explanation and apology to mollify the hot-headed and indignant Dicky Hamshaw and his friend Alec when they learned how all their energy, all their suspense and anxiety for the great airship and the safety of their friends had been unnecessary and thrown away.

"And—and you mean to tell us that the bombs are empty?" demanded the former, with some curtness, as soon as the fainting form of the rascal, Carl Reitberg, had been borne to his cabin. "I—this is no laughing matter."

"Precisely," answered the Major, with a little smile. "And, Dick, I'm not surprised at your anger. You see, we knew that those bombs had been rendered harmless."

"Then, sir, why not tell Alec and myself?"

The midshipman was almost boiling. But still, he had never been anything else but a good officer, and discipline was discipline. "Beg pardon, sir," he said. "But it makes a chap rather ratty. Here have I been hanging on to this chair, trying to keep cool and look it, when every instant I expected to be blown to atoms. I thought you must all be mad to go on so coolly with your dinners."

"While I'm in a horrible perspiration," confessed Alec, mopping his brow. Then he seemed to see some fun in the matter, and grinned at his comrade.

"All the same it was a good lesson for Mr. Reitberg," he cried. "Odious toad that he is. He didn't know that the bombs were empty, now, did he? He didn't look like it. That's why he funked. That's why he went under."

Mr. Andrew rose from his chair, and took each of the lads in turn by the hand.

"We owe you many apologies," he said earnestly. "I can't forgive myself for what has happened. But there are excuses. I did not know, Joe was kept in ignorance, even the Major and the Commander knew nothing of this matter till the very beginning of dinner. Then Sergeant Evans told us. We owe our safety to him, to his watchfulness—though I know you also have watched—to his cleverness, and to the experience he had in South Africa. There! I am sorry. But it was fine to see the manner in which you two behaved."

"Magnificent!" declared the Major.

"I shall report it," cried the Commander, gripping Dick's hand. "A fine example of the spirit which all naval men should show. Alec, shake hands."

"Now, tell us the whole tale, Sergeant Evans," demanded Joe, while Dick and Alec, now completely mollified, took their places at the table. Indeed, dinner proceeded much as usual, but for the fact that the Sergeant, while attending upon the diners, told them his tale crisply and shortly.

"I knew him, this Mr. Carl Reitberg," he began in the politest tones. In fact, you would not have imagined that he had any other but the highest opinion of the individual to whom he referred. Certainly his tones showed no trace of satire, of disgust, or even of anger.

"His name was different out in the Transvaal," he proceeded. "He was a suspected person, and as such came under the notice of the police, that is, the civil police. He was supposed to be an I.D.B., otherwise an illicit diamond buyer. But he was more. We military police suspected him of dealings with the Boers. We watched him, and he escaped, and left the country. It was natural, then, that I should suspect him when I found him here under another name. I watched him, gentlemen, watched him through a peephole cut in the wall of his cabin, which is next the pantry. He had a box with him, a suspicious box, filled with valuables as he said. I investigated the contents of that box."

"But, pardon for the interruption, Sergeant. That box was sealed," remarked Mr. Andrew, with a lift of his white eyebrows.

"Yes, sir—sealed. Red sealing wax, impressed with a seal hanging to the man's watch chain. I borrowed that seal one day. I opened the box, investigated the contents, removed the explosives, leaving everything else as it was, sealed the box again and returned it to its old position. No one was the wiser. Even Mr. Reitberg was unsuspicious when he opened the box this evening. He imagined he still had dangerous bombs, whereas I knew that they had already served their purpose."

"Served their purpose? How?" demanded Joe quickly.

"You remember the Pathans, sir? Well, Mr. Reitberg's bombs stopped their rush, and came in very handy."

The tale proved, if it had proved nothing else, that in Sergeant Evans the airship possessed a trusty and astute man. But it also proved to the hilt the rascality of Carl Reitberg.

"Of course," said Mr. Andrew, when the warm thanks of the gathering had been given to the Sergeant, "of course, we take no action. The ruffian is not worth powder and shot; his meanness will bring about its own punishment. When he recovers we will let him go, thankful that we are well quit of him."

It followed that late that night, he having then recovered consciousness, a gharri conveyed the disconsolate Carl to the railway station, where he took train for Bombay. But it must not be imagined that the man took with him any feelings of gratitude to those who had so handsomely dealt with him. No. They had made a fool of him. He realized now that the bombs before which he had been forced to sit, and which he had expected to shatter him to fragments in a few seconds, he realized that they had been rendered harmless. All his fears and terrors, all his squirming, the terrible exhibition he had made of himself were to no purpose. He had been fooled. The very people he had imagined to be so stupidly wanting in astuteness, who had failed to suspect him, had defeated his dastardly attempt with surprising ease. It made the magnate boil with rage and mortification. He fanned his heated brow as the train sped onward, set his crooked teeth and swore beneath his breath.

"Ah!" he grunted. "Made a fool of me. Know now that I am not the sportsman they imagined. Fancy themselves safe, and are sure of winning that wager. We'll see. There is still time. There is still Adolf Fruhmann."

Yes, there was still that unmitigated rascal, ready to attempt anything if sufficiently well paid. He was the man to come now to Carl's rescue. He was the one who must now attempt the wrecking of the airship. But how?

"I'll wire to him to meet me at Suez," Carl decided before he reached Bombay. "He'll be able to propose a scheme. Yes, there's time still. If I have failed, Adolf will manage to succeed. We'll show the folks aboard the airship who's best man in this matter."

Burning with anger at his defeat, and his vindictiveness increased almost in proportion to the distance he was steadily placing between himself and the great airship, Carl Reitberg boarded the steamer at Bombay in no enviable frame of mind. Indeed, what with the heat and his own stoutness he narrowly escaped an attack of apoplexy, and lay for some days in his cabin, his head swathed in bandages wrung out of iced water, a huge wind shute pouring the little fresh air there was into the compartment, while an electric fan shot eddies at his perspiring person. Indeed, to the average individual it was an uncomfortable season during which to visit the neighbourhood of Bombay. To Carl Reitberg, the pompous, fat, and rascally magnate swelling with indignation, hate, and all uncharitableness, it was a positive nightmare.

In this uncomfortable condition, then, we can leave him to his own devices, with the knowledge that, though he had failed once in his dastardly effort to wreck Joe Gresson's invention, he had by no means given up all hope of achieving success. For Joe and his friends, we can say that they gave scarcely another thought to their late guest, who had abused their kindness so disgracefully.

"It's a black page in the history of our trip," said Andrew, the morning following. "We will turn it over and seal it down. Ugly things are better as a rule when shut out of view. And now, Mr. Skipper?"

"Now, Joe?" cried the Commander. "We await orders. Do we remain here cooking in the neighbourhood of Delhi? Or do we seek a more balmy clime, where a man may sleep peacefully in his cabin, and must not necessarily spend the baking night restlessly pacing the open deck above dressed only in his pyjamas?"

"Yes—what next?" demanded Dick, his mouth still busy with the breakfast he was devouring. But what recked Dicky of heat? Mr. Midshipman Hamshaw carried an appetite wherever he went, and his breakfast this morning showed that heat hardly affected him. He was not even limp, whereas the Major, hardened soldier that he was, and accustomed to India, was as flabby as a wet rag.

"Which comes of modern invention," he laughed. "Send me to India in the cold weather, and leave me in the plains when the heat comes. I'll not turn a hair, for I've had time to become acclimatized. But set out from London as we have done on this new-fangled machine—apologies, Joe and Mr. Andrew—set out, I say, on this airship and plunge me suddenly from the heights, where one needs a fur coat, to the plains about Delhi in the hot weather, and I admit I become a limp, nerveless individual."

"While I for another shall be glad to move on," Joe admitted. "Well, now; we take in stores here—they are coming aboard already—then, following the plan agreed upon, we sail along over the all-red route. Naturally, this trip is not a true tour of the world, for then we should take a straight line, the shortest route possible. We are purposely lengthening our journey, and should we successfully complete it, we shall have flown many more miles than the twenty-five odd thousand which circumvent the globe. So our course lies east, parallel almost to the Himalaya mountains."

"Ah! A test of elevation, perhaps," suggested the Commander. "You could cross the Himalayas."

"Why not?"

"At their highest point?"

"I have reason to believe so," said Joe, with the quiet assurance of the inventor who has the utmost faith in the powers of the machine he has constructed. "Why not?"

"Because—well, because Mount Everest happens to be the highest peak," replied the Commander dryly. "Let's see; what is its exact altitude? Here, Dick, one of you youngsters, let us have the figure."

"Sorry, sir; can't. Forgotten—so long since I left school," answered the imperturbable Dick. "Ask Alec, he's the latest kid to leave."

He accompanied his remarks with a grin in his friend's direction, which became the broader as Alec shook his fist at him.

"Well, Alec? Dick's a dunce; he's like most middies," said the Commander.

And for a wonder Alec was able to supply the information.

"Twenty-nine thousand and two feet high, sir," he told them. "Highest mountain in the world. Cold as Christmas up at the top. Haven't been there myself, you know, but I'm guessing."

"In fact, rather more uncomfortable there than down here," laughed the Major. "Well, Joe, it's a stumper?"

"I cannot say. To cross above the highest peak we must ascend some five miles. That is a tremendous height; it will need special preparation."

But one could see that Joe was bitten with the idea of accomplishing that which no other person or machine had ever achieved before. He went to the engine-room forthwith, and for the next two hours closely inspected the gasometer and carburettor which supplied his engines. Then he took the temperature of the crude paraffin which, unlike other internal-combustion motors, not only formed the explosive charge, and conveyed power through those long, sinuous, cold-drawn steel pipes to the distant hydraulic motors, but also surrounded the cylinders, acting as an effective cooling agent. If one had watched him one would have seen the thoughtful Joe working out some pleasant little calculations, calculations which would have given Dicky Hamshaw quite a headache. But the result seemed to satisfy him, for he once more inspected his engines, made a small adjustment, and then went off to the saloon.

"Gentlemen," he said solemnly, "we have loaded our stores. If all are ready we will make for Mount Everest and there test the powers of this vessel."

It was one of the many advantages of being aboard an airship. There was no packing to be done, no cabs to call, no trains to be entered. Joe had merely to return to the engine-room and start his motors, so that within ten minutes the ship was off, followed by the cheers and shrill native cries of thousands. For a while she hovered over the city of Delhi, mounting and mounting steadily, till she was but a speck in the sky, a speck almost invisible because of the material of which she was constructed. It was an object lesson to many thousands also. For where in all India, in all the world, was there a gun capable of reaching her, of destroying the airship, of preventingher crew, had they so wished, from dropping bombs upon the citizens of Delhi?

"In war, an invincible arm," declared the Major with conviction. "A terrible arm, indeed, for here is a ship as secure, as handy, as manageable as any steamer. Let us hope that the report we shall take to War Office and Admiralty will not fall upon deaf ears. Or rather, let us pray that the authorities will test the truth of our statements by sending men aboard who are really qualified to form an opinion. Not amateurs, more or less filled with a sense of their own importance, and forgetful of that of others."

To those stepping the upper deck of the airship the view beneath was one of the greatest magnificence, for the brilliance of the sun brought objects beneath into unusual prominence. Then, too, owing to the elevation at which the vessel now floated, the heat of the day was no longer felt.

"Just like an English summer," Andrew murmured. "And the height, Joe?"

"Seven thousand feet or thereabouts; not a quarter the height to which we shall have to climb before crossing Mount Everest. For the moment I am satisfied. Now we will descend a little, for it will be cold when we begin to travel through the air. To-morrow, at about this hour, we shall have failed miserably or have added another honour to those already won by this ship. Don't think me boastful. I speak of things as they are, precisely as you have found them. I ask for nothing better than honest tests. Here is one. I shall strive to win in this encounter."

"But one moment," said the Major. "Excuse my ignorance. Mount Everest is twenty-nine thousand and two feet in height. Let us say that we must ascend to the enormous height of thirty thousand feet. Will that, then, prove a record? Is there a person who has before this date attained to such an altitude?"

"Certainly," came the prompt answer. "In the past many balloons have climbed to great heights, and I can instance a few such attempts. Coxwell is said to have reached the enormous altitude of seven miles in the year 1862. He lost the use of his hands, but contrived to open the valve with the aid of his teeth. His companion, Mr. James Glaisher, was then insensible. Then Dr. Berson and Dr. Suring ascended from Berlin in 1901 to the height of thirty-four thousand feet, contriving to maintain their senses by inhaling oxygen. And lastly, there is the recorded ascent of the *Albatross*, which, in 1909, set out from Turin, and reached the stupendous height of thirty-eight thousand seven hundred and fifteen feet.

"And what is the record of dirigibles?" asked the Commander eagerly. "We must recollect that they are a different sort of craft, and do not ascend by heaving ballast overboard—that is, as a general rule. This ship, we know, is influenced by her vertical screws."

"And will contrive to climb with them almost unaided," answered Joe. "But it may be that we shall attempt a record, in which case there is ample ballast to be thrown overboard. As to the height to which dirigibles have climbed, of that I am uncertain. But it is said that six thousand feet is the record for a Zeppelin, and we will allow that the Zeppelin is the last word in dirigibles."

"*Was*," Andrew corrected him quickly. "Was, Joe. The coming of this vessel annihilates the Zeppelin."

There was an air of suppressed excitement about the crew on the following afternoon, for the news of their coming attempt had leaked out. Moreover, the airship had driven her way steadily onward during the night, and all through the morning she had been steering a course parallel to the gaunt Himalayas, within easy distance of the snow glistening on the numerous peaks of this giant range, and within sight already of Mount Everest. The lofty peak raised its white head some fifty miles to their left, its snow slopes shimmering in the sun's rays. Its broad base also could be detected, merging imperceptibly with the mass of the range. But the centre portion was invisible, clad in a garment of white cloud, which seemed to warn all and sundry to leave that peak alone, and make no rash attempt upon it. But Joe Gresson was totally unaffected. He turned the ship's head directly for the mountain and waited at the tiller till those fifty miles were accomplished, till the airship was within a short mile of the mountain, looking a mere dot when compared with the mighty mass of rock thrusting upward.

"At this moment we begin our attempt," he told his friends. "Kindly observe our height. We are resting precisely seven thousand feet above sea-level. Now, I will start the elevating motors. When we are twenty-nine thousand feet up we will steer for the top of the peak. After that, if all are agreeable, we will ascend once more. I have a mind to accomplish a world's record. But we must take precautions. Let us don all the clothing we can find, and shut all windows and openings. Sergeant Evans has already taken out of store our cylinders of oxygen. You will find a mouthpiece attached to each one, and my advice is that you don them when we have reached a height of twenty thousand feet."

For a while there were bustling feet to be heard along the galleries of the airship. Men hastened to and fro carrying oxygen cylinders, while others made a round of the vessel to close all apertures. Then Joe set the aerial screws in motion, and, watching closely, Dick was able to detect the fact that the ship was rising swiftly. Indeed, before many minutes had passed they had plunged into the cold, white cloud surrounding the central part of the mountain. He strode off to the engine-room, to find Joe watching the barometer.

"Nineteen thousand feet," he read off. "Ah, we are mounting quickly! Twenty thousand feet. Now we throw our cooling fan out of gear, and make ready to cover over a portion of our radiator. In that way we shall be able to keep up the temperature of our motor and of its fuel supply. Now for the oxygen."

They were still mounting, mounting quickly too. Dick felt a queer sensation overcoming him. He was gasping, endeavouring to imbibe more air, eager for a greater supply of oxygen.

"Put on your mouthpiece and turn on the tap of the cylinder," Joe ordered. "You're grunting, positively grunting. And look at yourself in that mirror."

There was a tiny square which the engineer had secured to the side of the engine-room, and looking in it, Dick was positively startled to discover that his usually vivid and fresh complexion had gone. He was a pale, dirty-blue colour.

"Ugh! Hideous!" he grinned. "Now, let's try oxygen."

It had an almost immediate effect, as was to be expected, for within ten minutes he had regained his normal colour. Meanwhile, the cold had become extreme. Even there, in the heated engine-room, one felt it, while Joe anxiously placed his hand on the cylinder tops.

"Throwing the cooling fan out of gear will do it," he said, in tones of satisfaction. "I've still something in hand. Covering the radiator and so protecting it from cold will do the trick nicely."

"Twenty-seven thousand feet. Twenty-eight," he read out. "Are all feeling strong and well?"

They were gathered about the engine-room, some crowding in that chamber itself, some at the top of the ladder leading from it, grouped in the gallery of the airship. And a queer collection they were, muffled to the eyes, more than one already shivering with cold, for it must be recollected that this feat of clambering upward demanded no personal efforts from crew or passengers. Had they been on the snow-clad slopes of Mount Everest, amidst its glaciers and its crevasses, the path upward would have been one continual struggle, a struggle made all the more difficult by the increasing thinness of the air. Indeed this thinness of the air is one of the chief difficulties to be encountered by those who would ascend to huge heights above sea-level. Mountain sickness, the giddiness and nausea which attack people at great elevations, must also be overcome, though here, aboard the giant airship, not one of the members aboard felt so much as lightness of the head. It was the cold which troubled them. Why, Private Larkin's nose was positively blue! It peeped out from above a huge muffler which he had wound round his neck.

"I never!" Hurst remarked, grinning at him, and then taking another breath of oxygen. "You ain't handsome, not 'arf."

"'Ere," grunted Larkin, "none of yer lip! I'm 'avin'——"

But at that moment the need for more oxygen assailed him, and he buried his mouth in the apparatus affixed to each cylinder. Indeed, but for those cylinders this ascent would have been practically impossible. As it was, the ship climbed steadily, remorselessly upward. They were above the thick bank of wet cloud now. Of a sudden the cold became intense, while Dick found himself shielding his eyes from the glare. For the sun's rays were reflected from the virgin snow slopes with a brilliance he had never before experienced.

"Twenty-nine thousand feet. The summit of Mount Everest," called Joe, fingering the tops of his cylinders and the cooling surface of his radiator somewhat anxiously. "We will attempt a landing, and then we will ascend once more."

The big engine purred a little louder. Had an expert been there he would not have been able to detect a single alarming sound from the mechanism of the airship. For there was, in fact, little to go wrong.

"Freezing up does not trouble me," Joe had explained as they were ascending, "for my radiator is cooled by paraffin, and you may expose that liquid to extremes of cold with little effect. Even if there were danger of its freezing, the explosions of the engine cause heat, which is absorbed by the paraffin, and I have taken steps, by throwing out of gear the cooling fan, to retain that heat. As for the rest, the same fluid passing through those lines of steel tubes to the motors overhead is constantly in action. The pressure applied to it tends to add to its temperature, so that there again we can defy the cold."

The hum of the propeller told that the ship was in motion, for hitherto she had merely been ascending. Now the elevator screws were hardly rotating, while Dick and his friends could tell that they were advancing by the fact that the slopes of the mountain grew steadily nearer and nearer. The ship circled about the highest peak. She seemed to be looking for a landing-place. She even rested for a moment directly above the topmost pinnacle. And then Joe dropped her gently upon a smooth, level slope just beneath the summit.

"All explorers plant flags to show what they have done," he cried, laughing at those gathered about him. "We will do the same. Come, half a dozen of us will be sufficient."

They tore the door of the gallery open, for it was frozen fast, and struggled into the open, Joe and the Commander, with the Major, and Dick, and Alec, in close attendance. Bearing their oxygen cylinders strapped to their shoulders they trudged across the hard frozen snow, and within a few minutes had gained the summit. There they secured the staff of their Union Jack, pegged and roped it down, and promptly retraced their steps.

"And now for a record," cried Joe. "I advise all of you to don gloves if you have them and to keep moving about. I mean to rush the rest of the distance."

He covered more than half of his radiator, set the elevating motors buzzing, and then glanced anxiously at his barometer. They were rising, but very slowly. It

166

seemed to take an endless age to get away from the peak they had just visited. The tiny Union Jack, looking forlorn amid the snow slopes, appeared as if it would keep them company for ever.

"Turn that lever there," Joe commanded, pointing to one close to Dick's hand, for the midshipman was again in the engine-room. "If the outlet of my tank is frozen we shall have to halt for a while and apply heat. Ah, that's fortunate! Listen."

Above the gentle hum of the engine Dick could hear a gurgling, splashing sound, and looking downward discovered that a spray of water was falling from the airship, a spray which was caught by the breeze, whirled to one side, and transformed instantly into thin flakes of ice which went swimming through space to find a resting-place on the slopes of the mountain.

"Throwing out ballast," Joe explained. "Now we're moving."

The ship was clambering upward at a rapid pace, thanks to the weight rapidly streaming from her tanks. Joe watched his barometer now with smiling eyes.

"Thirty thousand feet," he stated solemnly. "Thirty-five thousand feet, gentlemen. Almost a world's record. But five more feet and I shall be satisfied." Had it not been for the mouthpieces which all were now compelled to keep constantly in use the crew would have cheered him. As it was they tramped the gallery, swinging their arms, beating their fingers, and muffling their faces in the first article of clothing upon which they could come. The cold was too intense for words, in spite of the heating arrangements aboard the ship. Indeed, but for active movement many of the crew would not have been able to bear it. And steadily, relentlessly, the ship ascended, while Dick, at Joe's bidding, emptied first one and then the remaining tanks aboard the vessel. It was with a shout of triumph that Joe announced that they had ascended to forty thousand feet.

"Kindly observe the barometer," he called. "Kindly bear evidence to the fact that we have gained this record."

Then began the descent. Joe arrested the elevating motors, and at once the ship began to fall. Not rapidly, as one might have expected, but slowly, imperceptibly, so smoothly that but for the barometer none would have known that she was moving. And now, as they reached the level of thirty thousand feet, and that tiny Union Jack came into view once more, but a stone's throw to their right, the mercury ceased to move. In spite of accelerating his motors Joe could no longer force the ship to descend.

"Dropped all the weight out of her," he said cheerfully. "Must now let gas escape. That's merely a question of operating the escape valves. See, they're all linked up to this lever."

He leaned over the engine, gripped a long handle and pulled upon it. It refused to move. It was firmly jammed, or rather, the linked mechanism beyond it was firmly frozen.

"Annoying," he exclaimed, though Dick could have sworn that an anxious expression crossed his face. "Try again."

He made several more attempts, but without success. Dick helped him without avail. Even the lusty Hawkins and Hurst together could produce no effect, while the screws now thrashing the thin air in an endeavour to force the ship downward made not the smallest difference to the height of the mercury. And meanwhile the cold was even more intense. In spite of the oxygen cylinders men were gasping. Indeed, all of a sudden, when at the summit of their success the crew of the airship found themselves face to face with disaster. They had climbed to this great height. They could not descend. Death from cold and exhaustion threatened them. Yes, death. For already Larkin lay inert in the gallery, blue from intense cold, his mouthpiece strapped to his face. Mr. Andrew clutched at the doorpost, looking as if on the verge of unconsciousness, while both the Major and the Commander had the appearance of men more than half frozen. It looked indeed as if here, at this enormous altitude, within stone's throw of the summit of Mount Everest, the voyage of the huge airship would be ended, and with it the lives of all aboard.

CHAPTER XVII

A Desperate Situation

A terrible five minutes followed the discovery that Joe Gresson had made, a period short enough as a general rule, but seeming almost unending under the tragic circumstances. For the great airship lay helpless in the air, turning slowly as if on a pivot, and dangling a thousand feet above that tiny Union Jack which marked the summit of Mount Everest. Then a breeze caught her and wafted her to one side, so that Dick, looking desperately from the window of the engine-room, could gaze down into India. But a swirling current from the opposite direction gripped her a moment later, swayed the ship which was rocking like a vessel at sea, drove her round and launched her northward, till the opposite slopes of the Himalayas came into view.

"Tibet—the road to Lhasa, the forbidden city," Dick told himself. "And that shining streak away over there must be the Brahmaputra. What's to be done? This is a nasty sort of hole in which to find ourselves. And I don't like the look of some of our friends. Larkin is as blue as blue, while Mr. Andrew don't appear much better. Where's Alec?"

That young gentleman was stretched full length at the foot of the ladder leading from the engine-room, and at once Dick stepped toward him and secured the mouthpiece of his oxygen apparatus to his face.

"Can't do more," he thought. "Wish I could. George! Joe don't seem too bright. He's as green as grass, and, 'pon my word, he's falling."

He was just in time to catch the leader of this attempt upon a world's record and snatch him from the engines. Catching him in his arms he sat him down with his back against the wall of the engine-room. Then, quite by the merest chance, he caught a glimpse of his own reflection in that same square piece of looking-glass.

"My hat! Dusky as a nigger! But never felt better in my life. Oxygen seems to agree with me, but not with my lovely complexion. Now, what the blazes is a fellow to do? This is a corker."

It was worse than that, for not only was the ship in danger of destruction, but without a doubt were her position at that altitude maintained, every soul aboard would be asphyxiated or frozen to death. Dick cast his eye at the barometer.

"Twenty-nine thousand feet. Dead level with the summit of the mountain," he reflected. "And ain't she rolling, just?"

That, too, was an obvious fact; for, relieved of the weight of the water which had filled her tanks, and which, like the engines, were disposed at the very lowest point possible, the ship now appeared to be a trifle top-heavy. In any case, she careened badly, swaying from side to side, till her decks presented steep slopes down which the figures of helpless members of her crew slithered. Yes, it was an ugly and distressing sight, for that loss of weight, and the fact that her elevating screws would not grip the air, had made the ship unstable in a fore-and-aft direction. To Dick's horror she began a new series of movements. The gust outside freshened of a sudden, just as gales do spring up at the height at which they floated, and at once the giant machine was swung round as if she were a top. Then she rolled heavily, till it was only by clutching at the rails about the motors that he escaped being thrown into them. Later she suddenly careened in the opposite direction, and hoisting her stern on high, projected her crew down the whole length of the gallery so that they were brought up against a distant bulkhead. Nor was that the last of her disconcerting gyrations. The breeze freshened again, till within a minute a whirlwind was singing and screaming outside. It caught the framework of the ship as if she were a leaf, and now that she was lying out of the horizontal, and Joe's curious design was therefore almost inoperable, it swung her to one side and sent her heading madly for the snow and rock-strewn summit of the mountain. Dick held his small remaining breath as the vessel bore down upon that rocky peak, and shivered as she missed it by a narrow margin.

"A miss is as good as a mile, sir," someone shouted in his ear, as if the person were a mile away. But Dick was deaf. His ears were singing and roaring, and when he let go his hold of the engine rails he was dreadfully giddy. But, in spite of his deafness, he was able to note two other things. The engine had stopped completely, no doubt because of the position of the ship, the fuel supply having been entirely cut off. Then Hawkins was beside him, not the Hawkins of old, with a clean-shaven face tanned to mahogany by exposure, but a sailor whose skin was of leaden hue, whose eyes were sunken and had lost their sparkle, whose shoulders stooped as if he found it hard to keep upright In other respects it was the old Hawkins.

"Orders, sir!" he bawled, whipping his mouthpiece aside for the moment. "This here's a fine old mess!"

"Must get those gas valves open and the engines started again. Here," Dick gasped in answer. "Make this cylinder fast to my shoulders. It's too loose for my liking. There's a bit of rope yonder. That'll do it. Quick!"

He had no breath for more; but Hawkins seemed to see his meaning in an instant, and soon had the cylinder of oxygen more secure on Dick's back. Then, with a dexterity which even this critical situation could not mar, he secured his own cylinder in similar manner. Dick gripped a hammer. Hawkins took a huge spanner.

"Now," said our hero. "We must get to the upper deck. Then start in the centre, each going in opposite directions. Force open every other valve. Even if you have to smash them to pieces you must contrive to open them. Come—no time to be lost."

His orders were given in short gasping spurts. But Hawkins understood and nodded. Then they clambered over the bodies of their comrades, won their way up the engine ladder, and raced as fast as they could along the gallery. Not that the pace was great, for each step seemed to be an effort. They gained the liftway, and stared upward.

"No motor working. Must climb," Dick managed to gasp. "Up we go."

He felt as if his heart would burst long before he gained the upper deck. That organ was indeed thudding heavily against his ribs, while the veins in his forehead, on his hands and face, were distended and purple. But there was pluck and determination to drive Mr. Dicky Hamshaw onward, while Hawkins was not the man to be beaten by an officer or to leave one in the lurch. And so, after a struggle which cost them dear, they won their way to the summit of that tiresome and never-ending ladder. A minute later, almost too fatigued to deliver a blow, they attacked the valves affixed to each of the many gas chambers, beginning with those at the centre.

"Frozen hard as rocks. Deck covered with frost and ice. The weight'll be an advantage. But how are we to get these valves open?"

It was difficult enough under that white covering to detect their presence, though, fortunately for all, both Dick and Hawkins had more than once examined the valves. Now they set to work with hammer and spanner, breaking away the coating of ice, and smashing the firm joint which the intense cold had formed round each seating. It was with a shrill, half-stifled cry of delight that Dick contrived to free the first of the valves.

"Wide open. Can smell the gas coming out," he told himself. "That'll fix her. A few more will do the trick. Wish to goodness she'd remain level."

Something shot past him at terrible speed, and brought up hard against the rail at the edge of the deck. It was Hawkins, pitched from his feet by a sudden lurch of the vessel, and saved from a dreadful dive into space by the rail against which he had cannoned. A second later his unconscious figure came hurtling back, and but for the grip Dick managed to fasten on him he would have shot over the side of the vessel in the opposite direction.

"Must go on alone, that's all," Dick told himself stubbornly. "Big job, but got to be done. I'll place Hawkins in the entrance to the liftway."

He dragged the unconscious figure after him, helped not a little by a sudden tilting of the vessel. Then, stowing him in a corner from which he hoped he would not be dislodged, he raced along the deck again, himself took a header as the deck sloped steeply, caught a stanchion to which one of the wireless supports was attached, and a moment later was beating frantically at a second valve. In ten busy minutes, in fact, he contrived to release no fewer than five, and had the satisfaction of smelling the gas which at once poured out of them. More than that, a glance at the summit of the mountain showed him that the ship had fallen already. She was resting just a trifle above that wet, cold blanket which enveloped the central part.

"And a chap feels less blown than before," thought Dick. "That's satisfactory. Now for the engines. Must get 'em going and way on the ship, for this gale is playing the dickens with her."

It was a way of expressing his meaning, and indeed, even now that he had accomplished his purpose so bravely, his work was likely enough to be defeated by outside influences. For the whirlwind had not abated, and three times while Dick worked had the ship been swept past the slopes of Mount Everest, at such speed that, had she struck, she would have crumpled up like a concertina. Now she was caught again, spun round like a top, sent twirling from the mountain, only to be driven back again till her bows actually collided with one of the slopes. But it was only a glancing blow, and the snow happened to be both soft and deep. Shivering, therefore, at the shock, she shook herself free, and shot off into the open.

As for Dick, he raced to the deck below, his respiration already decidedly easier. Stepping over the still unconscious figures of his comrades, he gained the engine-room and tackled the task of starting the engines.

"Must get way on her somehow," he told himself. "Let's see—engines stopped probably because of her pitching. You couldn't expect fuel to reach the carburettor when she was standing on her head. Wait a bit, I'll cure all that if once I can get those elevating screws going. How's that? Joe always turns that tap to make sure his fuel's flowing. There's paraffin there right enough. Now, will she start?"

He switched on the current from the starting batteries, setting the electric starting motor in action, and then moved the clutch lever, which threw this motor into engagement with the flywheel of the engine. Nothing resulted. Not a cylinder fired. There was not so much as the suspicion of an explosion. One might have expected Dicky Hamshaw to be flabbergasted and beaten by such a happening, and as a matter of fact he leaned against the engine rail and gazed hopelessly at the apparatus before him. Then he had a brilliant inspiration. They didn't often come his way, we confess. He was far too harum-scarum for flights of fancy or for patient investigation. But in his heart of hearts Dicky was quite the mechanic. As we have intimated, he hoped one of these days to be selected for submarine service, or for the naval flying school. Therefore it happened that facts and peculiarities about the mechanism of this huge airship had not escaped his notice. Indeed, they had attracted his attention and positively fascinated him. It happened, consequently, that he was well acquainted with the carburation.

"Got it!" he cried. "It ain't a case of a simple carburettor. In this case the fuel enters the carburettor, and to start the engines if cold, or when they've been rested for long, one has to fill the gasometer with gas. That's the ticket! I've seen Joe and the engineer making preparations. We just operate this geared fan, and force air through the carburettor. There it goes, and the gasometer's rising. I'll give it a little more and then try her. Afterwards the running engine automatically pumps air. Now. How's that for done it?"

He switched the current in again, and moved over the clutch lever of the starter. The engine spun round immediately, spluttered in one or more cylinders, backfired once, thereby throwing the starter out of action; and then, when Dick again pushed his lever over relentlessly, the engine fired, and went off at a speed that made the whole engine-room tremble.

Dick shouted. Or rather, he tried to shout, the mouthpiece and his own want of breath preventing much noise coming from him. His eyes sparkled. He actually danced, and then became very solemn. For after all the fate of his comrades and of this fine vessel still rested entirely in his two hands. Yes, entirely, for a glance along the gallery told him that not one of his friends was yet conscious.

"Set her going then. Wait—what's the elevation? Jingo—we've come down to twenty-two thousand feet. That's something; wish we weren't in this cloud though. It makes a fellow wonder which way he ought to steer. Ah, there go the elevator fans!"

He could hear them whirring, and looked up at the barometer. The ship was rising, and with a gesture of disgust he realized that he had set the elevators working in the wrong direction. Instantly he reversed them, and presently had the satisfaction of seeing that the vessel was descending. Then he started up the ship's propeller, and soon had her moving, but very cautiously; for the damp, white cloud hid everything. Indeed, he was within an ace of wrecking the vessel, and, but for a quick twist of his wrist and a sudden acceleration of his motor, he would have driven the airship against a rocky headland standing out from the mountain.

"A miss is as good as a mile," he grinned. "Oh, shan't I be jolly glad to get away from this Mount Everest? Not much!—not 'alf, as Hawkins would say. Anyway, that peep gave me the right direction. Now, I'll take her along at speed, and get clear out into the open."

"Eighteen thousand feet—what's happened?" the question came in weak tones from Joe Gresson. Dick nodded cheerfully at him. He had discarded his oxygen mouthpiece, though the cylinder was still slung to his back.

"You sit still," he shouted. "We're falling, and mighty quick now, I fancy. Stay there till you're feeling yourself, and then come and advise me. We're over on the Tibet side of the Himalayas, and I'm looking out for a landing."

One by one, as the ship descended, the unconscious crew regained their senses, and for the most part looked about them in the most bewildered manner. For they were piled indiscriminately about the gallery, crew and passengers mixed together inextricably. Nor had they entirely escaped damage, as might well be expected. Some were severely bruised by the manner in which the sloping deck had caused them to slide, while Larkin was quite angry. He was fully conscious, and had just dragged himself from beneath the somewhat ponderous frame of the grinning Hurst. His nose was bleeding, as was the case with many of them; but that was not the cause of his agitation. One eye was closed, and the cheek beneath beautifully swollen.

"Of all the mean tricks," he was growling, "of all the mean, dirty games to play on a fellow when he's fallen, this is it. What do yer mean, young feller?"

But Hurst still grinned placidly at him. He was, to speak the truth, barely more than semi-conscious. A delicious feeling of fatigue assailed him, and had he had his own way he would have lain there in the passage and fallen into a sound slumber. That is, as soon as he had finished with Private Larkin. He was sleepily admiring that hero at this precise moment. He didn't exactly know how it was that he and the noble Larkin had become so mixed up together. Perhaps they had been for a spree ashore, and here was the consequence. But this his addled senses could take in, and it afforded him huge amusement—Private Larkin's none too handsome face was swollen to the proportions of a pumpkin, and the distension beneath that eye was as green as possible. There remained but one orb then, a staring orb, which had fastened itself indignantly, even threateningly, upon the sailor, moreover Hurst could tell that it was the one that habitually squinted. What wonder that he could not take the angry Larkin seriously?

174

"If you don't look handsome, not 'arf," he interjected. "Jest you get movin' on yer two flat feet and take a squint at yer phiz in that there mirror. You'll see a sight there that'll scare yer. No, no! I ain't asking you to look away in the corner. The mirror's there, above yer ugly head, and lor, you just take care that you don't go right off and crack it."

The situation was becoming a little strained before the Major pulled himself together, helped the Commander to his feet, and separated the two who had been speaking. Then they went to Mr. Andrew, whom they found soundly asleep, breathing as gently as any child, and undoubtedly unharmed by his late experience. Joe, too, was on his feet now, while Hawkins had put in an appearance.

"I'm owin' one more to Mr. Dicky," he told his chums, as they clustered in the gallery and eagerly discussed this late happening. "I just did the most almighty skid you could dream of. I can remember the ship rolling and sending me quick right across to the railing. Then I slid back again, and I can feel now the grip that Mr. Dicky got of my collar. After that there was darkness, till of a sudden my eyes opened. Bless you, lads, that there Mr. Midshipman Hamshaw has saved the whole sitivation; by hisself he's done it. And if it hadn't ha' been for him, and his pluck, and what not, there wouldn't be a airship now, no, nor any of us covies. Larkin, you ain't called for to speak. I know what you was thinkin' of saying. That Mr. Alec'd have been as good. I agrees, so the wind's taken completely out of your sails, and there ain't no call for an argument. But though he'd have had the pluck, he didn't have the senses. It takes a hard chap to stand what we've been through. Understand me, lad; it takes a sailor—now, just you stop jawin'."

It was merely a passing pleasantry between the two services, and the pugnacious Larkin perforce closed his lips and sulked for a moment. But it was only for a moment; for within a little while the crew were gathered in their own quarters partaking of their evening meal, and so preparing themselves for the hard work now expected of them. In the saloon Mr. Andrew and his friends gathered about the table, while Sergeant Evans waited upon them as if nothing out of the ordinary had happened, and as if it were a mere uninteresting item in the day's performance that he himself, but two hours earlier, had been stretched senseless in his own pantry, his face a dusky blue, his nose and ears bleeding, and his pulse beating at a pace which would have alarmed the most hopeful of practitioners.

But if he said nothing, Andrew and Joe and their guests were full of praise of Dicky Hamshaw.

"'Pon my word, I'm proud of him as a brother officer," cried the Commander cordially. "Tell us all about it, Dick."

The bashful midshipman recounted what had happened, and how he had overcome the many difficulties which had, one after another, faced him.

"It looked like being all up at one time, sir," he said. "The ship was turning on her nose, making it difficult to get about and reach the valves. I'm afraid we've done a heap of damage. You see, one hadn't time to waste, nor breathe either. And so I laid in at the heads of the valves with my hammer, careless, so long as I could get them to open."

"And rightly so," said Joe warmly. "As to damage, it will be trifling, and of no consequence; for we carry aboard spare valves and seatings, and they can be fitted in a few hours. That reminds me to speak of our movements. We are now on the Tibetan side of the Himalayas, resting a couple of hundred yards above the ground, and in a totally uninhabited part. It will be necessary to refit, to take in water, and to set our gas-producer plant going. Now, why not a trip to Lhasa in the meanwhile? A trip to the forbidden city, there to call upon the Chinese Governor? It would be interesting and instructive both to the Llama priests and to ourselves, and it will be something to have accomplished."

Such a journey was a mere nothing to the aeroplane carried upon the broad deck of the airship, and as Joe required only a few of his staff to effect repairs and restock the tanks, quite a large party left the ship on the following morning. Nor is there much of startling moment to record as to their doings. For the city of Lhasa to-day is inhabited by beings holding different views from those living there but a few years ago. Then the place was sacred, travellers were forbidden to enter, while the very effort of reaching the city was more than enough to dissuade the average person from making the attempt. Those upland plains about the city are, in fact, a wilderness of inhospitality in winter weather, while the milder months are all too short for an expedition which entails going afoot, and demands strenuous exertions from the very beginning. But a welcome now awaits the stranger. The Llamas seek for outside guidance, and are no longer content with an existence unbroken by the smallest distraction. The European who cares to undertake that journey may expect some kindness, while Tibet to-day has sent her sons to Europe, there to gather something of Western learning and customs. It followed, therefore, that Dick and Alec had a merry and entertaining visit to record, and enjoyed the aeroplane trip immensely. Then they rejoined the airship, now complete and ready, and that same evening the vessel once more crossed the Himalayas and steered a course for Burma.

"Where we take in oil for our engines," said Joe. "Later, we will follow the red route down the length of Burma till we reach the Malay Peninsula. Afterwards there is Borneo to be visited, and then New Guinea and Australasia."

The delights of such a course need no elaborate description, and without a doubt they were put in the shade by constant admiration for the ship's behaviour. For it was not always fair weather, and that gale of wind about the summit of the mountain they had so recently left was as nothing to a storm experienced off Sumatra. Then, indeed, the true working of Joe Gresson's design was experienced and appreciated.

"I could not have believed it," the Commander shouted in the Major's ear as they stood on the upper deck clutching the railings. "A Zeppelin now in a gale such as this is would be torn to pieces."

"Smashed; her sides driven in without a doubt. Then she could never face a storm of this fierceness. She would be driven miles out of her course, if she were not wrecked instantly."

"While we merely head up to the gale and lay to, hardly even rolling."

Thanks to the water ballast which she had again taken aboard, the airship was wonderfully steady, while her capacity to withstand a gale was proved to the utmost. Even when turned broadside on to the wind the ship maintained her position, the sweeping aerial currents being cut asunder by those lateral keels, and passing harmlessly above and beneath her. But then she was possessed of those cross air-shafts in which powerful screws worked, a feature absent entirely from the Zeppelin.

It was a week later when the passengers on the deck above sighted the huge island of New Guinea, that inhospitable region, a great part of which is still unknown to white men, where jungles and swamps are inhabited by the fiercest of cannibals. And here it was that Dick and his friends came in for another adventure.

CHAPTER XVIII

Off to New Guinea

A purple sea from which the sun's rays flashed upward with all the iridescent colours of the rainbow; a gorgeous blue sky without a single fleecy cloud; and a medley of brilliant islets marked the course of the great airship as she stemmed her way towards the wild, uncivilized island of New Guinea. Stepping the broad, long deck above, and enjoying to the full a climate as balmy as that of Old England in the heyday of summer, one could peep down upon golden dots rising here and there in the distance, dots which grew from a purple haze and became more yellow, till at length the deep green of luxuriant vegetation began to merge with the yellow, till single objects became distinguishable, and until one could trace long lengths of smooth sand upon which white breakers roared, wide-sweeping coral boundaries of silent lagoons that appeared by their wealth of colour to be of vast depth, and groves of waving palms that invited those aboard the ship to halt, to descend and rest awhile amidst surroundings the peace and beauty of which none had ever seen an equal. But sometimes the picture was spoiled, for dark objects dotted the sands. Men raced out from amidst the trees, and puny bows sent equally puny arrows soaring upward in a feeble attempt to reach the leviathan overhead.

"Plucky of 'em," remarked the Major. "No doubt those islanders take us for some supernatural object, and are really shaking in their shoes."

"Shoes!" interjected the Commander, with lifting eyebrows, lowering the glasses which he had held for some while glued to his eyes. "I don't see anything to convince me that the people we have seen make use of such civilized attachments. Indeed, their clothing is chiefly remarkable by its absence. My dear Major, we are passing above islets seldom visited by white men, some hardly visited even by wandering Chinese or Dyaks. Those are nature's children we see below, many of them without a doubt wild heathen cannibals."

"Ugh! Supposing we were to fall," laughed Dick.

"Then we should be promptly enshrined as gods," grinned the Major. "I don't say, Dicky, my lad, that we should be allowed to keep this mortal state. The chances are that we should be killed out of hand and skilfully stuffed. Pleasant ending, eh? First the worthy Mr. Carl Reitberg, sportsman and magnate, does his best to blow us to pieces; then Joe makes a vain attempt to asphyxiate us all, or to plunge us for ever in an atmosphere likely to act upon us as would a refrigerator. Finally, there come these natives and a stuffing process."

"For them, sir, yes," laughed Dick. "If they're cannibals, and we're good eating, then there would be stuffing for them with a vengeance."

Sometimes fleets of canoes emerged from groves of palms or were launched from placid lagoons, while their crews paddled madly in the vain attempt to keep pace with the airship. And so as to encourage them, and because there was no danger of colliding with high ground, Joe set the ship at a lower altitude, till she was but a hundred feet above the water.

But such close acquaintance with this strange monster was too much for the nerves of the natives. It had been very well for them to discharge arrows at her when a thousand feet up. But now, when her vast proportions were more apparent, they took fright, and without a single exception bolted for cover, many of the passengers in the dug-outs diving overboard and swimming beneath water.

"Not that it'd help 'em much," the Major remarked. "With a rifle one could pick every one of them off as he came to the surface to breathe. Look! Did ever you see such clear water?"

It was positively fascinating to gaze downward and watch fish darting here and there, to follow the agonized movements of the natives who had taken to the water. For at that elevation the bed of the ocean was laid out like a map, a beautiful golden map, crossed by dull-red bands of coral often enough, marked by upheavals of rock in some places, and once, close to a rocky headland, showing on the sand at its foot the outline of a lost vessel.

"What a ship for treasure hunting!" cried the Commander. "No need to sound and dredge and send divers down in order to discover a wreck. There it would lie, beneath one's eyes, and one could set to work immediately. Joe, tell us like a good fellow, how far can a man see into other waters?"

"A hundred feet, sometimes more. In the Yellow Sea not nearly as much. But let us take the English Channel. I have carried out experiments there, and have detected the presence of a wreck in quite deep water. As to a submarine, from a ship such as this is one could drop a heavy mine over a submerged vessel without difficulty and without much danger to oneself."

"So that the use of submarines will become limited once such ships as this are built in numbers," ventured the Major.

"Exactly—or, rather, the risks to the crews of submarines will become even greater."

"Which leads one to ask where all this modern invention will end? As applied to engines of destruction, it has provided means whereby men may be massacred by the hundred; for modern guns and modern shell are capable of terrible destruction at distances never dreamed of but fifty years ago. Ships may be caused to founder not only by the direct gunfire of an opponent, or by torpedoes launched at her, but by the aid of submarines, the presence of which may not have been suspected. Add the modern rifle, with its high-muzzle velocity and consequent flat trajectory, and its vastly increased range, whereby troops may be slain at a distance of two miles from the firing point. Then, with wireless apparatus to enable one general to co-ordinate his movements with another, aeroplanes to spy out the land and report the presence of unsuspected troops, and lastly, airships such as this one, capable of almost anything—why, sir, where are we coming to?"

"Were I to say to a stage where nations agreed to limit armaments, to clear up their disputes by means of arbitration, and merely to keep sufficient fighting forces to collectively police the world, I should be considered a madman," said Joe deliberately. "But that era is coming. Not perhaps in our time, Major; but come it must, and not precisely for the reason that modern invention has made war more terrible than ever. No, sir. It is because ships such as this one, ships which plough the sea also, and better means of intercommunication amongst the nations, are making friends of the working people. Wars are made too often in the Cabinets and Foreign Offices of the nations. Then men are dragged from their homes to fight men with whom they would otherwise willingly have been friendly. They are sacrificed for an idea perhaps, for a petty dispute which the people will in future leave with every confidence to such tribunals as I have mentioned. Then, sir, there will be no war, save against savages who stand in the way of civilization."

Such a time may come—who knows? and it would be well for the peoples of the world undoubtedly. It is said that without war, without the strenuous effort to keep in ready condition, a nation suffers in morale, deteriorates, in fact. And one cannot but admit the value of the ordered life, the discipline, and the method young men encounter when enlisted in either army or navy. Still efficiency for war is not the only means of taxing the efforts of a nation. Peace demands its strenuous times, and commerce, the arts and professions, a thousand ways of living call for vigour, for brain and muscle, for all that is good in men, and thus keep up the morale of a nation. However, Joe and his friends were not the ones to embark upon such a discussion when sailing above such a delightfully purple sea as that lying beneath them. They hung over the rail of the vessel, eyeing each tiny islet as they slipped past it, and finally gave a shout of delight as New Guinea hove into sight in the distance.

"We'll mount a little so as to obtain a finer view," said Joe. "Then we can select a landing-place. It's already evening, so that I fancy it will be dark before we arrive over the island."

The tropical night found the ship floating directly over the island, across a great breadth of which she had rushed during the latter part of the evening. Then, having crossed a range of mountains, some of the peaks of which were of great height, Joe switched on one of his huge lanterns. Instantly the land beneath was illuminated, and as the vessel descended it was seen that she was directly above a huge plateau, which ran upward to the south, there to join with the foot-hills of the range they had just crossed, while in the opposite direction it fell away of a sudden, descending abruptly into a wide valley in which ran a roaring torrent. For the rest there was jungle everywhere, impenetrable jungle, save in a few places, one of which seemed exactly to meet the needs of the voyagers. At ten o'clock precisely the great airship grounded, settled upon her powerful spring arms, and then became stationary.

"And here we shall be able to overlook the engines," declared Joe as they chatted after supper. "Not that the motors want any particular attention. Still, a rest will do them no harm, while every engineer loves to make sure that everything is running as it should do. Therefore, to-morrow, gentlemen, the island is at your service, while I shall be seeing to the matters I have mentioned."

To say that the island of New Guinea was at the service of his passengers was to put the matter amusingly. For New Guinea happens to be an enormous place, and without an airship the crossing of it is almost an impossibility. Still, the neighbouring jungle and that broiling torrent down below offered many attractions, so that, when the morning dawned, it found Dick and Alec already dressed for an expedition and armed with shot guns, while the Major, the Commander, and Andrew stepped from their cabins dressed in rough shooting clothes, the latter with a rod in his hand, while the others bore sporting rifles. Larkin shuffled close behind the Major, bearing a basket of provisions, while Hawkins and Hurst had donned their service gaiters, and each with a haversack over his shoulder intimated that he proposed to keep watch and ward over Dick and Alec.

Then all trudged from the gallery into the open, sought for a path through the jungle, and finding none, proceeded to force their way through the matted trees and trailing creepers as best they could.

"We've agreed to make for the edge of the plateau," said the Commander. "Then Mr. Andrew can make his way down to the river, while we can follow or stay above—whichever appeals most to us. How nice it is to feel solid earth once more beneath one's feet."

"And smell the vegetation," chimed in the Major. "Not that jungles are always very savoury. Down below there, in the rainy season, I expect there's a miasma, and a European would quickly suffer from fever. Now, here we are at the edge. *Au revoir*, Mr. Andrew!"

They watched the white-haired but active Colonial descend the steep slope of the ridge, and saw him halt at the side of the tumbling stream to adjust his rod and prepare his line. Then the shooting party divided, Alec and Dick with the faithful Hurst and Hawkins striking off in one direction, while the Major and Commander, with the scowling Larkin, departed in another. And very soon rifle shots awoke the echoes, while our two young friends managed to bag half a dozen birds not at all unlike pheasants.

THE QUARTET SET OUT FOR THE AIRSHIP

"Do for the pot, and will come as a welcome change after frozen stuff," laughed Dick. "Wonder whether there are any alligators down in the river. If so I'd like to take a shot at 'em. Only we'd have to return for our rifles."

A close observation of the river revealed what all felt sure were the snouts of the beasts Dick had mentioned, while a number of log-like forms stretched on a mud bank were proclaimed by Alec to be undoubtedly the animal he was in search of.

"Then back we go to the ship," said Dick with his usual impetuosity, leading the return journey instantly. "Suppose there ain't no difficulty about finding her? Eh? It'd be mighty awkward if we lost our bearings, and you've to remember that she ain't like an ordinary ship. You can see right through her, and that don't help much when trying to locate a thing like that in these jungles."

As a matter of fact the task of returning proved extremely difficult, for whereas the path they had at first followed led them through a number of more or less open spaces, they now found that they had plunged into the densest of jungle. It called at once for the use of their knives, and even with their help progress was slow to the point of exasperation. Some minutes later they broke their way into a little clearing, across the roof of which trailed innumerable creepers, decked with wonderful blossoms, while the trees were filled with screeching parakeets, and, in the shaded parts, by myriad droning insects. Then there was a curious crisp, almost musical sound, a twang in fact, followed by the dull thud of a light object striking the trunk of a tree. Dick looked up. An arrow was quivering just above his head, and as he looked a second sped by him.

"My hat!" he shouted, thoroughly astonished. "See that! Arrows!"

"Niggers, sir!" cried Hawkins. "I catched a sight of one just through the trees. Best look for cover."

The words had hardly left his lips when Alec staggered backward and gripped the air helplessly. Dick seized him promptly and dragged him down behind a tree.

"Just keep your weather eye open there, Hawkins and Hurst," he sang out cheerily, "while I lay-to here and repair damages. Mr. Alec's hit. Ah! It's not much. He's conscious and says it's nothing. Now, old boy, let's see what has happened. Ah! Gone clean through the fleshy part of the arm and still transfixing the limb. Right! Break it off short and pull the piece out. Now, let's have a look at the head."

He held the end of the broken arrow up and inspected it carefully. It was armed with a piece of pointed metal of a yellowish-green colour.

184

"Copper," Dick announced. "A little corroded, but I'll swear it ain't poisoned. Anyway, to make sure, I'll suck the wound. That'll make a fellow feel easier."

Without hesitation he slit the sleeve right up above the elbow, using the sharp edge of the arrowhead for the purpose, and exposed the wounds and sucked them both in succession.

"Talk about cannibals," he grinned. "My—Alec, you taste too salt for anything! Feel better? Oh! Feel absolutely fit! Then let's see what's happening?"

Half a dozen arrows had meanwhile crossed the clearing, though but for the single native whom Hawkins declared he had seen, not another had put in an appearance, nor had there been so much as a sound from them. Merely the musical twanging of bows as the arrows were released.

"Put a charge into 'em, sir!" cried Hurst. "Them small shot'll soon clear 'em away. You'll hear the varmints holler."

It seemed to be a reasonable course to take, and at once Dick lifted his gun and sent the contents of two cartridges swishing amongst the trees. Not a cry followed, but the curious twang of bows was not again heard, while no more arrows flew across the clearing.

"Then we'll push on toward the ship. Now, Alec, feel fit for it?"

"Perfectly—never more so. I admit that at first the shock of the wound and the pain rather made me feel funny. But I'm right now. Go ahead. Sorry to have been such a bother."

In single file now, Dick leading, Able Seaman Hawkins immediately behind, and Hurst in rear, armed with his clasp knife, the quartet struck out for the airship. Once Dick imagined that he caught a fleeting glimpse of a native to his right. Then he thought he must have been mistaken. A minute later the wireless mast at the top of the airship met his view, with its tiny fluttering Union Jack attached to it.

"Hooray!" he shouted. "There at last. I'm beginning to wonder what has happened to the other three who set out with us."

He turned to speak to his comrades, took another step forward, and then disappeared into an enormous pit dug for that purpose. There he was received by a dozen or more active natives, and before Mr. Dicky Hamshaw could quite recover his senses, he was flat on his face on the sticky clay, his arms drawn up behind him, while the dozen natives already mentioned were busily engaged in winding green creepers about his ankles and knees and wrists and elbows. Not a sound escaped them. Not a blow was delivered, though Dick struggled fiercely. As to his companions he had no knowledge of them. They gave no shout, as one might have expected had they been attacked; there was not so much as a call to show that they had missed their leader. Only the birds still chattered above, while one could dimly hear the roar of the stream tumbling down the valley. Perhaps it was three minutes later when Dick, trussed like a fowl, was caught in the arms of a number of stalwart natives and pitched upward, so that he landed in the jungle. Then his weight was shouldered, and thereafter he only knew that he was being carried through the jungle, that often enough his body was bruised against overhanging branches, and that the most noticeable thing about his captors was their surprisingly strong odour. For the rest, they were tall, muscular men, exceedingly well made, and boasting of an abundance of hair, a regular mop, in fact, which covered their heads.

"Real beauties," thought Dick, still rather breathless after such a surprise, but not in the least downhearted. "Handsome chaps, without a doubt, but, my word, they do just smell a trifle. Seems to me that they must anoint their bodies with something composed of dead fish and glue. Ugh! 'Pon my word, it makes me feel quite giddy."

He tried wagging his head and calling to his captors. But not one took the smallest notice of him. Then Dicky made a second attempt, shouting loudly. At once a huge native who was leading this silent party turned, scowled at the midshipman, and prodded him with the blunt end of a spear.

"And looks as if he'd use the business end next time," thought Dick, eyeing the ruffian. "This is a turn up. And I wonder what's happened to Alec and the others?"

But he was destined to be kept waiting, for those silent natives still forged their way through the jungle, and when they had been moving for some time and had unceremoniously pitched Dick to the ground as if he were a bundle, it was only for a momentary rest. Another batch of men who till then had been hidden in the jungle picked him up upon their shoulders, and the same solitary dispiriting march was continued. At length, however, it came to an end. The jungle became thinner, and the trees more scattered. Then they suddenly emerged into the open and entered a village built by the bank of a river. Natives swarmed from the low-built huts, women, men, and children, and danced about the captive. Their chatter and their cries came as a positive relief to our hero after the deathly silence of the others. He was carried across to one of the huts, the door was opened, and a moment later Dick was sent rolling.

"And jolly nearly broke my arm in the fall," he growled, beginning to get angry. "A nice way in which to treat a captive, to treat a fellow they may be thinking of devouring."

That was Dicky Hamshaw all over. He couldn't help a joke, even at his own expense, and there he was actually smiling in the darkness of this native cabin. But comfort is a great thing, even in the midst of adversity, and at once he rolled over and managed to prop himself upright against one of the plaited walls.

"Wish they hadn't been so free with these creepers," he grumbled. "A chap can't move, while my hands and feet feel absolutely numb. Now, how does a fellow tackle an ugly job such as this is? Of course, if there was another here, Alec, for instance, or that beggar Hawkins, we'd try our hands at gnawing. No, not hands; teeth, of course. But I ain't an acrobat, and can't twist my head round to get at this binding."

He could hardly move, in fact, and as the minutes passed the numbness of the hands and feet became more apparent. It was clear that if he were to make no effort now he would not have the strength to do so if he delayed much longer. And for that reason, and because the midshipman was a good plucked 'un, as Hawkins had often and often asserted, he managed to get to his knees, though they were lashed together, and slowly jerked himself across the floor of the hut. The movement brought him to the opposite wall, close to the part where the door was situated, and there he discovered a crevice through which he could look.

"The village street, and niggers hopping about everywhere. Still excited at their capture," thought Dick. "Hallo! A procession. More parcels being carried. Why, if that isn't Mr. Andrew!"

It was that gentleman without a shadow of doubt, with the Commander and the Major following. He recognized Larkin with the greatest ease, for that individual's face was gnarled and twisted, and his squinting eyes threatened all and sundry. Hawkins and Hurst followed, borne on the shoulders of eight natives, while Alec's trussed figure brought up the rear.

"All prisoners! What a turn-up for the airship and for Joe!" thought Dick. "There go some of 'em into a hut. Yes, Mr. Andrew and Hawkins and Hurst into one. Now, Larkin and the two officers into another. Jove! They're carting Alec in my direction. Better get back where I was thrown."

That was easily done by the simple process of rolling, so that when the door of the hut was thrown open his captors discovered Dick lying on his face, as straight as a plank, seemingly unconscious. There was a thud as Alec's frame landed, the door went to with a creaking bang, and again there was silence.

Dick rolled across to his friend at once, struggled to his knees, and then manœuvred so as to be able to bend over him.

"You lie still," he whispered. "I'm going to try my grinders on those lashings of yours. My! Ain't this a turn-up?"

He did not wait for an answer, but sprawled as best he could across Alec's body. Then wriggling to the best of his ability, he managed to get his mouth down to the creeper lashing which secured Alec's wrists and elbows. Nor was the task he had set himself so very difficult, for those creepers were fresh and green, and only a bare half-inch in diameter. The teeth, too, which played upon them were strong and healthy, with splendid cutting edges. So that within ten minutes the hands were free, while a second effort cut through the lashings holding the elbows.

"Buck up and get feeling into your hands," gasped Dick. "I know how they are, as numb as possible. But be quick with it! Then dive into my pocket. I put that arrowhead there, and know those ruffians haven't moved it. There! Rub your hands together. Feeling better, eh?"

Alec beat his hands together, and rubbed them vigorously. But in spite of that fully five minutes passed before he could use them. Then he dived into Dick's pocket, fished out the arrowhead, and soon had the lashings which bound the midshipman lying loose beside him. To cut his still remaining bonds was an easy matter, so that very soon both were free.

"And now comes the easiest part of the business," whispered Dick, his old assurance undiminished. "Alec, we've got to get a move-on this instant. See those two huts opposite? Well, our friends are lying there, and we're going to 'em. Now, come along, and look lively. If you meet a nigger give him what for instantly."

It was a simple matter to force a hole through the wattle walls of the hut, so that within a very few minutes the two had emerged from it on the side facing the river. Bending on all-fours, they crept away till they had passed three other huts, and had reached one of larger dimensions.

"Kind of courtroom, I expect," whispered the midshipman. "Anyway, it seems empty, for I've squinted in. It's the kind of crib to suit very well, and happens to be exactly opposite the huts in which they've put our comrades. Now, in we go. Who says we're grumbling?"

He was a splendid fellow to follow, and heartened Alec wonderfully. Indeed, the latter was almost enjoying the adventure. But care was needed, and dash into the bargain, while the hardest task of all remained before them.

"Easy enough to crawl about behind the village, and to hide up in this courthouse," said Dick, scratching his head. "But there's the main street to be crossed before we can join the others, and that street happens to be swarming with smelly natives."

No doubt it was no ordinary difficulty. But then Mr. Midshipman Hamshaw was not altogether an ordinary individual.

"Hang the danger and the bother of it!" he exclaimed testily. "There are the huts with our friends in 'em. Well, I ain't going to be kept here by a parcel of niggers."

CHAPTER XIX

Saved from the Natives

"They're getting ready for the entertainment. My word!" whispered Alec in his chum's ear, when the two had been secreted for some little while in the huge hut to which they had managed to gain admission. "Preparing for the ceremony, and a fine hullabaloo they're making about it."

"And propose to conduct matters with full rites and customs and ceremony. In fact, a full-dress parade," said Dick, smiling, though there was an anxious look about his eyes. "Full dress, Alec, not that there's much dress about these niggers. That's where the difficulty comes in."

"What difficulty? How? Don't follow."

"Well, if they were decent, civilized sort of savages they'd wear cloaks, wouldn't they? They'd cover themselves with something better than the plaited girdles they have about them. That's where we'd come in. We'd borrow a couple of their wretched blankets, smuggle ourselves across the way, and then—well, there you are."

"Wish we were. But crossing the street here is no easy matter. What are these wretches doing?"

"What I've said. Holding a full-dress parade. Making ready for a ceremonial. Preparing for dinner."

There was still an excited grin on the midshipman's lips. But he was by no means happy. Who could have been under the circumstances? for there he and Alec were, free for the moment to be sure, but separated from their friends, while the latter were bound hand and foot and imprisoned in the huts opposite. As to the natives by whom they had been captured, they were an ill-smelling, murderous-looking lot. Tall, and extremely athletic, their bodies covered with knotted muscles, they were now parading the street, coming past the courthouse in a body, led by three dreadful individuals who wore ugly masks, and to whose persons hung a hundred different items. To a clattering dirge played by some twenty musicians, a dirge that boasted of no traceable tune, the three natives in front were dancing wildly, extravagantly throwing their limbs about, twisting and writhing and foaming at the mouth.

"Hideous brutes. Men of mystery, I suppose," whispered Dick. "Medicine men, sorcerers, or whatever they call 'em. Look at the chaps behind with clubs in their hands, and the rest with bows and arrows and spears. This is a precious pickle!"

It was worse. It was a desperate situation in which to find themselves, and the trouble was that Dick and Alec, though burning to do something active, could see their way to do nothing.

"Couldn't reach the ship. Impossible," muttered the latter. "First thing, we don't know where she is. I couldn't find my way to her for a fortune. Then I'd be so long over the job that I'd arrive too late. Eh, Dick?"

"Got to work this little business out ourselves," came the answer. "You're right about the ship. Those beggars carried us a long way, for they walked very quickly. Besides, there ain't time, as you say. We've got to get a move-on ourselves, for, if I'm not mistaken, that band ain't working for nothing. Look at the village folks following. They turned out in force to see the fun."

And fun it must have been to those untutored savages, though to the prisoners it was an agony. For those three horrible medicine men halted opposite the hut in which Dick's friends had been incarcerated and began another dance, if possible more frenzied than the last. The band, too, made the most of the occasion, each instrumentalist beating his parchment-covered gourd, or his wooden native piano, as if he wished to outdo his comrades. Then stakes were brought, fresh cut from the jungle, their ends pointed, and to the sound of the instruments, to the wild yells of the natives and the dancing of those three wretches, they were driven into the ground, three in front of each hut, and two before that so recently occupied by Dick and Alec. Then firewood was brought by the women and children and laid close to them.

The two young fellows looked on at these preparations with sinking hearts, their spirits oozing in spite of their courage. For the reason for such gruesome preparations was obvious. Dick knew, Alec knew also, and explorers have declared it to be a fact beyond contradiction, that the natives of New Guinea are addicted to cannibilism. Horrible as the thought may be, yet there is proof positive to support this affirmation. And here were Alec and his friends faced with this desperate situation. No wonder that the young fellow had gone white to his lips, and that Dick's fists were clenched and his brows knitted.

"I'm not going to stay and look on any longer," he said all of a sudden. "I'm going higher up the street, where I shall make a dart across and so try to reach the other side. Coming? or staying? You haven't any need to take risks."

Alec blazed out instantly. He found the excuse for temper a positive relief, and though he answered little above a whisper his words were bitter ones and angry.

191

"Taking risks! Who's a right to take 'em more than I have? Who are you to talk about risks to me—to ask if I'm coming or funking?"

"Didn't say funking," snarled the middy.

"No. But you meant it. It was as good as saying it. I'm jiggered if I'll stand——
"

"Sorry," said Dick lamely. "Chap doesn't always think when he's speaking. I knew you were game. Only it's a desperate sort of thing to try, and I suggested the business."

"That's why I'll come, willingly," was the handsome answer. "There, shake hands on it, and let's move. But we want a weapon of some sort. Let's hunt round here."

The result of this effort was the discovery of a bundle of arrows, half a dozen formidable clubs, the blade of a spear, and an old cutlass.

"Showing they have had something to do with outside people," said Dick.

"It's rusty, but it'll do. Now, I'll take a couple of the clubs, and you bring as many as you can carry. We want 'em for the others. Now, out we go. If we're going to cross, it'll have to be pretty soon or never."

Never, one would have said, seeing that the narrow street was packed with individuals, with women coming and going, and with shrieking children. But the two young fellows were determined, and at once forced their way through the same opening by which they had entered. They were now on the river face of the village, directly behind the largest hut of all, with other dwellings extending to right and left of them. A few paces away there was a thin fringe of jungle, and then a broad river. Dick looked at it swiftly.

"Ground falls towards it," he whispered. "The trees, too, would help to hide us. Let's creep down to the water."

They were there in a few seconds, and found themselves treading a muddy bank, upon which lay a dozen or more dug-outs. Dick did not hesitate for a moment. He placed his clubs and the cutlass in one of the boats, the nearest to the water, signalled to Alec to do likewise, and then began to lift her. Alec helped him instantly, and together they carried it down the bank and floated it in the river.

"Step in," said Alec.

"Right! Got a paddle?"

"Yes—up stream; I saw something."

What it was that he had seen Alec did not venture to tell his comrade; together they struck their paddles into the water, and sent the boat running upstream.

"Keep her close in," whispered Dick. "What's this you noticed?"

"Water away to our left, at the top end of the village. I caught the reflection through the trees. It may be only a pond of sorts, or it may communicate with the river. If it does, they're diddled."

"Jingo, the very thing! If only we're so lucky. No—yes. I do believe there is a stream. Steady does it. Now, round with her head. Hooroo! We're in good luck now, and we'll be able to stir up those niggers. Yah! Listen to the brutes howling."

Fierce cries came from the village at this moment, and made them think that their own escape had been discovered. But it was not that which had aroused the natives. It was the production of one of their captives. One of the huts was opened, one of the lashed bundles lifted and dragged out, and then the door was shut firmly. It was Larkin who was brought into the light of day and sat upright. The lashings about his knees and feet were cut at once, while a couple of the warriors began to knead his limbs with the hard palms of their hands. No doubt they were merely restoring the circulation, and Larkin himself was by no means misled by their action.

"Hof all the smellin', ugly, dirty critters!" he exploded. "And what's this they're up to? Has if I didn't know as well as possible. Jest give me a chance one of these fine moments, and if I get at one of them three fuzzy-wuzzy dervishes, why, I'll make 'em fuzzy."

They dragged him to his feet at last, only to find that he could not yet support his weight. Then the massagers made a second attempt, while a few amiable individuals, seeing the helpless Larkin once more lifted, held the points of their spears beneath him, a gentle hint that he was to remain standing. A little later they bound him to one of the stumps driven into the ground, and commenced an impressive dance about him.

Meanwhile Dick and Alec had not been idle. A few strokes of their paddles had taken them from the main channel of the river, and soon they guessed, though they could not be sure of the fact, that this stream enclosed the village, and discharged itself into the river again somewhere lower.

"Of course, I remember now. The fellows who were carrying me waded through water," said Dick. "That proves it. Let's get ahead, for that'll take us directly behind the spot we're aiming for. Then we'll creep through the jungle."

Digging their paddles in till the blades were submerged, they sent the light craft swishing onward, and very soon were sure that they had reached the correct position. Then they leaped ashore, drew the boat up on the bank, and shouldered their weapons.

"Come on!" said Alec. "If we can break into the huts we'll put a different sort of complexion on this business. But wait, there are two of 'em."

"You take one, I take the other. Then we join hands. Better still, if they don't spot us, slip back into the jungle. Jingo! Listen to their howling. Hope the business hasn't begun already."

It looked very much as if it had, for as they emerged from the thickness of the jungle and approached the village they could see an enormous crowd assembled—that is, enormous for such a village. Perhaps there were three hundred people there, blackening the street, dancing madly. And a glimpse between the huts showed one solitary figure lashed upright to a post. It made Dick's heart leap and Alec's blood boil. They sped onward at once, keeping under cover, but careless of brambles and creepers, tearing their way through the underwood till they were breathless with their exertions. But haste was not likely to be all in their favour, and, recognizing this, they were soon creeping on all-fours, worming their way through reeds and long grass to which the jungle had now given place. At length, when their pent-up feelings were almost too much for them, they reached the back of the huts, which fortunately were close together, and promptly proceeded to operate on them. Indeed, one lusty slash from Dick's sabre made a cut to be proud of. A second sliced an opening within a foot of the first, while a little quick handling converted the slits into a wide opening. He was in within a second, slashing at the creepers binding three figures which lay helpless upon the mud floor. Nor was there need to caution the friends whose limbs he had so unexpectedly set free.

"Guessed it must be you, sir," whispered Hawkins, sitting up and flapping his helpless hands to and fro. Indeed it was pitiable to see the powerful man reduced for the time being to the weakness of a child. Dick seized Mr. Andrew and rubbed his limbs with energy, while Hurst began to kick his heels against the floor and wave his hands after the manner set by Hawkins.

"Now," whispered the latter hoarsely, when at length the feeling had returned to his limbs, standing in the semi-darkness of the hut opening and closing his huge hands, and fashioning formidable fists of them. "Now, Mr. Dicky—beg pardon—now, sir, let a man get at them 'ere 'eathen. Let 'im 'ave a say in this here matter. Swelp me, but I'm game to take on the whole pack of black-'earted 'eathen."

If he were, there was likely to be every opportunity, for outside the roar and shrieks of the natives were appalling in their intensity. Dick stepped to the front face of the hut and peered through one of the many crevices, for in New Guinea draughts of cold air are rather to be desired than otherwise, the heat often enough being extreme. Through that peephole he saw something that almost turned him livid, rooted him to the spot, and for a moment held him helpless. For directly beneath his ken was the figure of the unfortunate Larkin, strung up to one of those stumps driven into the ground, surrounded by a gesticulating and evil-smelling mob, and with those three foul, over-dressed sorcerers close to him. They were dancing now with a different movement. They were sidling from one point to another, as far as the pressing throng would allow, twisting this way and that with sinuous, snake-like movements, but never once taking their eyes from their victim. And each one of these brutes was armed—the tallest and most hideous with an enormous club; a second, a fat ruffian of particularly evil type of countenance, with a curving knife; while the third waved a flaming torch.

As for Larkin, he at least showed his mettle, and reflected credit upon the service to which he belonged. For he did not wince, not even when each of those sorcerers in turn sidled in his direction and brandished his weapons at him, while the third made pretence to set on fire the wood littering the ground at his feet. Larkin addressed them in a manner common to the barrack-room. There was the strong flavour of the canteen about his speech; while his two eyes, no doubt each addressing itself to some different point, fixed upon the rascals dancing there, scowled at them, threatened them, but never flinched.

"They're—they're going to sacrifice him, Larkin," Dick managed to blurt out at last.

"The black-'earted 'eathen," came in a growl from Hawkins, now at his side, while Hurst joined them, muttering deeply beneath his breath. "What'll you do, sir?"

"Wait for Mr. Alec and the officers, then rush 'em. Get hold of those clubs."

But a second later there came a disturbing noise from the adjacent hut, just at the precise moment when that hideous tall sorcerer danced his way back to Larkin, and, swinging his club overhead, brought it down with a thud on the top of the pillar to which the unhappy fellow was lashed. Even then the brave soldier did not flinch. They heard him growl loudly and angrily as the club thudded on the top of the stump.

"That's one fer you," they heard, "one fer you, yer ugly son of a gun. But jest you wait till I get a whack in. Then I'll make yer feel sorry you was born, I will."

There came a shout from that adjacent hut. The door flew open, and in a twinkling a forlorn little band dashed forward, Alec at their head, the Major and the Commander following. Hawkins and Hurst and Dick acted on that signal. They flung themselves upon the frail walls and door of that hut, bursting it open as if it were constructed of paper. Then, followed by Mr. Andrew, they launched themselves at the natives, Dick wielding his rusty sabre, Hawkins with an enormous club, whilst Hurst and Andrew were similarly armed.

195

"The black-'earted 'eathen!" shouted Hawkins, springing to the front, for he was a huge fellow, and extraordinarily active. "That's fer you, you smelly sea serpent!"

It was the big sorcerer, he with the club, who had made such fine practice round Larkin's head, and looked as if he would at any moment crack his skull. But he was too late now. Hawkins was not the kind of man to deal a blow that asked for repetition, not at least when in anger. And he was furious. His club beat down that of the native, broke it, in fact, and then descended with a crash full on his woolly pate. The dull crushing sound that followed, and the manner in which this man of medicine fell in his tracks, told a tale there was no mistaking. Meanwhile Dick had run through a second sorcerer, while the gallant Alec had dived for the waist of the third, he with the torch, had handled him as he would a man breaking from scrum and likely to get clear away if not securely collared. Yes, Alec seized this wretch, and, exerting an abnormal strength, lifted him, swung him in the air, and then tossed him to the ground. By then the Major had cut Larkin free, and the latter individual burst upon the enemy like a torrent. Seething with indignation, he selected the fellow whom Alec had tackled, and who had now risen to his feet. Larkin launched himself at him, seized him by neck and shoulder, and shook him as if he were a rat. Then he pushed him away a foot or two, drew himself backward in time to escape a lunge and a blow from a knife which the rascal had suddenly produced, and then struck out with tremendous force, sending his fist against the point of the sorcerer's chin.

"And he won't get askin' fer more, I don't think," declared the furious soldier, looking about him with those pugnacious, wandering eyes. "No, I don't think; and so here's something for some of the other fellers."

There might have been no such thing as weapons, and certainly the angry and gallant fellow had no fear of them. Unarmed himself, save with the weapons with which nature had provided him, he again flung himself at the enemy like a rocket, and was seen striking out to right and left, sending the natives flying. Hurst was there too, Hurst bursting with righteous indignation, and Hawkins, a force in himself. While the two officers and their junior, the gallant midshipman, were already in line with them, Andrew and Alec forming two of the force also.

"Rush 'em," shouted the Commander. "Now, at 'em, hammer and tongs, but don't go too far. Hooray! They're bolting."

The mass of natives had, indeed, of a sudden taken to their heels, and no doubt the dash and daring of Dick and his comrades had scared them wonderfully. But there was something else to account for this sudden *volte-face*, and a sharp report and a loud detonation from the far end of the village told its tale instantly. It was the airship. There she was swooping down upon the place, one of her deck guns in operation. Pop! pop! pop! The quickfirer sent shot after shot amidst the fleeing natives, while someone located on the very nose of the ship, on the tiny, narrow gangway which led to that exposed position, waved frantically to our friends. It was Joe without a doubt. Joe in the seventh heaven of delight at the sight of his comrades.

"Stay where you are," he bawled through his megaphone. "We're landing. Those niggers have gone scuttling over the river."

The ship was down in their midst in the space of a few seconds, and for a while there was violent shaking of hands amongst the friends.

"Thought I should never see you again," declared Joe, mopping a very fevered forehead. "Missed you after a few hours had passed and rose at once to inspect surroundings. Couldn't find a trace of you, and so began to swoop backward and forward. By chance I saw this village, and with a pair of glasses made out the situation. No, no, Larkin, not a punitive expedition this time. We've better things to do, and, after all, these natives only acted according to their own lights."

The pugnacious Larkin was positively boiling, and strutted about the little group, his two fists doubled, his arms waving, his head a little forward, and his eyes turned towards the flying natives.

"Just one little turn at 'em, sir," he asked. "Just one little one, if only to get a bit of me own back."

"Not a step," replied Joe firmly. "Come, gentlemen, aboard, and let us be moving."

It was obviously the best course to pursue, as there was nothing to be gained by attacking the natives. But as a warning to them to leave Europeans alone in the future the village was fired and the numerous dug-outs lying upon the bank of the river broken to pieces. One, however, was taken aboard the airship as a trophy, as well as sundry clubs, knives, and utensils, while Dick carried away that useful cutlass.

"Just to show Mr. Reitberg, the sportsman, that we've been here," he told his chum. "But even when he sees the canoe he won't believe. However, there are other ways of making him do so."

As a matter of fact Joe and Andrew had been extremely careful throughout this momentous trip to leave records of their arrival in various parts, and that document which they had obtained from the foreign office had been *viséed* by a variety of officials in a variety of countries.

Thankful to have escaped from the plight in which they had found themselves, Dick and his friends now embarked, and the great airship promptly swooped upward.

"From New Guinea to Australia is but a step," said Joe with a smile. "We will spend a little time in calling on our friends at the Antipodes and then speed onward, for time is drawing in. We must now pursue a straighter course."

Ambling across Australia, where her presence caused a huge commotion, and where both passengers and crew came in for a large share of the proverbially warm-hearted hospitality of the colonials, the ship called in at the north and south isles of New Zealand, and then, speeding up her engines, steered for the south. It was with sad and yet proud hearts that a week later those aboard manœuvred the huge vessel directly over the frozen South Pole, and there gazed down upon the relics left by Amundsen and Captain Scott, records of the daring and persistent bravery of men whose names will go down upon the roll of fame for future generations to observe.

"We will land and ourselves walk across the Southern Pole," said Andrew. "Then we will visit that tragic spot where Captain Scott and his comrades, caught by that fatal blizzard, and delayed by a sick comrade, lay down in their tent and died, died the death of heroes."

One does not need to recount how they descended, nor how they found that cairn of snow heaped upon the bodies of the fallen. Here crew and passengers left the ship and stood silently about the cairn reading the inscription left upon the rough cross erected above it.

"This cross and cairn erected over the remains of Captain R. F. Scott, C.V.O., R.N., Dr. E. A. Wilson, and Lieutenant H. R. Bowers, R.I.M., as a slight token to perpetuate their gallant and successful attempt to reach the goal. This they did on the 17th January, 1912, after the Norwegians had already done so on the 16th December, 1911."

"And we must not forget their sick comrades who perished on the same journey," said Andrew solemnly. "They were Captain L. E. G. Oates and Petty Officer E. Evans, R.N. Truly has it been said of these heroes that hereabouts died some very gallant gentlemen."

From those cold and forbidding Antarctic regions the airship rushed towards sunnier climes, and was very soon over Cape Horn. Thence she traced the whole length of South America, passing over the Pacific coast of that enormous continent. She threaded her way above the isthmus of Panama, where the Spaniards of old extracted wealth from the Incas and from the natives of Mexico, and where Drake and men of his adventurous stamp won riches from the Spaniard. Thence the vessel paid a visit to the States of North America, her coming being heralded by the discharge of fireworks in thousands and by signal rockets. Indeed, a warm welcome was given to passengers and crew, and invitations to stay longer. But time was pressing. Canada, too, was calling, so that that long frontier between North America and Canada was crossed, a frontier, be it noted, devoid of forts and guns, across which Canadians and Americans fraternize.

"And now we turn our faces homewards. This is the last lap," said Joe, when a round of festivities had been enjoyed in various Canadian cities. "We have proved this ship to be capable of a world-circling trip. She has safely ridden through tempests which would have destroyed a Zeppelin. Let us now return to London, there to show the people of England that we are still in existence, and there to hand over this ship to the authorities."

It was with light hearts that they sent the vessel eastward. Hovering for a while over the historical city of Quebec, where French and English had once contested matters, and where their sons now live in amity together, Joe sent the aerial monster scudding over the length of the mighty River St. Laurence. Then they sailed above the vast Gulf of that name, and swept seaward between Newfoundland and Cape Breton Island. It was in that neighbourhood that the lookout man sighted a tiny speck upon the ocean.

"Boat adrift, sir, I think," he reported. "I can see a man waving something."

Joe fastened his glasses upon the spot, a movement which the Commander copied.

"Man adrift on a piece of wreckage," sang out the latter. "Waving his shirt as a signal. Lucky for him that we were crossing."

They steered above the castaway and sent Dick down upon the lift, with Alec and Hurst to help him. Then they hoisted them again and brought aboard a man seemingly in the last stages of exhaustion. He was almost speechless with thirst and black with exposure. A beard of ten days' growth was on his face, while his hair was long and matted.

"Fisherman," he gasped. "Driven off the land. Been drifting to and fro for days, and without food and drink for many. Water! water!"

Aboard the airship this unlucky wight received the kindest attention, and indeed was soon snugly curled up in a bunk in the men's quarters. No one suspected he was other than he pretended to be, an unfortunate fisherman from the shores of Nova Scotia. No one aboard recognized the man as Adolf Fruhmann. But it was he, Carl Reitberg's rascally lieutenant, and once more crew and passengers and airship were in imminent danger.

CHAPTER XX

Adolf Fruhmann's Venture

Never perhaps was there a more exaggerated example of base ingratitude, of trickery, of cunning, and of calculated rascality than that instanced by the presence of the ruffian, Adolf Fruhmann, aboard the great airship. Snug in his bunk, feigning exhaustion and illness after exposure and privation, the wretch successfully evaded the ken of Joe and his friends while sending messages of the profoundest gratitude to them.

"All so much dust," he sniggered beneath the bed-clothes, for only the top of his head was showing. "Just a little more dust in their eyes to blind 'em. It just makes me roar when I think how the scheme acted, and Carl saying all the while that it wouldn't. Well, he pays, pays all the more handsomely."

He went off into a paroxysm of silent laughter, which shook the bunk and brought the tender-hearted Hawkins to his side within a moment.

"Eh, mate?" he asked gently enough, for your sailor or your soldier attendant is the very best of fellows, as gentle as any woman, and often almost as clever where nursing is necessary.

"Eh, mate? Got the shivers? Fever? Well, I've had it, and it ain't too agreeable. But Mr. Andrew'll put you right. He's the doctor aboard this ship, and a good 'un. I'll send along for him."

"Please," gurgled the wretch in the bunk, still keeping his head hidden. "Please, I'm as cold as an icicle at times, and then boiling hot. I'm dying."

"Not you, mate," came from the encouraging Hawkins, who hastened away at once so that he might save this derelict fisherman some suffering. And Mr. Andrew was equally solicitous.

"Come, let us have a look at you, my friend," he begged, arriving in the men's quarters. "Show your face and so let me judge what is the matter."

The crafty Fruhmann complied in a measure. He roused himself on to one elbow, and then fell backward as if the effort had weakened him. Then he pushed the clothes back from his face with one hand, keeping the other firmly across his eyes.

"Can't see," he mumbled. "Almost blind after those days and nights in the open. Don't dare to open my eyes."

Andrew left him with a draught, and a caution to Hawkins to see that the wide windows of the men's quarters were curtained.

"Shade the electric light when it gets dark," he said. "No doubt he is suffering with his eyes. I've known the same with men lost in the backwoods of Canada in the winter. There, my friend, a few days will put you right. You'll be fit to travel back once we get to England."

"But not aboard this ship, no," smiled the artful Fruhmann, burying his head again once Andrew was gone, just as if he were a frightened ostrich. "Not aboard this flying vessel, mister. 'Cos she won't be flying then if Adolf Fruhmann has anything to do with the matter. And to think I'm here, and so easily, when Carl was in a funk all the while that I'd miss 'em!"

That set him off into another smothered giggle, which again shook the bunk and called Hawkins over to him. Indeed, that big-hearted fellow was decidedly ill at ease, till the arrival of Andrew's promised draught and its administration to the patient produced an apparently instantaneous effect.

"Take the shivers out of yer," said Hawkins. "Make yer easy and send yer to sleep. Sing out when you're wanting anything. There's soup here that'll make you fit for anything, and lemonade and what not."

Fruhmann thanked him with his tongue in his cheek, disappeared again beneath the blankets, and gave himself up to scheming and considering matters. Indeed he was a cunning, clever fellow, and by adopting the excuse of sickness was entirely freed of suspicion. More than that, there was no danger of recognition, and the hints and information which the rascally Carl Reitberg had been able to give him had showed this wretch that there was little need for caution.

"That beard and the dirt and so on fooled 'em finely," he told himself. "Not that there's a one to be feared save Sergeant Evans, the man who worked with the police in South Africa. But he's a saloon man, and didn't catch sight of me. If he had he'd have been bothered finely. But if I was to use soap and water and a comb, not to mention a razor, well, the tale'd be different. And so here I am aboard, a sick and exhausted fisherman, cared for and molly-coddled by that thundering lout Hawkins, left pretty much to myself because I'm supposed to be extra sleepy. Ho! ho! This'll make Carl laugh fit to hurt himself. It's a tale that'll help to make him pay up extra handsome."

It was, in fact, just the sort of story to go down with the rascally magnate. All the sporting instincts and ideas as to love of fair play which he may have possessed in his youthful days were gone entirely. And even had he still retained a few shreds and remnants of honest feeling for others at this period he threw them overboard when dealing with Joe Gresson, Andrew Provost, and the crew and passengers of the great airship.

"We're bound to beat them," he had told Fruhmann, when the latter had hurried away from England to meet him at Suez. "We're bound to follow the ship and break her somewhere. There's money in it."

"I hope so. That's why I'm here. That's why I'm ready to take risks," his rascally hireling told him.

"And we've got to find a way to get about the business. Now, I've failed with the bombs."

"And got scared mighty badly," grinned the other. "Well, it's my turn. You leave this to me. How will I do it? You listen. See here. The papers wherever the ship goes are crammed with columns full of her history, her wonderful powers, her beauty of outline and construction; not to mention photos. And there's something far more important."

"Eh, yes? What?"

"There's always a list of places she's intending to visit. For instance, here's the latest telegram from India. Let's read it."

Fruhmann lolled back in his cane-work seat on the veranda of the hotel and unfolded a paper. "Listen," he said, taking his cigar from his lips and admiring the cloud of smoke he sent upward. "Here it is. The cable companies are making a fortune over this airship."

"As I hope to do," sniggered the magnate.

"As you will do if you trust things to me. Now listen. 'Departure of the great airship. Huge excitement in India. Mr. Joseph Gresson confident of successful ending to his trip. Proposes now to steer for Borneo and New Guinea; afterwards for Australia and New Zealand. Will cross the South Pole direct for Cape Horn, and may be expected in North America. Will visit Canada finally and make a triumphal return by way of Quebec and the Gulf of St. Laurence. Those who wish to see the last of her must hasten to Newfoundland or the Island of Cape Breton.'"

Fruhmann took to his cigar again, looking sharply at his master. Carl meditated deeply. He was not brilliant at any time, and was now dull to the point of exasperation.

"Yes," he drawled sluggishly. "But—er—I don't quite see where this helps us. You can't, for instance, hope to come up with the ship at the South Pole."

"Stop fooling!" growled his amiable lieutenant. "Who is talking of the South Pole? You want me to get aboard. Well, Canada's as good as Australia, and it's possible. I couldn't reach the first before the ship had passed. But I can reach Canada. There's a steamer leaving the Canal this very evening. She's a pleasure cruiser direct from New York, and she steams straight home from the Mediterranean. Now, I board her. Never mind if they won't take passengers. I'll smuggle myself aboard and your money'll do the rest. From New York the train takes me quick to Nova Scotia, and from there to Cape Breton Island it's a mere step."

"Ah!" The fat magnate began to follow. "But——" he gasped, turning in his chair. "Then?"

"Easy. I steal a boat and put out to sea just before the ship leaves Quebec. I've built a sort of raft already. I sink the boat and take to the raft, while I've been growing a beard from this very instant. I signal the ship——"

"Stop!" cried Carl. "It may be night-time when she comes over."

"But I have a lamp. Fortunate, ain't it? It's all I've saved from my boat. A mere lamp! No food. No drink. Just that lucky lamp, and I signal. I'm taken aboard. I'm ill, desperately bad. I lie up in a bunk, and——"

The fat magnate laughed till he coughed, and then became positively purple.

"You—you're a boy, Adolf," he wheezed. "It's a fine scheme. But—but supposing it fails. Supposing the ship changes her course? Then it's too late. You're leaving the attempt to the very last instant."

"And all the better. It won't fail. Besides, at the end the folks aboard won't be suspicious. They've been looking out for you since you planted those bombs aboard. They've had a wary eye open for sportsmen. But I'm merely a poor, exhausted fisherman. I don't count. I'm too ill to be interviewed, and I——"

"How'll you do it?" asked Carl eagerly.

"Ah, that's telling!"

It was a matter on which Fruhmann had been absolutely silent. But he had his plans. Indeed, his scheme had been completed long ago in every detail, and as he lay in that bunk, sniggering violently at times, he was a proud and happy scoundrel. For his plans had carried so far wonderfully. He was in the camp of the enemy, but as a friend. He was a pampered, unfortunate fisherman, at whose presence no one could feel suspicion. In fact, he was on the verge of a triumph. Nor was he the one to hurry.

"Let 'em settle down to the feeling that I'm aboard," he told himself. "To-morrow night'll do. I ain't going to spoil things by hurrying."

And so till the following night he lay inert in his bunk, still a prey to those extraordinary attacks which alarmed the honest Hawkins. It was after midnight when he crept from the men's quarters, leaving them all slumbering, and made his crafty way along the gallery. Nor, strangely enough, did he need a guide.

"Got Carl to draw a sketch of the ship, and studied it," he smiled. "That's the way to do this sort of business. Ah! That's the engine-room. I have to go for'ard to find the ladder. Wonder who's on duty?"

He could hear the soft purr of those motors so beloved of Joe Gresson. He halted just above the place and stared in through the transparent floor of the gallery. One light was burning, a shaded light, and close to it sat the man in charge of the engines. He was asleep. Fruhmann almost whistled.

"Got him!" he hissed. "Easy as smoking. Slip down there, keeping the motors between me and him. There's enough noise to keep him from hearing. Then— then I do it."

A pair of socks were his only foot covering, and made not a sound as he placed a foot on the first rung of the ladder. If anyone could ever creep like a cat it was this scoundrel. He seemed to slide down the ladder while never once did he take his eyes from the form of the sleeper. Then he went on hands and knees and crawled down one side of the range of motors.

"Better than bombs, far," he was saying. "Must work things so as to make the ship helpless. Just now her automatic gear's steering her upon the course they've set. But there won't be any automatic movement when I've finished. And the best of my scheme is that it don't endanger life, that is, my life. It's blowing tidyish now, and of course the ship'll feel it. She'll get sent this way and that, and be wellnigh wrecked. But she's got wireless, and we're over the track of ships. That's handy."

How the cunning rascal had schemed it all out. Whatever he proposed to do now he reckoned would render the great ship helpless, and would wreck her. But not on the instant. No. He was not attempting desperate methods such as Carl had chosen. The ship would be helpless, and become a wreck in time, but her wireless would enable some steamer to be called before the last fatal moment.

"It's grand and so easy," Fruhmann gurgled. "Now, we remember the description. There's a large valve on the left of the engines. That empties the water tanks. But we're on the other side, and the valve just here sets free the paraffin. It drains their tanks, runs away with the fuel supply of the engines, empties the radiators, and taps every drain from the hydraulic distributors. In fact, just this little, gentle turn makes her as helpless as a child, robs her motors of power and lets the breeze play goodness knows what with her. How very simple!"

The villain, smiling at his own cleverness, steadily turned the lever controlling that valve and heard on the instant the gurgle of fluid running swiftly through the open orifice. Then he crept to the ladder, clambered it cautiously, and faced for the men's quarters. It was at that precise moment that a hand was laid heavily on his shoulder.

"You're a slinkin', mean-faced, scheming hound," came in gruff tones from no less a person than Hawkins. "I was took in with yer tales at first, I own I was, took in nicely. But I'm all alive-o now, and don't you forget it. Here's just a sample of what'll happen."

He gave the man a terrific buffet, a buffet which sent him giddily against the wall of the gallery, while it awakened the sleeping mechanic. "You just look lively and turn down that paraffin valve," sang out Hawkins, "and next time you wants to sleep call in a mate ter relieve you. Now, you, I'm a goin'——"

Precisely what the angry Hawkins proposed to do there is no saying. But Adolf Fruhmann had no intention of giving him the opportunity. To give this rascal his due, he had courage, a greater store than possessed by Carl Reitberg. And now that he was taken in the midst of his attempt, and saw prison before him, he formed the desperate resolve of fleeing.

"Get to the liftway and keep 'em off," he told himself swiftly. "Yes, there's an aeroplane up there. You press a lever and the machine rises to the deck. A button sets the engine going. You can't upset. It's safe, safer than staying here. I'm off to try it."

He broke away from the sailor and went racing along the gallery. A moment later he was at the liftway, where, guided by his memory of what Carl had told him, he stepped upon a platform and touched a button. But that action was disastrous. A piercing shriek instantly awoke the sleepers aboard the airship. For Adolf Fruhmann, adventurer and scoundrel, had for all his cleverness made one vital error. He had stepped upon the wrong platform. That button which he had pushed released the well through which that twirling lift was wont to descend beneath the vessel. It opened with a sudden clatter, and in one second the ruffian who had hoped to wreck Joe Gresson's fine vessel was precipitated into space. Nor could he be discovered when the searchlights were turned upon the surface of the Atlantic.

"Then forward!" cried Joe, "and let us be thankful for such a deliverance."

"Forward!" repeated Andrew. "Surely no further dangers can threaten this vessel."

"None," declared the Major. "You may say that we're almost in home waters already. Let's ask the engineer to put on speed. It would be nice to lunch to-morrow over Old England."

But it was early morning two days later when Dick sighted the white cliffs of Dover, for a strong head-wind had made rapid travel difficult and undesirable.

"Port in sight, sir," he said, saluting the Commander.

"Then we'll send 'em a Marconi."

"To whom?" asked Joe, smiling now, for was not this a triumph?

"Er—well, why not to Mr. Carl Reitberg?" gurgled Dick. "Compliments, you know; happy greetings. Just arrived to claim that money, and sorry about that fellow you sent to see us off the St. Laurence."

"Send this," said Andrew, laughing at the midshipman. "Great airship in sight of England. Making for London where all may see her. Owners present hundred thousand pounds deposited by Carl Reitberg to hospitals."

"And the ship?" demanded the Major.

"To King and Country," said Andrew promptly.

The End

www.ingramcontent.com/pod-product-compliance
Lightning Source LLC
Chambersburg PA
CBHW060620290526
45793CB00001B/88